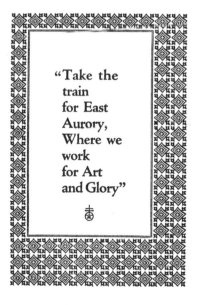

"Take the
train
for East
Aurory,
Where we
work
for Art
and Glory"

Art & Glory

Elbert Hubbard in 1914

Art & Glory

The Story
of
Elbert Hubbard

by

Freeman Champney

The Kent State University Press

Copyright © 1968, 1983 by Freeman Champney
All rights reserved.
Library of Congress Catalog Card Number
ISBN 0-87338-295-1
Manufactured in the United States of America
Published by The Kent State University Press,
Kent, Ohio 44242

CIP

Library of Congress Cataloging in Publication Data
Champney, Freeman.
 Art & glory.

 Originally published: New York: Crown Publishers,
1968.
 "Major publications in the Elbert Hubbard output": p.
 Includes index.
 1. Hubbard, Elbert, 1856-1915—Biography.
2. Authors, American—19th century—Biography.
3. Publishers and publishing—United States—Biography.
4. Roycroft Shop. I. Title. II. Title: Art and glory.
PS2043.C47 1983   700'.92'4 [B]   83-14863
ISBN 0-87338-295-1 (pbk.)

Preface to the Paperback Edition

I AM delighted to see this book back in print. Though it didn't reach as large a market as its first publisher had hoped, the enthusiastic letters which still arrive from people who have found the book for themselves suggest that the Elbert Hubbard story continues to absorb and illuminate. I am also glad to have this opportunity to apply a little hindsight to the book twenty-odd years after it was being researched and drafted.

Several reviewers noted that my treatment of Hubbard-Roycroft gave scant attention to their place in our arts-and-crafts history. This gap is especially noticeable today because Hubbard-as-popular-philosopher has been in deepening eclipse for some years, while the arts-and-crafts movement has had a large revival. To find recent Hubbard-Roycroft references, you turn to such books as *The Arts and Crafts Movement in America, 1876-1916*. (Robert Judson Clark, editor, 1972, Princeton University Press.) And you do find them. This handsomely printed catalog for an exhibition—organized by the Princeton Art Museum and the Art Institute of Chicago—states in its Introduction to "The Roycrofters": "Elbert Hubbard had charisma. It contributed to making him a brilliant salesman . . . and established him as a cultural messiah to thousands of Americans." The Winterthur Portfolio III, 1967, has a comprehensive and beautifully illustrated article by Prof. Robert Koch on "Elbert Hubbard's Roycrofters as Artist-Craftsmen."

As I see it, the vogue of the Roycroft "art goods"—the handmade pottery, copper and leather items, and furniture, as well as the books with their flowery initial letters and limp leather bindings—was temporarily obscured by a wave of "modernism." We went through a large cultural shift—spectacularly in architecture, painting, and sculpture, but also in furniture, crafts, and interior decoration. Such slogans as "form follows function" were "in," many family antiques went into the attic, and "gingerbread" became a swear word. And in the graphic arts, those silly little serifs came off many of the new type faces, and "dynamic symmetry" began to replace the old printer's rule of "center all display lines."

In a sense, this modernism was a utopian movement. Life could, and should, be clean, sharp, and functional. The new vision took over in the academy and among the intelligentsia. As Tom Wolfe has uproariously documented in *From Bauhaus to Our House*, architecture led the swing.

But after we had lived with all that clean design and those glass walls for a generation, we began to realize that human critters don't respond very well to such an environment. People are crotchety, playful, and often sloppy. In other words, people are human, and their humanity doesn't flourish in controlled and purely functional surroundings. So: use a spray-can of paint on that poured concrete, and let's play around with ornament and chisel marks and cross-stitches.

When I wrote about the Roycroft art objects, I was probably reflecting that modern deviation in taste. But also, I had found no evidence that Hubbard himself played any large, creative role in the fashioning of this part of the Roycroft output. He was the boss, to be sure, and he *had* brought the William Morris message back from England. And he did nurture the procession of "honest Roycrofters" who were doing the work. But even in the bookwork, when the young Dard Hunter came to East Aurora (well into the new century), his reminiscences tell us that after Hubbard put him to work designing books, " . . . I made drawings for title pages and initial letters. He seemed pleased . . . but he had no more knowledge of design than I." As a longtime printer and book designer, I was probably turned off on this aspect of my subject. If Hubbard himself hadn't worked on these things, they weren't central to my study.

So, in the craftwork, Hubbard was more of a catalyst than a creator. But he *was* quite a catalyst. As Milton Brown says in *American Art* (Abrams, 1979): "Hubbard was a guiding spirit, neither artist nor designer, who could nonetheless breathe spirit and vitality into an artistic enterprise."

And when we turn our hindsight to Hubbard's role as "General Inspector of the Universe," we don't find much accurate prophecy of the future in which we are now living. Hubbard's espousal of feminism was ahead of its time, but today it may seem outrageously partial and patronizing. Similarly, his celebration of the man who carries messages to Garcia, and his later attempts to glorify big business and to defend it from the muckrakers, look rather irrelevant in this time of multinational corporations. Hubbard saw business as personal, creative, and entrepreneurial. And this *was* a large part of the picture at the time. In some areas it seems to be coming back. We seem to be rediscovering the "work ethic," or at least lamenting its scarcity. And there will always be messages which cannot be computerized.

So it is not as a prophet that Hubbard is notable today, but rather as an articulator of the feel and flavor of many aspects of his time. As Gerald Carson noted in his review of *Art & Glory* in the *New York Times Book Review*: "Hubbard's mind was a kind of wind harp, activated by all the ideas that were in the air at the time. In slangy, racy vernacular and outrageous metaphor, the sage of East Aurora gave voice to social protest, gibed at preachers and professors—and shook up the self-educated, of whom he was a conspicuous example."

How-things-were is something to understand on the way to coping with how they are now and how we hope they will be tomorrow. And I believe that the Elbert Hubbard story offers a lively and many-faceted heritage.

Freeman Champney

Merritt Island, Florida   Summer, 1983

The  Philistine

A Periodical of Protest

The only man who makes money following the races is the one who does so with a broom and shovel

---

Vol. 30
No. 3

Printed Every Little While for the Society of the Philistines and Published by Them Monthly. Subscription, One Dollar Yearly ✄ Single Copies, Ten Cents FEBRUARY, 1910

The cover of the February, 1910, issue of *The Philistine* (exact size). The covers were always brown paper, with black type and red decorations.

Acknowledgments

I owe thanks to many people for help, suggestions, and information used in the shaping of this book. (A nonprofessional, I suspect, owes an unusual measure of gratitude to more people than does a scholar, or an author, who works at his trade all day and every day.) First, to Miriam Hubbard Roelofs and Elbert Hubbard, II, for generously supplying information and material. To Bruce Thomas, then Assistant Librarian at Antioch College, for professional assistance and friendly interest. To Miss Inez Robb and the McLean County Historical Society in Bloomington, Illinois, for courteous assistance. To Harold Igo, John Cornell, Garth Cate, and W. B. Pleadwell for material on Elbert Hubbard. Paul Bixler, Antioch College Librarian, and David Jolly, Assistant Librarian at Northwestern University, were also helpful.

All this assistance was received during and shortly after the academic year 1955–1956, when I was on sabbatical leave from my job of managing the Antioch Press and used part of the year for the first round of Hubbard research. (Thanks are also very much due to Antioch College for its policy of giving faculty status and sabbatical leaves to its administrative people.) Paul Rohmann, then my assistant at the Press, now its director, made it possible for me to take the year away from the Press, and his continuing interest in the Hubbard study has been important.

During this period, Professor Bernard Weisberger, then an Antioch colleague and a historian of the Hubbard period, was helpful and encouraging (we were working in the Library of Congress during the same summer). Professor Brom Weber, who was completing his doctoral dissertation on Hubbard at the University of Minnesota when I was working on my first draft, was generous with sources, suggestions, and comments.

Grateful acknowledgment is made to the following for permission to quote from published works to which they hold the copyrights: The Bobbs-Merrill Company, publishers of *Royal Bob: The Life of Robert G. Ingersoll,* by C. H. Cramer, copyright © 1952; E. P. Dutton & Co., publishers of *Romantic Adventure,* by Elinor Glyn, copyright 1937; Alfred A. Knopf, Inc., publishers of *My Life with Paper: An Autobiography* by Dard Hunter, copyright © 1958; Liveright Publishing Corporation for permission to quote from *Tramping on Life,* by Harry Kemp, copyright 1922 by Boni & Liveright; William H. Wise & Company, publishers of *Elbert Hubbard of East Aurora,* by Felix Shay, copyright 1926. And again to Elbert Hubbard, II, for permission to use material covered by the Roycroft copyrights.

The rethinking and rewriting of the book, which have gone on in odd moments since 1962, owe much to another group of people who encouraged its completion—often by simply showing interest at times when the job seemed endless, and perhaps pointless. Willard Lockwood, director of Wesleyan University Press, made detailed criticisms of the earlier version, and suggestions for redoing it, which were perceptive and useful. Special thanks go to Rietta Gantter, Janet Weinandy, Richard Underwood, Katharine MacCarthy Champney, and Ellen Offner for their interest during the rewriting. And the forces that contrived a fifty-inch snowfall in Syracuse, in February 1966, are to be thanked for the three days of leisure they provided at a critical time.

Special tributes are gratefully tendered to two special people. My wife, Marjory Winner Champney, has a high order of talent and skill in areas quite different from history and writing. But throughout the work on the book, her perceptions as to what was right and what was wrong with it have been clear and sound. She has also had the wisdom and patience to let its author find his own way. I have also been extremely fortunate in my agent, Carolyn W. Stagg, of Lester Lewis Associates. Herself a native of East Aurora, with memories of her neighbor Elbert Hubbard dating from her childhood, she has gone a long way beyond professional duty and cost accounting in her efforts to arrange publication of the book, in both its earlier version and its final form.

Finally, the large and small details of editing and publication have been handled with skill, taste, and unfailing judgment by Millen Brand of Crown Publishers. I have been lucky beyond my deserts throughout this project, not least in my editor.

FREEMAN CHAMPNEY

Syracuse, New York

Contents

	Acknowledgments	*ix*
1.	Introduction	1
2.	Family	7
3.	Boyhood	13
4.	Success Story	25
5.	Rebirth	37
6.	Growing Pains	53
7.	Fra Elbertus	71
8.	Messages	87
9.	How Can Sin Be Sin?	99
10.	Mortgage-Burning	109
11.	Art & Glory	123
12.	Because I Could	139
13.	The New Woman	153
14.	Big Business & More of It	167
15.	Vestibule to Paradise	181
16.	Last Journey	193
17.	Afterword	209
	Sources and Leftovers	*215*
	Notes to Chapters	*217*
	Major Publications in the Elbert Hubbard Output	*243*
	Index	*245*

"If you want to get the Work done, select the Busy Man -- the Other Kind has no time!"

❡ "Let's see! Let's see! What is it they pursue in Boston? Culture! That's it! In East Aurora we don't have to pursue Culture ❧ She feels at home and abides with us!" ❧

Some of Elbert Hubbard's favorite mottoes published by The Roycrofters. Note the colophon.

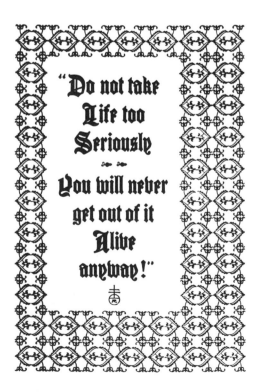

"Do not take Life too Seriously -- You will never get out of it Alive anyway!"

❡ "Get your Happiness out of your Work ❧ or you'll never know what Happiness is!" ❧ ❧

1

Introduction

WE HEAR a great deal these days about the "search for identity." This search seems to be the thing people used to have in mind when they said that someone was trying to "find himself." It is slippery to define, but it does imply that people have a choice of selves—some false and some real, some that fit and some that pinch.

Often, the search for that self, or that identity, means a bruising rearrangement of the intricate ties between the self and the Others—not only people close at hand, but the congealed accumulation of other selves in laws, mores, and religions. And then there are the brute facts that mold and limit selves—such as geography, status and wealth, skin color, physical constitution. Also, the search takes many forms—or may not take place at all—at different times and other places. In some societies, the self seems to be part of the package delivered at birth. There is no agonizing search and very little choice—you either belong or you don't exist. But there are also periods in the lives of separate people and of nations when all the doors seem to open. The clutch of the Others weakens, and choices appear in every direction. At such times there can be a great flowering of selves—perhaps more so than later, when the whole business becomes more self-conscious, and a phrase like the "search for identity" becomes part of our sophisticated small talk.

This book deals with a man who lived in one of these open-door periods, a quite recent one. It was a time when a great many things began to be possible, and a great many more seemed equally possible. Not only things that puffed and clattered and spun and gave off sparks, but new ways of living, seeing, and thinking, and new answers to the weary paradoxes and naysayings of the ages. Or so it seemed. This man was involved in one way or another with most of these new things and new ideas. He came, by devious routes, to a considerable celebrity and a catalytic effect on many people. He was both worshiped and hated. He was a tangle of passionate contradictions, and a prophet of the simple life. He was a rebel, a heretic, and a front man for big business. He was a prolific writer, full of brilliance, bombast, sentimentality, calculated sincerity, pretense, and self-revelation—and sometimes he was straightforward and vivid. As "General Inspector of the Universe," he had something to say about nearly everything that went on in his time—and often what he said on one day contradicted what he had said the day before. His contemporaries saw him (when they weren't seeing reflected images of themselves coming from his direction) in many different shadings of light, and angles of perspective. Few people were indifferent to him, and practically everyone had a try at finding a pigeonhole in which he would fit and stay put. All in all, he was a man in search of his identity on a scale, and to a degree of public involvement, difficult to match today. He lived in, around, and outside of a society that was also in search of an identity, a national image, or a real self. Like him, his America had its public false faces, its mythologies, its inner struggles, and its moments of truth.

It is more than fifty years since Elbert Hubbard went down with the *Lusitania.* Although many people living remember him, and remember the excitements that clustered around him, the Elbert Hubbard niche in the history books has become smaller and shabbier with the years. For nearly twenty-three years a bronze plaque appeared on the wall of a building in the business district of Bloomington, Illinois. It stated:

ON THIS SITE

ELBERT HUBBARD

WAS BORN JUNE 19, 1856

HE WENT DOWN WITH THE LUSITANIA

OFF THE COAST OF IRELAND

MAY 7, 1915

The plaque had been installed, with ceremony, in 1931. There had seemed no necessity, when it was being cast, to go into detail about who Elbert Hubbard had been. In 1954, a building was being torn down in Bloomington and, at some point in the demolition, the proprietor of the Courtesy

Corner Parking Lot walked to the McLean County Historical Society a block away to inquire if they had any use for this thing he had picked up. It is there now, in the Society, tacked to the end of a display case.

We *could* leave it there, along with the man it was meant to commemorate. Most historians of the period have done just that. But there is a story here, of a man and his times, that has never really been told. It has become lost somewhere between the worship of his disciples and the scorn of his critics. One key to it, I believe, is that Elbert Hubbard never did "find himself," never achieved that certain identity which is such a Holy Grail today. To place and judge a man—now or in history—you have first to plot his position. Then or now, Elbert Hubbard didn't stand still long enough for such a procedure to work. (As he said himself: ". . . life is unrest, and its passage at best a zigzag course, that only straightens to a direct line when viewed across the years.") He makes sense only in motion, and since he never came to rest short of the bottom of the Irish Sea, there was a lot of motion. And he wrote perhaps seven million words while he was in public orbit, which provides substantial data for tracking.

Many of the externals of American life have changed beyond recognition since Hubbard's time. But some things have changed less than we might think. Who we are and how we shall live—jointly and severally—are wide-open questions, as they were then. The answers that Elbert Hubbard came up with were many, often contradictory, and never quite adequate, even for him. But they are often illuminating, and they are seldom dull.

Some of the readers of this book will have firsthand memories of Hubbard and his times. More will have impressions deriving from their parents, the books in the attic, or their own reading. Others will associate little or nothing with the name of Elbert Hubbard. To give all readers some approximation of an even start—and to indicate some of the puzzles inherent in such a study—we will sketch the highlights of his public career before looking at him in detail.

From 1895 to 1915, Elbert Hubbard was an American celebrity, in an extensive variety of roles. As a public tastemaker, he crusaded for studied simplicity, and arts and crafts, in the American home. He was a disciple, in his fashion, of William Morris, and he preached (sometimes) an approximation of Morris's neomedievalism. From Hubbard's Roycroft Shops in East Aurora, New York, solid and arty Morris chairs and other furniture were carted into the better American parlors. Library tables proudly bore Roycroft books, with tooled leather bindings and hand-illumined pages.

As an opinion molder and popular philosopher, Hubbard had many themes. At various times he called himself an anarchist, a socialist, and a defender of big business. He agitated for feminism and women's rights, for liberal divorce laws, and greater marital freedom. He was a major prophet to the self-educated and the "culture gulpers," and he carried on a long feud with the Brahmins of New England. He took up Colonel Bob Ingersoll's campaign against religious orthodoxy, and he chivied the clergy in season and out. He added formal education, lawyers, and doctors to his prime targets, and so made a clean sweep of the learned professions. He preached a health-and-salvation gospel of his own that featured fresh air, honest toil, individualism, and positive thinking.

Hubbard's gospel reached his public through several channels. Thousands of people heard him lecture, in nearly every major and minor city in the country. One season he did two turns a day in Orpheum Circuit vaudeville. His monthly magazine—the *Philistine*—was a torch flaring in the murk of orthodoxy and stuffiness for more thousands. Variously astringent, preachy, and boisterous, it was one of the few survivors of the "little magazine" explosion of the 1890's. For fifteen years, Hubbard published his monthly biographical "Little Journeys to the Homes of the Great," and another of his overlapping publics got many of their notions about history, art, music, philosophy, great men, and love from these pamphlets. He also wrote five novels, a life of John Brown, and innumerable essays and oddments. Still more thousands of people came to visit his headquarters at East Aurora. Here he had another cluster of roles: as a combination of lord of the manor and father and prophet to his employees; as a one-man Chautauqua program, host, and innkeeper to the pilgrims, honeymooners, and tourists; and as disturber of the peace and proprieties, giver of work, and unpredictable neighbor for the East Aurora population.

He had subsidiary roles that grew out of the major ones. As a writer, he was one of the first to make a colorful weapon and a vivid prose style out of the vernacular. In his last years, he became an unofficial court jester and elder statesman to big business. As a businessman himself, he introduced some very cute tricks into direct-mail merchandising, and he had a large share in turning advertising from stodginess to the foxy sell. As an employer, he brought benevolent paternalism to its fanciest level since the time of Robert Owen. And finally, he came to be a sort of licensed eccentric: his everyday outfit included a large Buster Brown cravat, baggy corduroys, flannel shirt, farmer's brogans, and a western Stetson. His hair was naturally curly, and he let it grow to his shoulders, giving a page-boy effect.

During the vaudeville tour, Harry Lauder said, "Elbert is the only one of us who wears his makeup on the street."

This description is a flamboyant one. It was a flamboyant time, and Elbert Hubbard's livelihood and the maintenance of his multiple roles depended on keeping his place in the public eye. He was a household word and a focal point of reference—whether in admiration, worship, scorn, or amusement—for a great many people. This personal involvement was reflected by the more than forty thousand letters of condolence, appreciation, and reminiscence that poured into East Aurora after his death. And that there was magic in the Hubbard writings is indicated by their market's steady expansion for nearly fifteen years. A process of selecting, excerpting, and reissuing Hubbard's words continued into the 1930's. It kept the Roycroft printing plant going, and William H. Wise & Company (which handled the marketing) claimed over a million copies combined sale for the ultimate paste-up job—*The Note Book of Elbert Hubbard,* and its companion reader, *The Scrap Book of Elbert Hubbard.*

Most of this public performance took place after Hubbard was forty-four. Up to the time he was about thirty-six, his life had been outwardly unremarkable. His father was a country doctor; and Elbert, as the only surviving son in a family of five children, had grown up with chores to do, a district-school education, and with the Baptist Church nominally in charge of his soul. In his teens he became a drummer for a soap manufacturer. He prospered, married, had children, and rose to a partnership in a rapidly expanding firm. In 1892, he sold out his share in the business, for reasons which were clear to few people, perhaps not entirely so to Hubbard himself. From this time on, his life was swept into that semipublic search for identity. He began to shed the roles and the selves that made up his visible existence, and reflected the expectations of his family, friends, and neighbors. He moved out into a fast-running tide, social and personal. It was to be quite a voyage.

Dr. Silas Hubbard
about 1881

Juliana Frances Hubbard
about 1881

2

Family

THE YEAR 1856 was a difficult one in the lives of Elbert Hubbard's parents.
The previous fall, they had left friends, relatives, and a promising medical
practice in Buffalo to ride the day coaches to Bloomington. It wasn't covered-
wagon westering, but it was a sufficiently long and precarious move for Dr.
Silas Hubbard, his young wife, their frail, hunchbacked son Charlie, and
two-year-old Hannah Frances. Bloomington was settled country, but it was
raw and new, with successive dust, mud, and the biting prairie blizzards.
In the ramshackle house where they spent their first winter, the wind came
under the door in gusts that lifted and shook the carpet. And Juliana Frances
Hubbard was pregnant again.

In Buffalo, the Hubbards had lived in a two-story brick house. The
doctor had worn kid gloves and a high silk hat, and carried a gold-headed
cane. A mahogany table with a china dish for the calling cards of visitors
had stood in the entry. No one in Bloomington brought calling cards, so the
table now supported the family Bible, and the cane, the kid gloves, and the
hat were put away. A Bloomington cousin of Dr. Silas had encouraged them
to make the move. But they found there were more doctors in Bloomington
than the town could support, and the competitive battle for patients had
little trace of Eastern gentility.

It was a hard time. But in the spring they found a better place to live,
and in June, Elbert Green Hubbard was born. A year later, the family
moved a few miles north to the village of Hudson. There was no doctor in
Hudson, and the town's Baptists were organizing a new church. The Hubbards settled on a small farm on the edge of the village—soon given up for

a house across from the new Baptist Church. Here the doctor and his wife were to live for forty-three years.

Dr. Silas Hubbard came of a solidly Yankee line dating back to a George Hubbard who had come to Massachusetts from England early in the seventeenth century. Silas was the youngest of nine surviving children, born in 1821 when his mother was forty-nine. His father died two years later (singing "Am I a Soldier of the Cross?" on his deathbed). After seven years of trying to carry on the farm in Chautauqua County, the widow sold out and moved to Buffalo to be near her grown children. The oldest son, Elias, undertook to see to the schooling of the young ones, Solomon and Silas. They were sent to a Methodist boarding school at Lima, and Silas prepared for college at the Academy at East Aurora (a coincidence, as things turned out). In 1838, he went to Allegheny College at Meadville, Pennsylvania.

There is one letter from Silas in the record from his Meadville days. Writing to Solomon, he acknowledges that he is "well and doing as well as any other fool of my size," and expresses a proper familial devotion: "My mind often wanders home & I think about you & all the folks every day, about the kind actions of you & them, especially of my obligation to Brother Elias. These meditations never cease to interest me very much." Solomon had apparently been urging the study of human nature, and Silas replies, "I study it every day, Phrenologically, for I have found that great and important information can be found in that science." Finally, Silas gets to a principal reason for writing: "I have put off mentioning one thing until nearly the close of this letter, not because it is of less importance nor that by putting it off until the last will help the matter is plain, but I am again obliged to have recourse to Brother Elias's kindness & I wish you would represent to him that I need $10 (ten) dollars to pay my tuition. I would be very grateful if you would send it in your next letter. *I will be as prudent as I know how.*"

With this out of the way, the letter relaxes a little, with a glance at student high jinks of 1839. "The faculty are not so strict here as they in Lima. . . . They never expell except in extreme cases. The President even took great delight in seeing the boys take eather before the collage the other day. There were about 20 students took it & all manner of capers you might well imagine were performed." The letter goes on to refer to older brother Justus who had been having troubles and "bore his affliction with Christian fortitude. It is a wise thing to make our affliction as light as possible by resignation if it cannot be helped. If there are rewards in another world & if afflictions in this life are counted as an expiation, there is no doubt that he will get to heaven. Tell him & all the folks that I am glad to hear from them as often as I can. I am occasionally afflicted with the tooth ache like the rest of you."

College days for Silas were something other than carefree luxury. He sometimes walked to nearby towns to lecture on phrenology, closing the evening with head readings, and with a collection which might or might not buy him a meal. In 1842 he got his medical diploma at Castleton, Vermont, and, perforce, walked back to Buffalo. Here he opened an office and waited for patients. They were slow to come, but among them were the parents of Juliana Frances Read.

"Frank" was a lively, healthy girl of fourteen. She had been born in New York City and had come to Buffalo by Erie canalboat when she was three. Her father, though his family had lived in Philadelphia since Franklin's time, looked very Irish, and had the personality to match. When he visited the Hubbards in Illinois as an old man, the children were strictly ordered not to let slip the information that there was a saloon in the town. Grandpa's merry ways were a puzzle to his grandchildren. Elbert's sister Mary recalls that "When he saw us, a long way off, he took off his wide-brimmed straw hat and *whooped,* which startled us, for it was not the solemn, heavy-hatted way in which grandfathers usually arrived." And he embarrassed them dreadfully on Christmas by dancing them around the tree, singing, "I wish you a Merry Christmas, and a Happy New Year. With your pockets full of money and a belly full of beer." (Two taboo words in one sentence.) Grandmother Read, on the other hand, had been "an austere Puritan, pious, intolerant, and a shrewd business woman."

Frank was an irrepressible youngster, frightening her schoolmates by eating the supposedly poisonous "love apples," and annoying the pompous father of one of her girl friends by getting the giggles at the table. (This father was a Baptist elder, and raised objections to Frank's becoming a church member when she was sixteen because he thought her too worldly. This same elder was the great-grandfather of Harry Emerson Fosdick; in her old age, Mother Hubbard had her own, unshakable convictions about the personality of the great-grandson.) All her life, Elbert's mother was both Irish and Puritan (her daughter Mary said she was "a creature of moods which varied from profound melancholy to excitable gayety"), and more than a little of this mixture passed on to her son.

When Dr. Silas began his professional calls on the Read family, he once had occasion to reprove Juliana Frances for throwing snowballs with, and at, the boys of the neighborhood. A few years later, she taught school at the Indian Reservation south of the city. Since the doctor had patients in the same area, he often invited the girl to share his buggy when she was going back to work after a weekend at home. On one such trip he proposed marriage; and, in 1849, when Silas was twenty-eight and Frank was twenty, they were joined together in matrimony. The match had been approved, even urged, by the bride's mother, but it was a marriage of respect rather than love for Frank. This was considered neither remarkable nor tragic. Marriage was woman's proper destiny. A good marriage was justified by its fruits and its transcending of the merely personal. If the doctor's wedding gift to his bride (a locket on a gold chain, enshrining his picture and a lock of his hair) seems today a little chill and patronizing, it probably accurately symbolized his side of the contract. As a professional man of parts and sobriety, he was committing himself—as much of himself as was committable—to a permanent union.

For her part, the bride has been raised in piety and obedience. She had never danced, played cards, or been inside a theatre, and her Calvinist training had stressed the strength to bear and forbear, to carry the cross of duty and affliction, and to accept the Lord's will. It was not a lighthearted agenda, and it seems—even for its time—a rather grim confine for a young girl who was "gay, witty, sensitive, and quick tempered." But there were compensations, too, in the strength and dignity that such a life style could bring forth.

Dr. Silas had kept his relations with God a private matter, and never joined the Methodist Church of his upbringing (not even for Brother Elias). But as a married man, he gave in to the urgings of his new wife and her pastor and was baptized by the Reverend Henry Kirk Green, of the Niagara Square Baptist Church. (Juliana Frances had been baptized by a Reverend Elbert Clarke, and the third Hubbard child was to be named Elbert Green Hubbard. Years later, the pious origin of Hubbard's given names was considered a very funny joke.) Once he had made this move, Silas seems to have accepted the bleak dicta of Calvinism without fussing about them and to have maintained them all his life. Mary remembered that whenever Silas and Solomon (who was an Arminian, with less stringent beliefs about God's grace) visited each other, "though they may have been separated for twenty years, they resumed their arguments on these beliefs within fifteen minutes after a reunion . . . pounding their knees and shaking their fists at each other, as they hotly discussed God's plan for our salvation."

The Hubbards' first child was Charlie, who was to twist his spine permanently in a fall before the Hubbards left Buffalo. In 1853 the first daughter (Hannah Frances, known, like her mother, as Frank, and later to be Mrs. John D. Larkin) was born. Their mother studied landscape painting between babies, and the doctor took an active part in the founding of the Buffalo Medical School, and contributed to the professional journals. Just what caused this tentatively established family to leave Buffalo for the prairies is not clear. Mary ascribes it to "the blood of pioneers" in her father's veins; that, and urging from the visiting cousin from Bloomington. Neither the other Hubbards of Silas's family, nor Silas himself after this one move, seem to have had any urge to wander. The move seems particularly out of character for Silas. It was certainly not for wider moneymaking opportunities—Silas could never be brought to collect from his patients, and he left a city practice for a country subsistence. It might have been a forlorn hope of health for Charlie, away from the city and the long, snowbound winters—though southern Illinois doesn't seem that much healthier. Possibly some sharp family crisis precipitated the move, but there is no evidence for further speculation.

Those early years in Illinois were not easy. There were plenty of patients, but they were scattered over six or seven townships, and many did not pay in cash (but in firewood, pork and beef at butchering time, oats and hay for the Hubbard cow and horses, and corn and garden truck in season—sometimes a daughter came to the Hubbards for a few weeks to work out a bill for which there was no money). There were no drugstores, and the doctor was his own pharmacist, often assembling his own and the neighbors' children to assist in a pill-rolling ceremony. In the summer he covered his rounds in a two-wheeled gig. In the winter he wrapped himself in furs and rode horseback, often coming home with sleet-covered beard and eyebrows. Like other country doctors, he set bones and amputated limbs, pulled teeth and delivered babies. All without benefit of X rays, lab tests, or anesthetics. His wife went with him when there was need, to nurse the very ill, swaddle the new babies, and lay out the dead.

Those were difficult years for Mother Hubbard, too. Two years after Elbert's birth she lost premature twin boys, and nearly died herself. When Elbert was three and a half, his nine-year-old brother Charlie died. Crippled since his fall in Buffalo, Charlie's life had been that of an invalid child: an indoor life, frequently sick and in pain, knitting and crocheting and making baskets on his good days, or reading the sermons and theological commentaries that made up much of the family library, always sustained and cherished by his mother, who was "wild with grief" when he died.

Charlie's only recorded reaction to Elbert was that the noisy, bumptious baby made him tired. At the funeral, seated beside his mother, little Bertie kept mumbling to himself. When his mother leaned over to hear what sad wisdom he was absorbing from the ceremony, she found he was repeating to himself all he could remember of "Pop Goes the Weasel." His mother kept Charlie's slippers and gloves among her special keepsakes for the rest of her life. Mary Hubbard has written that he was "the most precious of her children."

A second girl was born a year later and named Anna Mirenda. When Bertie saw the baby, he said, "Oh, Ma, isn't she just a little daisy?" and no one in the family called her anything but Daisy thereafter. Before the next daughter (Mary) was born, in 1864, the doctor had tried to enlist as a surgeon in the Union Army, but had been turned down because of varicose veins. It was a great disappointment to Silas, hardly that to his wife, who was pregnant with Mary.

Silas was a strong Union man, and wrote Solomon that "so far as I am concerned there is no occasion for me to cry 'Peace, peace' so long as there is an armed rebel in the land. . . . I think the Lord loves this nation yet and that He is only chastising it for its good." Silas had once sat through a malpractice case in the Bloomington courthouse, listening to a lawyer named Abraham Lincoln conduct the defense. Many of the Hubbards' Bloomington friends knew the Lincolns well, and Mother Hubbard had heard much women's gossip about Mary Todd Lincoln, "her temper, her extravagance, and her erratic ways." When Lincoln was killed, the Hubbard sitting room was filled with mourning neighbors and quiet, wondering children. The doctor rode a handcar to Bloomington, hoping that the report was false, but found the courthouse yard "filled with silent, weeping throngs."

The Civil War and its aftermath made up a large part of the early memories of both Elbert and Mary. Most men, including their father, wore the blue Army overcoats, with their red flannel linings and brass buttons. New graves, new tombstones with military credentials, were in every cemetery, and "every family cherished quaint daguerreotypes and tintypes of brave, dead, young soldiers, proud in their uniforms." The Hubbard house was constantly full of "gaunt and bearded men in uniform, some invalids, some drunkards and broken by vice," who needed the doctor's help with their pension applications.

In 1868, when Elbert was twelve, the last girl was born, and named Honor. This completed the family constellation. An older sister and three younger ones. A crotchety and abstracted father. An emotionally volatile mother, whose favorite child was the dead Charlie.

3

Boyhood

SOUTHERN ILLINOIS has a violent climate. During summer thunderstorms, Mother Hubbard would hold the children to her on a featherbed placed in the middle of the sitting-room floor. Sometimes there were long droughts, and when the rains did come they were often cloudbursts—one such left the Hubbard yard dotted with tiny, living fish. In the fall and winter, winds shook the houses and bent the trees. Little Frankie was sometimes chased down the road by tumbleweeds, which she was sure were alive.

The area was a mixture of peoples. From England and Scotland, from New England and upstate New York, from the deep South and the border states, the Hubbards' neighbors and the doctor's patients were a sampling of classes and cultures. (To the doctor's family there was one top-drawer category—the "good pay" patient.) A group of poor whites from Money Creek supplied Mary with an authentic bogeyman—a large, stubble-faced man who called her his "gal" and was always vowing to steal her away. He frightened her into fainting on the attic stairs once. She hid from his visits after that, but she must have told Bert about the experience because a similar type turns up in several places in the mature Elbert's writing—always loud, bewhiskered, brutal, and named "Mudsock."

In the Hubbard household, the days generally began with the doctor's ablutions. He gave himself a rubdown with a "flesh brush," followed by buckets of cold well water. Throughout the operation he prayed aloud for guidance and grace, for himself and his family, calling the roll by name as he directed divine attention to individual needs and shortcomings. The doctor's days were busy and often interrupted. Called from the table, he would embarrass the children by asking a second blessing on the food when he returned. Family prayers were usually limited to the visits of the Baptist preachers because, as Mary says, her father's "methods were sketchy, often leaving us on our knees when he was hunting for his hat."

The district school was a two-room frame building, next to the village graveyard. Lessons were suspended for all funerals, and the children became experts on burying technique and the mores of public mourning. The schoolrooms were typical of hundreds. "The seats and desks were of unpainted pine, carved liberally with many initials, and the ceiling was adorned with a great number of spit balls. The heat came from a big stove in the center of the room which alternately froze and roasted us, and the air was aromatic of slates washed in spittle, dirty, thumb-marked books, chalk, smoke, unwashed clothes and bodies and the dust of ages."

The three "R's" and very little more made up the curriculum. The McGuffey *Readers,* with their piledriver inculcation of the moral virtues, were standard fare in the Midwest. Spelldowns were weekly sporting events. (Bert went down early; Daisy was a champion.) "Speaking pieces" was a public agony for most of the children, including Bert. Mathematics was workaday computation, and the physical sciences were almost nonexistent. There was a little geography, usually consisting of the memorizing of boundaries, capitals, and rivers (often as rhymed chants, voiced by the whole school, since maps were rare). Physiology might be touched on incidentally in warnings against alcohol and tobacco. This was all.

By the time Mary graduated to "the big room," her brother was one of the big boys. (The teacher kept, and used, a hickory stick to maintain his authority over these big boys.) After school, the big boys "rastled"—a "cause of great agony" to Mary, who was convinced that Bert "would be killed by those awful boys." He seems to have held his own, and to have growled at Mary for her tearful interference, though once, when the big boys were playing catch with a kitten and Mary was weeping about it, Bert intercepted the kitten, handed it to Mary, and told her to "skeedaddle" with it.

Nearly thirty years later, Hubbard summed up this part of his boyhood in his *Little Journey to the Home of Daniel Webster:*

Those were splendid days, tinged with no trace of blue, when I attended the district-school, wearing trousers buttoned to a calico waist. I had ambitions then —I was sure that some day I could spell down the school, propound a problem in fractions that would puzzle the teacher, and play checkers in a way that would cause my name to be known throughout the entire township.

The only indication of things to come in Mary's memories of her brother's schooling is that he "annoyed his teachers . . . occasionally by roaring inappropriately when his too-responsive sense of humor was tickled."

For the children, public schooling and the Protestant Church were parts of the same process—to turn young ones into god-fearing grownups as quickly as possible. This was the standard pattern. As Mark Sullivan saw it, "in every section of America, education started as a religious conception, was regarded as a part of religion almost as much as baptism . . . sole purpose to enable children to read the Bible." And of the two, the Church was the more powerful and pervasive influence. Mary Hubbard was one of those who felt sin and damnation as personal realities. She tells of the fiercely competitive revivals that Baptists and Methodists conducted every winter, early in the new year. The village children were excused from school, assembled in the churches, and "told that we were all sinners in the sight of God, and that the time had come when we must repent and seek conversion. An emotional appeal was made, and we all began crying. Our parents were called upon to pray, which they did one after another, and my heart grew hard and bitter for I felt that we had been trapped and that our parents were aiding and abetting the ministers to make us unhappy . . . we were called upon to say something about the state of our souls. Most of the children . . . asked for prayers in the glib language of their elders, but my lips were sealed and I could only shake my head. . . . I was set down as an incorrigible child, and when the last sermon was preached on the text, The harvest is past, and ye are not saved, I was sure they meant me. . . ."

Children were given full exposure to the Sunday sermons "dealing largely with the doctrines of the church, with salvation, hell fire, and the judgment." As Ingersoll put it, "every little brain becomes a menagerie filled with wild beasts from hell." Mary was especially susceptible to "passages describing the Judgment Day . . . the scenes of Gabriel coming in the clouds of Heaven, the blast of his trumpet, the separation of the sheep from the goats, and the awful sentence to the left hand of the throne of God." She "became obsessed," and kept watching the sky, "my heart beating wildly and my face pallid if there were some strange arrangement or color of clouds. The shriek of the railway whistle in the night would wake me to a numb terror, the taste of brass in my mouth."

Elbert underwent the same treatment and pressures, but he seems not to have taken it as hard as Mary (she had to be led out of church when such a sunny and joyful hymn as "Hark, from the tombs a doleful sound" was announced). Bert went through "Mrs. Coy's Bible Class" of boys, and he excelled in a popular parlor game of Bible questions and answers (though

Silas was the family champion), but, "Some fundamental honesty in his nature made him resist conversion as it was represented to him, and he respectfully refused salvation, season after season." In spite of her earlier resistance, Mary joined the Church when she was twelve, and "was baptized in the icy waters of Six Mile Creek on a snowy February day, while the congregation sang on the banks, 'Oh, happy day that fixed my choice.'" But Elbert was never converted. Mary gives no indication that he openly rebelled, but he was the only holdout in his Bible class—"a seeming impossibility, considering his training and uprightness." But there it was, and the "ministers sorrowfully shook their heads." What he felt about the whole thing turned up frequently in print twenty to forty years later. One good sample is in the *Philistine* for October 1908. "The entire intent of the evangelist is to kill in the man his sense of self-reliance—to destroy his self-confidence—to make him think less of himself. . . . When you make a man doubt himself you injure him. The evangelist assumes that man is born a failure—a damned, despicable, and lost thing—a derelict on the tide of eternity, drifting straight to hell. In law what a man does in terrorum is not valid, but in theology that is the only thing which counts."

The ferment of science, evolution, and "the higher criticism" was soon to be at work in the cities, and immigration was bringing people of strange customs and faiths to the prairies. But in towns like Hudson there was very little life or being outside of the Baptist and Methodist churches. Theology was the principal substance of intellectual life for a great many people, and the Hudson schoolchildren sometimes battled with sticks and stones in gangs of Baptists and Methodists.

As in most middle-class families, the Hubbard family Bible was an elaborately bound and illustrated volume, standing in massive dignity on its own table. Its violent chromos fascinated and awed the children. The illustration on the page for family births had been erased, and Mary wondered if it might have pictured the mystery of childbirth. It was only after she was grown that she learned that her mother had expunged the picture because it showed an infant being sprinkled instead of immersed.

For the Hubbards, the church was "the center of all our social life," and it maintained watchful discipline over personal conduct at all ages. Though the Baptists "took a righteous pride in having no man-made creeds, . . . they venerated something vaguely known as Baptist Usage upon which Mother was an authority." The Church trials "seemed very terrible" to Mary. In spite of his Calvinism, "Father usually voted 'Nay' when it was put to vote to withdraw fellowship from the guilty one. I was torn between sympathy for the sinner and shame for my father because he would not act with the popular majority." Dr. Silas was once indignantly ordered from the house of a neighbor when he diagnosed pregnancy in an unmarried daughter. He was vindicated by subsequent events, but he took no pleasure in it, and was again in the minority when the Church expelled the wretched sinner. Those Church trials are not easy to imagine today, when much of the business of the Protestant Church is the easy-does-it assuagement of the anxieties of a hedonistic generation. Seventy years ago, the Church not only brandished a very vivid hell in the hereafter; it could, and did, punish violations of the mores with the immediate hell of social isolation.

But young Bert's life was not all hellfire. He had chores to do and wild countryside to explore when he could escape. He later rhapsodized about his boyhood:

I knew all the forest trees, all wild animals thereabout, every kind of fish, frog, fowl or bird that swam, ran or flew. I knew every kind of grain or vegetable. . . . I knew the different breeds of cattle, horses, sheep and swine.

I could teach wild cows to stand while being milked, break horses to saddle or harness; could sow, plow and reap, knew the mysteries of applebutter, pumpkin pie, pickled beef, smoked side-meat, and could make lye at a leach and formulate soft soap.

That is to say, I was a bright, strong, active country boy who had been brought up to help his father and mother get a living for a large family.

I was not so densely ignorant—don't feel sorry for country boys: God is often on their side.

Horses were a lifelong passion with Hubbard. The first twelve dollars he saved went for a horse, and he seems to have never been without one thereafter. Though there is some fantasy in his yarns about his youth, he probably had to stretch very little in a passage such as this: "At the tender age of six, Mozart was giving concerts and astonishing Europe with his subtle skill. At a like age I could catch a horse in the pasture by baiting him with a nubbin, climb his back, and without saddle or bridle drive him wherever I list by the judicious use of a tattered hat. Of course I took pains to mount only a horse that had arrived at years of discretion, matronly brood mares or rundown plough horses, but this is only proof of my practical turn of mind."

Baseball, of an informal yarn-ball and barrel-stave kind, was another lasting Hubbard passion. Playing ball often interfered with his boyhood chores; even in his business days he carried a softball on his trips on the

chance of an occasional game of catch. At least once he organized an
impromptu game of "one ol' cat" among passersby on a Manhattan vacant
lot while he was waiting for a train. And ball games were to be a constant
diversion of Roycroft life.

There were other sports for the young Hubbards. There were no
television sets, no radios, no comic books, no jukeboxes, no hot rods, no
movies; there were only people. And their games took a lot of activity and
ingenuity. Taffy pulls, bobsledding, sleighride parties, " 'Clap in and clap
out,' 'Going to Jerusalem,' 'Happy's the Miller that lives in the mill,' and
'Blind Man's Buff,' boisterous, happy, romping games." Also "Forfeits,"
which was apt to lead into kissing games. Quieter sports were checkers, the
"Bible" game, or dominoes (cards and dancing were strictly taboo, but
dominoes and kissing games acceptable). The only deck of cards that Mary
remembers seeing in the house was being put in the stove by her mother
(with the tongs).

Silas took the children to the circus sometimes, but only to the
menagerie and selected sideshows, the performance itself being considered
wicked. This was a common distinction. In *The Damnation of Theron Ware,*
Harold Frederic tells of the fine line drawn between "ladies in tights on
horseback" and "cages full of deeply educational animals," and mentions
"painful episodes, connected with members who took their children 'just to
see the animals,' and were convicted of having also watched the Rose Queen
of the Arena, in her unequalled flying leap through eight hoops, with an
ardent and unashamed eye."

Reading was limited by the Baptist taboo on novels, but there were
the *Baptist Standard,* the *Weekly Pantagraph,* and later *The Youth's Companion.* In addition to the doctor's medical books (which the children in-
vestigated on the sly), the household contained such standard items as
Belcher's *History of Religious Denominations,* a life of Washington, Mat-
thew Henry's *Commentaries,* Josephus, *The Pilgrim's Progress,* and *Robinson Crusoe.* There were also bound volumes of the *Western Literary
Messenger,* and the family kept scrapbooks of stories, poems, and pictures.

On a typical winter evening, Silas might be reading aloud (to himself)
from the *Commentaries.* Mother Hubbard would be knitting, or darning
socks, while daughter Frank did crocheting or tatting. Elbert would be
"growling and puffing over his arithmetic." When the little girls, playing
with their dolls on the carpet, got into squabbles, the doctor would address
his wife, "Mother Hubbard, *won't* you make those children behave?" Her
standard admonishment to the girls was "Let *dogs* delight to bark and bite!"

If neighbors dropped in, the men slumped in their chairs and talked weather, politics, and religion, while the women knitted and gossiped and the children passed apples, cider, and doughnuts.

In the good weather, picnics on the Mackinaw River were organized, with wagons and carriages loaded with people, babies, baskets of fried chicken, hams, rolls, pies and cakes, jellies and pickles. Swimming (with old clothes as bathing suits) might be undertaken, or hook-and-line fishing, or searching the river gravel for Indian arrowheads. Bert and Silas hunted for quail, prairie chickens, snipe, ducks, or wild turkeys. The little girls mourned over the victims and buried the uneatable remains in their pet cemetery.

Mother Hubbard made as much as she could of Christmas for the children. When she had been a girl, any frivolous celebration of the day had been frowned on as popery, and it was still not the custom for parents to exchange presents or for children to give to parents. A stocking for each child, with such rarities as an orange, candy sticks, and nuts, with rag dolls for the girls and a pocket knife or knitted mittens for Bert, was enough to make the day miraculous. Visiting and entertaining were the order of the day. Mothers and daughters were busy in the kitchen all morning. There were horses to unhitch and stable. There were gossip and talk, and finally there was the dinner. Often there was no room at the table for the children, and they waited in the bedroom for their turn. "We tried on all the bonnets and wraps . . . mauled the babies, and peeked at intervals to see if the meal was finished. We . . . shook our fists at the slow diners and called them under our breath 'Greedy Pigs,' but at last our turn came."

In the spring, the wood stove was moved out of the sitting room and the rag carpet was taken up for its seasonal beating on a clothesline in the yard. Silas always took this occasion to suggest that, really, floors should be bare, with a few throw rugs that could be shaken out as they needed it. His wife always disposed of this "preposterous theory" by asking, "What would people think of us?"

Silas said and did what made sense to him, and that was reason enough. Like many other such men, he was considered an eccentric, and was a constant subject of mimicry for the village children. On his horseback rounds in the winter, the doctor would pray aloud, talk to himself, and flap his arms to keep his circulation moving. When he was questioning a patient, or absorbed in a discussion, he would rub his hands together and repeat "Ah, yes, just so, just so, just so." Mary and the other girls were dreadfully embarrassed by the amusement their father caused, and Mary could be sent "into angry tears" by her friends saying "Just so, just so," or by her school-mates bouncing in their seats and flapping their arms when her father rode by. Mary "early vowed that when I married, it would be to a man so exactly like every other man that nobody would ever take any notice of him whatsoever."

As has been noted, Silas was usually on the losing side of mercy and forgiveness in the Church trials. There were other ways in which he walked with God in his own way. Sometimes he worshiped with the Methodists or with the Dunkards and their sacramental foot-washing. When he was called upon to pray in public, he quietly repeated the Lord's Prayer. This could put quite a damper on a revival of shouting Methodists.

Silas's passion for phrenology had been partially domesticated by making it into a parlor game. He would be blindfolded and set to reading heads at parties and Church sociables. Even so, he got out of hand at times, as on the occasion "when he thought he had the most detestable and conceited young man of the town under his hands and proceeded to tell his faults, but upon being unbandaged, met the coldly reproachful eyes of the Baptist preacher." In his bachelor days, Silas had "discovered two new bumps, and had a plate made picturing the human skull, adding his own discoveries to Dr. Fowler's and he had his map copyrighted, and ordered such preposterous quantities that he used them for book plates the rest of his life." In middle life, Silas became a partisan of the germ theory of disease, and would go on and on about it. Mary remembers seeing a "young farmer sweat under his prolonged demonstration, and other doctors smile with tolerant amusement." The rest of the family would team up "to keep the conversation away from bacteria on social occasions." There were those who thought that "too much learning had made him mad." He also insisted on wholesale vaccinations when there was a smallpox scare.

According to Mary, her father's eccentricities "were an unmixed joy to Elbert, who did not suffer our embarrassment. He delighted in father's queer ways . . ." Elbert's "delight" was probably more complex than his sister realized. In his years as a pundit, the medical profession was to be second only to the clergy as a target for ridicule (often with a doctor saying "just so, just so"). But it was assumed, while Bert was a boy in district school, that he would grow up to "read" with his father and become a doctor himself.

There is nothing in the record to indicate that the young Bert had any great interest in either medical books or any other kind of book. He wanted to be a farmer. He slept on a roped bed in the attic and shared his space with the flour and meal barrels, the bunches of drying boneset, pennyroyal, tansy, and hops, the bags of dried apples and peaches, and the boxes of old clothing and candle molds. He had a money box, the same one in which he saved coins for his first horse. Some of the items in Bert's room were more special. A box under his bed contained the doctor's collection of human bones (Bert used them to frighten his playmates). The Hubbard family was custodian of the Church's baptismal robes, which hung in their black majesty along one side of his bed. The children surreptitiously played "Baptizin' " with the robes, and cracked their shins on the strips of lead that were sewn into the hems. (Immersion has its own techniques for maintaining the proprieties.)

When he was about thirteen, Bert went briefly into business for himself. He invested some of the contents of his money box in a mail-order home product called "Glutina." After proper mixing, boiling down, and processing, it was supposed to produce a miraculous adhesive, easily packaged in the handsome green wrappers that came with the kit, and sold to housewives for several times the original investment. Bert enlisted his sisters in the manufacturing, and together they made a fine mess of the Hubbard kitchen. The product turned out to be unusable, unsalable, and practically indestructible. The experience was not a happy one, but possibly it taught him something about which side of a mail-order transaction is apt to be more rewarding.

A year or so later, Bert and his mother carried out a much more successful business operation. The Hubbard house was intolerably small for the growing family and the medical practice. They had no money, but they had the unpaid accounts in Silas's ledgers. Since the doctor himself absolutely refused to dun his patients, Bert and Mother Hubbard set out to collect the makings of an enlarged house (labor and materials, mostly) from the patients in arrears. This took a lot of time and negotiating, but they carried it through, and the Hubbards finally had enough bedrooms, and an office for Silas.

This, his regular chores, school, and his hiring out as a farmhand, seem to have been the solid realities of Bert's early adolescence. Mary remembers him as "a happy contented boy" who "really loved to work, for he had abounding health and unlimited energy." This was not light work, either, and it had its quota of chapped hands, stone bruises, and chilblains. He often fell asleep over his schoolbooks in the evenings, and sometimes he went sleepwalking when he was overtired. He had an enormous appetite, and his mother sometimes fed him full before the family went out to a dinner party so that he wouldn't embarrass her with his bottomless capacity.

Bert's father presented him with a copy of Gray's *Anatomy* after he left school. According to Mary, he tried to read medicine, but before he got through his first volume he threw the book across the room. He was going to be a farmer, not, most emphatically, a doctor. But an unexpected visit at about this time turned the sixteen-year-old in an entirely different direction.

In the spring of 1872, the Hubbards were visited by Justus Weller, a nephew of Silas. His wife was Mary Larkin. Her brother John was "Uncle Jet's" partner in the making and selling of soap, with a factory in Chicago. Uncle Jet seems to have been quite a "card," with a beard and a silk hat, "full of pranks and fun." By a coincidence, he arrived on the day the Hubbards were doing their annual soapmaking. The leached-out lye from the winter's wood ashes, and the carefully saved fats, were boiled up into bar and soft soap. This all-day family job was combined with a cleanup of the grounds, and made a sort of spring festival. But the custom was dying out in the Midwest (and by so doing was to make the fortunes of men like Uncle Jet). The Weller-Larkin-Hubbard families began a "visiting" association leading to the marriage of John Larkin and Elbert's oldest sister. Elbert himself made quite a hit with Uncle Jet, and was offered a job as a salesman. He painted the family spring wagon in bright colors, with "J. Weller & Company—Practical Soaps" prominently displayed, and shortly picked up his first consignment of the commodity that was to dominate his working life for over twenty years.

"IS HE SINCERE?"

Drawn by W. W. DENSLOW

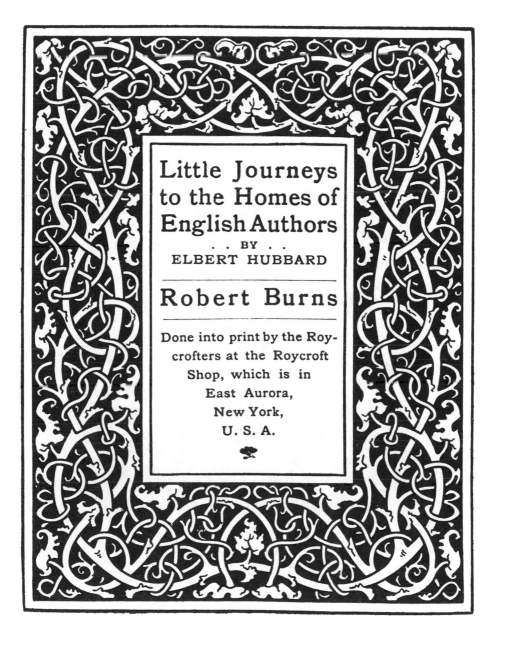

Little Journeys to the Homes of English Authors

. . BY . .
ELBERT HUBBARD

Robert Burns

Done into print by the Roy-
crofters at the Roycroft
Shop, which is in
East Aurora,
New York,
U. S. A.

The title page (exact size) of one of the *Little Journeys* books.
The decorative design varied from title to title. The cover
was either brown or gray paper with a quite simple typographical
layout, printed in two colors. The layouts and the colors varied
from title to title.

Elbert Hubbard,
soap salesman extraordinary,
about 1884, age twenty-eight

4

Success Story

FOR THE next three years Elbert saturated large areas of the Midwest with Weller's Practical Soaps. The method was a simple one: towns were canvassed door to door, and a twenty-pound box of soap was left for trial wherever the housewife was agreeable. After the town was covered, the rounds were repeated and the soap either collected for or tossed back in the wagon. By that fall, Elbert had covered Normal, Bloomington, and Peoria successfully, and the Hubbards' spring wagon was retired from the operation —trains and hired teams being used from then on.

From Peoria, Bert wrote home: "DEAR MA, Your letter was duly rec'd & I was glad to hear that they had commenced the barn and that the colt was no worse. I have been to three political meetings here—heard Gov. O. P. Morton of Indiana speak—he is a Grant man & a very good speaker, then U.S. Senator Thos. A. Hendricks, a very eloquent speaker, but a rascal in principle, and Lieut. Gov. John L. Beverage of this state. I thought I had better go for it is only *once in a lifetime* I would have a chance to hear such men." The letter continues with sightseeing details, and assures his mother that he attended Baptist services, ". . . a very nice church & it is well furnished, *the floor is carpeted,* and *the seats are cushioned.*" The sixteen-year-old closes, "Yours affectionately. E. G. HUBBARD."

Uncle Jet's visit had broadened the world for the other Hubbards, too. Daisy had gone to St. Louis with her new-found uncle and had written home daily of the marvels of travel and city life. Mary and her mother spent two weeks in Chicago that were equally memorable, even though it was only a year after the great fire. Mother Hubbard could not be persuaded to enter a theatre, though a few years later she allowed herself to be taken to see Jo Jefferson as Rip Van Winkle. She was "so carried away and fairly intoxicated by it that when she came home she rehearsed it until we too could see Rip and the goblins. She did not see many plays in her lifetime, but a few good ones . . . were as wine in her veins."

Elbert had another Hudson boy with him as a helper on the Peoria trip. The boys returned in "brightly colored pea-jackets which they wore to the Saturday evening Lyceum in the schoolhouse, making them the envy of all the other fellows, and making pea-jackets stylish in our town for some time to come." As he covered more distant states, Elbert wrote often to his mother and his sisters, usually enclosing money in his letters to his mother. If he wrote to his father, it is not recorded. In May of 1874, he was home for the wedding of his sister Frank to John Larkin. By now he was considered "a commercial traveller . . . . not a mere soap slinger, and his clothes were fashionably cut and very elegant." By this time, too, "he had a sweetheart in every town, and their pictures came back in his letters for our praise or disapproval, usually the latter, for we were terribly jealous. . . ."

Maybe he wouldn't be a farmer. He was discovering that he could handle people as well as horses and that the world was a larger and more interesting place than McLean County. He was young, handsome, and, as Mary said, "had a rare gift for making friends." Also, he "acknowledged relationship with every one who claimed a Hubbard connection. Knowing nothing of genealogy, and caring less, he got us into difficulties which to this day I cannot correct."

Elbert was a good salesman and a hard worker. Years later, Felix Shay quoted "a Western businessman" who had been in one of Elbert's sales crews as a boy. Each morning at six, "Hubbard would kick his feet up towards the ceiling to get rid of the covers, and land feet foremost in the middle of the room with one bound. In the next five seconds the covers were off me! . . . I never saw such energy . . ." And Hubbard was to rhapsodize in the *Philistine* about those days. "I used to have a new vest every trip, and it was a miracle in chromatics that spoke for itself. But this was nothing to my smile—my smile was contagious, also infectious, as well as fetching. When I arrived in a town everybody smiled, and invited others to smile. The man who dealt out White Rock splits smiled, the 'bus-driver glowed, the babies cooed, the dogs barked, and the dining-room girls giggled, when I came to town. I scattered smiles, lilac-tinted stories, patchouli persiflage, good cheer, and small silver change all over the route. . . . And I sold the goods . . ."

As a drummer, Elbert was on hearty and joshing terms with his customers, fellow salesmen, and all the draymen, freight agents, hotel clerks, and waitresses that the day's work brought into his orbit. But he seems never to have adopted the traveling man's more customary ways of filling up his spare time. Alcohol, tobacco, and cards he never touched. He attended political meetings, explored the countryside, visited state fairs and museums, collected souvenirs and curiosities for the folks back home. He called on onetime Hudson neighbors and relatives, including his mother's only brother, in Oshkosh—the Read family eccentric, who was a Democrat and a Unitarian. He also acquired the reading habit. He broke the Baptist taboo on novels by sending home cheap copies of Dickens and George Eliot. (It was finally decided that the girls might read them, except on Sundays.) And Emerson seemed to have been written especially for him. Though he was to grow a little patronizing toward Emerson later, as a boy on the road he read those "neon-sign sentences" with an intensity that he seldom equaled later. Elbert's reading during these years seems to have had a strong sense of purpose and he did a lot of note-taking and cross-indexing. But apparently he felt little identification with others who were doing the same sort of thing. He made a patronizing reference in the *Philistine* in 1898 to "the Library Loafer . . . wherever the Free Library exists there does he gather . . . reads and reads and reads and mouses . . . yet no one ever calleth him learned . . . harmless and would be unobjectionable were it not for the fact that he never bathes and smells like a Jury Room."

Sometime during this period, Bert attended a lecture by Bob Ingersoll. It is not recorded whether this was one of the lectures in which the Colonel invited the Almighty to deliver a rebuttal by striking him dead on the platform, but both the content and the flavor of this experience greatly impressed young Elbert. Words and ideas could be exciting, too, and another way to move people. Ingersoll became one of his first heroes.

We tend to think of Elbert Hubbard's nineteenth-century prairie world as one of very limited literacy. Which it was. But in an important sense, the word—spoken or written—had an urgent reality then that we seldom feel today. The whole common life of the time—to put first things first—was based on the one Book. The Bible was infallibly and literally God's Word, and it supplied everyday practical guidance, solace in times of trouble, assurance of the cosmic importance of life, moral absolutes, history, poetry, philosophy, and prophecy. Much of the intellectual content of life was in finding the proper application of the Word to the immediate situation, and in contending with those who mistook its plain meaning.

Words were not cheap in this society, and those who could manipulate them
into magical combinations had power and respect.

In 1907, Hubbard reminisced about the "argufying" of his boyhood
and its theological framework. "Forty years ago no town in America was
free from joint debates where the disputants would argue six days and nights
together concerning vicarious salvation, baptism, regeneration, justification
and the condition of unbaptized infants after death. Debates of this kind
set the entire populace by the ears, and at post-office, tavern, grocery, family
table . . . reasons nice and subtleties hairsplitting were passed back and
forth." The Protestant mixture of righteousness and individual judgment
made for some lively times. As Hubbard said, "These eyes have seen a
camp-meeting where singletrees, neck-yokes, harness-tugs and scalding
water augmented arguments concerning foreordination as taught by John
Calvin and freewill as defined by John Knox." There was a nice balance
in the situation. Absolute certainty was there, on every parlor table. No one
need feel adrift in a world without authority. At the same time, there were
denominations and subdenominations offering a great range of interpreta-
tion. And the man who found none that fitted his scheme of things often
went out and started his own.

At the time Hubbard left district school, the tools and the techniques
used in the Hubbard home and the prairie economy were pretty much the
same as they had been a generation earlier (except for sewing machines
and kerosene lamps). But by the time he pulled out of the soap business
(1893), telephones, incandescent lamps, typewriters, adding machines, and
linotypes were coming into use in the cities, and reaper-binders, corn cutters,
and combines were moving onto the farms. (That great symbolic device, the
cash register, was still to come, but soon.) The generations that followed
were to equate these wonders with science. But a good case can be made
for the notion that science—as a radically new way of looking at the world
—came into American society during Hubbard's boyhood, and came as a
set of ideas with practically no tangible referents. For most people, it was
Lyell, Darwin, Spencer, Huxley, and their popularizers who shattered the
total authority of the Book and opened the doors of men's minds for all
that was to follow. If the Creation had not taken place literally as set forth
in Genesis, what man could henceforth know what was real and what was
right? Heresies beyond numbering or imagining would arise; how could
they be refuted? These were the sorts of questions that were asked. Those
who tried to answer them usually invoked the name of science.

The theory of evolution was an overwhelming event, and it was so perceived. It was a mortal threat and it was a great liberation. The interesting thing is that the popular battle over it was verbal and abstract. The tangible evidence for the doctrine was something no one but an occasional naturalist could put his hands on. The mechanisms involved in the evolutionary process were highly inferential and speculative. For many people— perhaps for most Americans in the latter part of the nineteenth century —science came into their lives, not as an objective, communicable method of exploring reality, but as a great abstract idea—that there might *be* a reality other than God's Word.

Orthodoxy was simple and literal. Much of the excitement stirred up by Ingersoll, and his enormous influence on popular thinking, came from his examining the Bible on the same everyday level. People might be emotionally outraged by his threat to faith, but no great mental effort was required to follow his amiable speculations. Take a look at Adam, he would invite his audience, lonesome in that garden and wandering about "as if waiting for a train." The Lord finds this restless creature is getting on his nerves, so He decides to make a woman. But He had used up all the "nothing" out of which He had made the world, so He borrows a "cutlet" from Adam. "Imagine the Lord God with a bone in his hand with which to start a woman, trying to make up his mind whether to make a blond or brunette!" As for the end product, he observed gallantly, "Considering the amount of material used, I look upon it as the most successful job ever performed." Ingersoll's treatment of other biblical puzzles was similar. "What a picture! Jonah sitting on the edge of the lower jaw, wiping the perspiration and the gastric juice from his anxious face, and vainly looking through the open mouth for signs of land!"

Ingersoll also had stock answers for all the stock questions. When a woman presented him with a bouquet, and asked, "Colonel, who made these beautiful flowers?" he was right on cue with "The same, my dear young lady, that made the poison ivy and the asp." And when challenged to suggest a single improvement in Creation, he said, "I would make good health catching instead of disease." Unlike the later Elbert Hubbard, Ingersoll seldom bit off more intellectual substance than he could chew, and his gospel was serene and free of complexities. "Happiness is the only good," he trumpeted. "Demons and gods exist only in the imagination . . . knowledge consists in ascertaining the laws of nature, and wisdom is the science of happiness."

In 1875, the Larkin-Weller partnership came to an end (Uncle Justus and Mary Larkin Weller were being divorced). An agreement was reached

under which Weller was to keep the Midwest territory; John Larkin was
to set up a new plant in Buffalo, and have all the sales territory east of
Detroit. Both ex-partners wanted to keep Bert, but he decided—with the
help of a family conference—to go to Buffalo with John Larkin. He wrote
later of his arrival in Buffalo: "I was nineteen years of age, and had been
earning my own living since I was twelve. [Fifteen is more like it.] In my
own mind I was considerable of a man. I wore spring bottom pants, a
dinky derby, a warm vest and had a fairly good opinion of myself." In
addition to the sporty clothes, the physical Hubbard stood five feet nine
and a half inches, and he made the most of his height by an upright carriage
and an easy, graceful walk. His face was handsome and open, with a broad
forehead, a strong nose, and luminous dark eyes. In his later years he was
sometimes mistaken for William Jennings Bryan.

After he became a public figure, Hubbard claimed a fantastic variety
of working experience between the time he left district school and the time
he moved to Buffalo. During this period of a little over four years, if we
were to take his remarks at face value, room would have to be found for
"went westward like the course of empire and became a cowboy; tired of this
and went to Chicago; worked in a printing office; peddled soap from house
to house; shoved lumber on the docks; read all the books I could find; wrote
letters back to country papers and became a reporter; next got a job as
travelling salesman; taught in a district school; read Emerson, Carlyle and
Macaulay; worked in a soap factory; read Shakespeare and committed most
of *Hamlet* to memory with an eye to the stage." There is more of this
passage, but this is enough to show the pattern. He made other claims about
these years ("When I was in the drug business . . ." "When I was a country
doctor . . ." ". . . that summer I was seventeen and herded cattle on the
Kansas prairie"). In his obituary, the New York *Times* credited him with
"farmer, laborer, shepherd, miner, printer, . . . reporter, . . . dramatic critic."
The Encyclopedia Americana gave him four years as a journalist in Chicago
(1872–1876). During this period, the only verifiable item—the one thing
he did for his living from about 1872 to 1875—was to peddle soap. There
is no evidence to justify such mythology as ". . . when I did the Book, Music,
Art & Dramatic Page on the Chicago 'Times.'"

One of Hubbard's associates commented in 1915: "Hubbard was rather
late in coming to literature—he had stopped on the way to pick up an
honest fortune. . . . No reproach in this surely, but the Fra was needlessly
concerned to suppress it, preoccupied always with the construction of a
fitting legend, and he at times romanced extravagantly in order to hide

the real facts of his early career. He used to tell a yarn of his life as a cowboy in the west, which part he dressed very well, having furnished himself with a regular broncho buster's outfit to make the thing good. I remember I once laughed at this when he had given a rehearsal for my special benefit in his barn at East Aurora. He never quite forgave me."

The reliability of Hubbard's autobiographical remarks is a question that pops up every time we touch a Hubbard statement about himself. Two somewhat opposing compulsions are noticeable: to display himself, to boast and confess; and to befog the record with inaccuracy, fantasy, and invention. We find innumerable bits of self-revelation, in the most unlikely contexts, but they have to be measured against the part he was playing at the moment. This pattern has elements of defensiveness, of mischievous humor, and of a need both to draw others to him and to keep himself untouchable. In his occupational mythmaking, there was probably a need to compensate for the shallowness of his background, which he felt more acutely than he ever admitted. When the English *Who's Who* asked for his pedigree, he listed "the University of Hard Knocks" under education (along with "Hon. degree of M.A. from Tufts College," which was true, and "LL.D from the Auditorium Annex, Chicago," which was pure spoof), and he was tickled when his concoction was printed verbatim.

The new plant was set up in Buffalo, and Elbert took to the road again. He had eastern cities to cover now, and he managed a full sightseer's tour of Washington, and a stay in Philadelphia during the Centennial Exposition. This was the exposition—with its Corliss engine in Machinery Hall—that caused Henry Adams to speculate at length on the relative powers of a Virgin and a Dynamo to evoke civilizations. This period of American history (while Elbert was cultivating a moustache and sporting his spring-bottom pants) was one of public corruption, business depression, and misgivings about the future. But little of it seemed to touch Hubbard. He was young, the time when "to seize the world by the tail and snap its head off seems both easy and desirable." His visit to Washington was in the final, disgraced days of the Grant administration. Breadlines were forming in many cities, commercial failures were at a new high, and the countryside swarmed with tramps. But Elbert was impressed by the stuffed animals and birds in the Smithsonian and the live plants in the White House conservatory. He also saw Congress in session and "had the pleasure of looking down on the bald head of a man I sold a box of soap to in Dayton, Ohio—Gen. Garfield."

Mary was sent to Buffalo for a year's stay with the Larkins when she was thirteen. She had a violent attack of homesickness at first, but recovered to enjoy the change and the city. Bert took her to Niagara Falls, where they "ran the gauntlet of yelling, importuning hackmen, who followed us to Prospect Point, Bert hectoring them all the time with the most absurd remarks, so personal that I was embarrassed for them." On the Suspension Bridge, "Bert terrified me by pretending he was going to push a workman . . . into the green, swift treacherous current beneath."

Between a father who embarrassed her by being himself, and a brother who got the same effect by putting on an act, Mary had an emotional girlhood. At this time she was desperately anxious that Bert not be ashamed of his country sister, and it bothered her that "he did not take the pains to charm me that he did with other older girls." There seem to have been a lot of these. "Young girls and old maids simpered and preened for him, and he left in his wake a trail of broken hearts. 'Why are girls so silly?' I would ask, and I would grow furious with him when he rolled his black eyes at them and twirled his little new moustache, and sat close to them, listening sympathetically to their tender confidences, making each one think for the time being that she was the object of his most devoted interest."

In addition to this genteel lady-killing, Bert was still experimenting with his physical image, "wearing only the best and most stylish clothes. If pants were wide, his were the widest and flappiest, if they were tight, his legs looked like sausages. . . . His cravats were wide and stiff with brocade, . . . his collars were high and widely pointed, and his cuffs were long and proudly linked. Silk underwear was not too good, his hosiery was an artistic display—his shoes were sharply pointed or roundly blunted according to the mode, and were kept immaculate and shining."

Bert continued to be a prolific letter writer. A few of these letters have survived, and they show the development of the playful prose and the "preachment" form that were to be typical of his later output. Two of his parody sermons found their way into print anonymously. One took as its text, "Jack and Jill went up the hill." Much of it was adolescent word foolery, but some of it could easily have come out of the *Philistine* later:

Jill was the loved and loving wife of that most noble character, Jack. . . . What a beautiful lesson of marital felicity is here taught. Jill was not one of those short-haired women who like that society which has for its motto the pernicious adage, "If singleness is bliss, 'tis folly to be wives," sometimes marry because they cannot support themselves, and who always endeavor to usurp authority over their husbands. No, bless the Lord! She was not one of these. Had she been, the text would have read, "Jill and Jack." . . .

But, my beloved hearers, what did Jack and Jill do? *"They went."* Listen while I read it again. . . . Jack and Jill went. They did not say, "We guess we will go," "We will go if it doesn't rain," "We will think about it," no postponement on account of the inclemency of the weather, they waited not for a more convenient season, no dalliance, no wavering, no procrastination, no hesitation, but firm determination, perfect faith! They decided to go and *went.* . . .

What did they go for? A pitcher of beer? *No.* A flask of Jersey Lightning? *No.* What then? "A pail of water." Glorious temperance lesson! . . . Why did they not go *down* the hill instead of *up?* Because, up on the hillside the water springs pure and clear, while in the valley below is the sluggish stream where the snake wriggleth, the crawfish crawfisheth, and the miasma miasmates.

These sermons were not written for his parents (who considered them irreverent or worse) but for Daisy, who was then teaching high school in Morris, Illinois, and for Mary, who was soon to be doing the same thing. Besides their foolery, the sermons give more than hints of what their author had on his mind. In this one, he seemed strongly concerned to strike a blow for masculine authority. "'Jack and Jill,' blessed words! How they point that bundle of inconsistencies, that alphabet of hieroglyphics, that unguessable riddle, that angelic idiosyncrasy which we call woman, to her proper place. . . ."

And sure enough, in 1881, the same year as the Jack and Jill sermon, Elbert married Bertha Crawford, of Normal, Illinois. The Bloomington *Leader* announced the "elegant wedding event," and noted that "the presents were expensive and elegant." Elbert had met Bertha when the Weller soap crew was working downstate Illinois. She was pretty and feminine. She dabbled with watercolors, and she potted her garden flowers and brought them indoors for the winter—there would be over four hundred of them on the Hubbard premises in 1885. She was to bear Hubbard three sons and a daughter and to get on his nerves dreadfully before the marriage came to an end.

The Hubbards settled in Buffalo, and their first son, Elbert II, was born there. They lived in the city for nearly three years. There is very little in the record about these years. They were filled with work at the soap factory and with domesticity. But the reading and the self-exploring were still going on. One letter to Mary showed a considerable progress in its style and form over the "sermons":

In the days of yore when I was an innocent soap peddler, I approached a large house in Boston, on which the legend of "Hubbard" was engraved on a big brass plate covered with verdigris. A rather portly woman in a grease-covered gown (a Mother Hubbard gown) came to the door and I made known my errand and told her my name. Because her name was Hubbard, I forgot her greasy gown, and forgave her for having her shoes unbuttoned. We talked about what nice smart people all the Hubbards were and she was so well pleased with me that she gave me an order for a dozen crates of soap, and as her pocket book was upstairs, she requested me to call Saturday . . . for the money. I called but she was not in, so I called Monday but she had lost her pocket book. Tuesday she had just given her last X to a superannuated preacher, so I called again, Bill called, Dan ditto, and suffice it to say that I am 12 crates of soap poorer than I would have been had I not had the pleasure of meeting this Mrs. H . . . . . . and would often be saved the pain of having Dan or Bill remind me of what nice smart people the Hubbards are.

Apparently Mary had written that teaching was hard, unappreciated work, and her brother replied with a lengthy preachment on the text of "the seeming ingratitude of your scholars." It went on and on, with a quotation from Andrew Johnson, and this: ". . . the lack of being grateful is not ingratitude—it is thoughtlessness. The gratitude may come—it will come later. . . . to make my meaning plainer, it is the Why-for-ness of the As-it-were, as we say in Concord. . . . The actions of children are spontaneous; they act from impulse on the instant not thinking who will be annoyed. . . . Bertie this morning put his mamma's new stockings in the 'chamber mug' and in a very orderly manner placed the cover on. When she came in . . . and searched for the missing stockings he assisted in the hunt, by looking under chairs, tables, and lounge in the most innocent manner possible. . . ."

In 1884, Hubbard bought a large house with an acre of land in East Aurora. The village was on the railroad about sixteen miles southwest of Buffalo. At that time it was a center for the breeding and training of trotting horses. After his day at the soap works, Elbert often exercised trotters on the private tracks or the roads around the town. He did some speculative buying and selling of trotters himself. The time was to come when Hubbard and his East Aurora neighbors would have some very nasty things to say about each other. But when he wrote to Mary about the new house, he was Domestic Man and Good Citizen without qualification. "The neighbors began to call before we got up our cook stove, and have kept it up ever since, nice people too, well dressed, modest, own their own homes, and have an interest in maintaining an orderly well-kept village."

J. D. Larkin & Co. moved into a new factory in 1885, and the junior partner was a very busy man. A second son, named Ralph, was born. Mary announced her engagement to the principal of the Gardner, Illinois, high school where she was teaching and her brother wrote his congratulations. "Marry forsooth! Odds bodkins, and why not? Ain't you good looking and confectionary and capable of making some good man happy? . . . As the financier of a large manufacturing concern, let me say that the move you have made is a good one. To have an interest in the principal is well. To have the principal *and* interest is better. . . ." It was to be a long engagement, since Mary's intended left teaching to go to law school in Chicago, and they were not married until 1888. Shortly before the wedding, Mary received a long letter from Elbert ("You have been expecting to receive advice from your brother, and as I would never have disappointment cross your pathway, here goes.") There were probably echoes of his own domestic frustrations in the Emersonian harangue that followed:

Men and women look forward with joyous anticipation to having a *home* but how oft and many a time do they consider a home (a divine word) to consist of a convenient and beautiful house in an aristocratic location—nicely furnished —pianos, velvet carpets, carved furniture, hot and cold water, marble washbowls, pictures, rich and rare books and bric-a-brac. . . . *But this is not a home*—these things by themselves are the veriest trash . . . Yet since the days when Mother Eve complained of having nothing to wear . . . men and women have staked their soul's happiness on the possession of *things*. Now *things* are valuable only just so far as you can utilize them, and no more. *Things* must be a means and never an end. . . . immense numbers of women in cities have homes for mere show . . . he or she who sets too much store on the possession of things forfeits health, moral and physical, as well as spiritual. The *end* of life is the formation of character; some say that we are laying here the foundations of a structure that is eternal. "Build thee more stately mansions, Oh my soul!"

Mary was a little bored, since "I was marrying a penniless, briefless, caseless young lawyer and our immediate concern was just the bread and butter we needed for our subsistence." She decided she was being used as a practice audience, since it was a little hard to see herself as the subject of "Let us not think too much about the hardwood polished floors, and when you write me, tire me not with the accounts of your tapestries, and servants but tell me that you are trying to be an example of industry and economy, heroic cheerfulness and fidelity to duty to mankind. . . . Tell me that your house is the home of 'plain living and high thinking.' "

Shortly after this letter, Hubbard sold his prize trotting horse for "near a thousand dollars," and explained the transaction in a letter to his mother.

"I must confess that I have a weakness for horses, but I do not crave the
notoriety that comes with association of one's name with that of the stud
horse (pardon). This fact is causing me to go out of the horse business. . . .
Fast horses, I admire, but sad to relate, if one keeps a fast horse, fast men
with tight pants, and diamond pins are continually forcing their companion-
ship on one. They ask, 'What will you take?' and are ever anxious to treat
and be treated (for the man who treats is always insulted if he is not
treated) so *hic jacet speedy equine,* or words to that effect. . . ."A third son,
named Sanford, was born to the Hubbards in 1888.

Larkin soap sales were expanding rapidly, with much of the business
coming from direct-mail sales to consumers. An early offer featured a "combination box of 'Sweet Home Soap' . . . laundry soap, toilet soap, a washing
compound and a bottle of perfume—all for $6." Soon the pitch moved to
a "guess-what" premium in each box—anything from a pair of collar buttons
to a picture of one of the Presidents. Sales continued to climb, and the
premiums became more and more elegant—"six solid silver teaspoons"
(German silver, *not* so stated). But the real supergimmick came in 1888.
This was a Club Plan by which a Larkin customer could order soap in
wholesale quantities, peddle it to friends and neighbors, and earn really
impressive premiums—a silk-shaded Chautauqua Lamp, a Chautauqua Oil
Heater, a Chautauqua Desk.

In the stodgy and straightforward merchandising of the time, such
razzle-dazzle was rare. And it paid. It was to make John Larkin a millionaire
—and incidentally to enable the Larkin Company to commission one of
Frank Lloyd Wright's early masterpieces for its administration building.
But these glories were to take place without Elbert Hubbard's participation.
He had been traveling a main road, clearly marked, and Success was just
ahead. But he was about to turn off the highway.

5

Rebirth

SOMETIME DURING 1889, Hubbard met a young woman named Alice Moore, then teaching in the East Aurora High School. Born in Wales, near East Aurora, Alice had grown up in small-town orthodoxy very much like that of Hudson, Illinois. Like Hubbard, she had discovered books and ideas for herself (in her teens, she had quite a battle with her family over her right to read the notorious and "unwomanly" George Eliot). It cannot have been easy, but Alice had gone to Normal School and established herself as a teacher—one of the very few independent callings open to women. Unlike Hubbard, Alice knew exactly who she was. She was a New Woman, and there was little ambivalence in her defiance of respectable society when matters of enlightened principle were at stake. There was a quality of dedication and intensity in Alice, and a radiance. William Marion Reedy was later to refer to her as "a woman with a fine, clear eye, a most pleasing smile, and a carriage that bespeaks celerity of thought and action."

The impact of Alice Moore on Elbert Hubbard was not to become public knowledge for about thirteen years, but the story emerges unmistakably from the things he did and the things he wrote. In the things he wrote, the record is full of gaps, flashbacks, and evasive confessions. It was to be a long time before Hubbard could say, simply, that Alice had "caused me, at thirty-three years of age, to be born again." Before that, there were to be many hints. In the *Philistine* for July 1901, Hubbard was ostensibly telling of a lecture he had delivered in Philadelphia. "Suddenly my eyes looked straight into the eyes of a Personage. She was twenty-nine in June, I think, or thereabouts—rather tall, plain, but with a face that beamed intelligence, insight and good nature. She was not coy, affected nor abashed and she smiled the frankest kind of smile of welcome . . . I smiled back . . . It was all in an instant, but we had met, this fine, strong woman and I in a soul-embrace, and there was a perfect understanding between us." He went on to say that this exchange of smiles was all of the meeting; "have not seen her since, and do not know her name. Yet she will never forget me . . . And I can never forget her." The June birthday was authentic, and since it was not the kind of detail normally absorbed from such a meeting, we may take it as a private sort of teaser in this very public message.

There were to be many more of these public-private playings with revelation before the secrecy exploded. Alice Moore seems to have been Bertha's friend before she was Hubbard's. In 1899 the current *Little Journeys to the Homes of Eminent Painters* was discussing Rubens who, according to Hubbard, "had a wife of his own, to whom he was fondly attached; and this wife was also the close and trusted friend of the woman whose husband was off to the wars. . . . I give the facts just as they appear, having canvassed the whole subject, possibly a little more than was good for me." And a year later, Robert Burns served as the excuse for this: "Love is progressive—it hastens onward like the brooks hurrying to the sea. . . . The only kind of love that is blind and deaf is Platonic love. Platonic love hasn't the slightest idea where it is going, and so there are surprises and shocks in store for it. The other kind, with eyes wide open, is better. I know a man who has tried both."

Although there was some ordinary yearning by an overdomesticated and unappreciated husband in Hubbard's reaction to Alice Moore, this was only part of it. As those letters to his sisters show, there was a lot of show-off male in his thinking and writing. A feminine audience was something he had to have. Alice was something more—a woman with ideas of her own, who could provide a challenging feedback. We may speculate that, in effect, she listened approvingly to his dreams of a larger life than soap peddling, smiled acceptingly at his boyish vagaries, looking him in the eye, and asked, "What are you going to do about it?"

The answers were to be a while shaping up, but in 1890 Hubbard wrote a novel. He seems to have kept the whole thing a secret, then and later. (Almost a secret. He sent part of the manuscript to Ingersoll, who was intrigued, and offered to comment on the whole book.) It was published in 1891, titled *The Man: A Story of Today*. The putative author was one Aspasia Hobbs. There was quite a subtitle: "With Facts, Fancies and Faults Peculiarly Its Own; Containing Certain Truths Heretofore Unpublished

Concerning Right Relation of the Sexes, etc., etc." The publisher was J. S. Ogilvie of New York, who issued it as Number 47 of the paperbound "Sunnydale Series," issued monthly at thirty-five cents a copy, $3.00 per year, and entered as second-class matter. The inside front cover carried an ad for Van Houten's Cocoa; Beecham's Pills had the inside back.

It is curious that Hubbard never publicly acknowledged the book. By any standard of well-constructed fiction, it was pretty bad—but so were his other novels and stories. "How I Found My Brother" was even worse, and that one was his pride and joy. Possibly he was afraid of what the scholars and critics would do to it, since it had a story-within-a-story that purported to tell the real life history of William Shakespeare. But he was not diffident later about his "life" of another historical character, one John Brown. Probably he wrote it as a trial run for his dreamed-of life in Letters, and kept the basic facts—that he had done it, and that it had been published —stored away for his own reassurance. Once he had publicly launched his literary career, he seemed to have a built-in insulation against criticism, but he may have been much more vulnerable while he was still officially a soap-business executive.

The booklet is revealing. Aspasia Hobbs is "an old maid, aged 37," left a foundling on the Hobbs doorstep, her foster-father later going "bust." She is self-supporting, self respecting, and "homely and angular, and can pass along the street without a man turning to look at me." She works for "Hustler & Co.," manufacturers of glue, and their John Bilkson is not a sympathetic character. Aspasia is wiry; for five years she has been pounding a "caligraph," and she can "walk twenty miles a day, or ride a wheel, fifty." On one of her cycling tours in the country around Buffalo, Aspasia gets lost and a storm comes up. She is sheltered by The Man—who sounds like a housebroken Walt Whitman, full of wise saws and massive virtue. "I knew, down deep in my soul, that this man possessed a power and was in direct communication with a Something of which other men knew not."

Aspasia comes out weekends to visit The Man, who, it soon develops, is not only in touch with a special Something but is three hundred years old and has a Message for which Aspasia is to be the willing vehicle to mankind. As the Message unfolds, much of the philosophy with which Hubbard captivated a large portion of early-twentieth-century America is shown being developed.

Health is of the mind. ("Fear is the great disturber. It causes all physical ills.") Death is similarly a product of wrong thinking. ("Men die only when they are not fit to live.") Most of women's troubles come from being pampered. Women are the carriers of all human good, but old maids are apt to be better women than are wives. Lawyers are scoundrels, and misfortune is a blessing in disguise. Controversy and argument are death to truth. Messiahs are always crucified, and "to work for popular applause is to court death." Fresh air and positive thinking are essentials of health and wisdom. Among these general propositions are such small-scale wisdom as, "sensible people do not talk baby talk to children, nor do they talk down to people who they imagine ignorant."

The Man's principal secret has to do with making full use of the subconscious mind, and Shakespeare is the prototype of how this is to be done. Shakespeare was "not technically a scholar," and his achievement was "not to clip and measure and adjust . . . but only to cast asunder the gates of the human heart." Further, "no four walls of a college could have held him . . . only teacher was nature, his only need was freedom. Who gave him this?—*a woman!*" The woman was Harriette Bowenni, with whom William carried on quite a love affair before she learned that he was married to Anne Hathaway (who was "whimsical, ignorant, fault-finding, jealous" and a "slovenly housekeeper"). "Shakespeare should have been frank with this girl and told her his story at once." But the mischief was done and anyway she was the liberator of his creative powers. She, it seems, wrote the first twenty-six of the sonnets ("To Mr. W. H." means William Harriette). The Man, to give authentication to all this, is the natural son of William and Harriette.

Along about here, a raucous and bloodthirsty mob (representing Ignorance and the Fate of Messiahs) bursts into The Man's cabin. He and Aspasia are threatened with lynching and dragged to the lockup, from which they are ultimately freed by the bucolic wisdom of a judge. This final attempt to give action to the tale is a good deal more painful in the full text than in this summary. In all of Hubbard's fiction, the plots are fantastic and the characters are cardboard. They are there as background for the preachments, which are often eloquent. But both plot and characters are transparently revealing of their author. Almost every Hubbard novel, for instance, has an Alice figure front and center. The whole pattern suggests that the pretense of fiction may have fooled the author more than it was supposed to fool the public.

Alice's reactions to *The Man* are not in the record. Just possibly, her reactions might explain why Hubbard never acknowledged authorship. The description of Aspasia Hobbs did not make a romantic image, even for a New Woman. (Perhaps Hubbard had to make his heroine unattractive to quiet his own qualms about what he was heading toward.) And the book started with an "Open Letter" from Aspasia to "Martha Heath." It celebrated the acceptance of the book by the fifth publisher who saw it (". . . has written me that the story does not amount to much; in fact, that I have no literary style, but as the book is so out of the general run they concluded to accept it. . . ."), and then it said, "You say you dislike awfully to see those last five chapters in print, and so will I, my dear." Speculation aside, Alice Moore entered the Emerson College of Oratory, in Boston, in 1890. Whatever her further contribution might be to Elbert Hubbard's rebirth, the initiative was going to have to come from him.

A second "Open Letter" in the front matter of *The Man* was to John Bilkson of Hustler & Co. It was not a friendly letter, and concerned Aspasia's departure from the company. This may have been a trial run, too. Mary Hubbard Heath said of this period, "It was apparent throughout all of his correspondence that a struggle was going on." Toward the end of 1892 he burned his bridges. He arranged to sell out his interest in J. D. Larkin & Co., and he began taking Latin and Greek lessons from the Episcopal rector in East Aurora. A letter to his mother puts his case and is worth quoting in full:

MY DEAR MOTHER:

Next to the selection of my parents, I have completed the most important move of my life. In fact, my death can not be a matter of as much importance— or fraught with greater moment. So, that to you, above all others, I write it first—I have sloughed my commercial skin. That is to say, I have sold out my entire financial interest in the Soap Business. My last share was transferred today and the money is in the bank to my credit. Why have I gone and done this thing? Because, dear Mother, I have all the money I want and there is a better use I can make of my time.

That excellent man, S. Hubbard, M.D., and myself are probably the only men in the whole U.S. who have all the money they desire.

The next question is: What do I propose to do? I am going to Harvard College, and it is my intention to take a full four years' course. I also hope to spend a year in some university in Germany as well.

John and Frank look upon my plans as a mild form of insanity, but I am at peace with them and all the world besides. I have not paddled away from a sinking ship; the business here has never been more prosperous.

I have concluded that he who would excel in the realm of thought must not tarry in the domain of dollars. Another thing, I believe that he who would live long and well must live like a poor man, no matter what his income is. We must be warmed and fed, of course, but we must wait on ourselves and work with our hands a certain number of hours each day.

Many men want to lay up enough money to give their children a start. Money will do it all right, but it is on the down grade. If my boys can not get along without my financial aid, they can't with it.

I wish you and father would both write giving me your blessing to my new arrangement.

With much love, as ever

E. H.

No replies to this letter are in the record. Nor is there any indication of what Bertha thought of her husband's plans. During this pre-Harvard interim, Hubbard was working on several new literary projects, and this time he was not keeping them secret. The first book-length writing to carry Hubbard's name was a fictional sketch, called *One Day: A Tale of the Prairie,* which he completed at about this time. The story concerned a delicate girl-child in an Illinois farm family—poor, stupid, and devout. The father says of his conversion, "I've 'sperienced a change, an I don't keer a gol darn who knows it." The family does not encourage little Edie's queer, bookish ways. This "skylark in a crow's nest" (she is a foundling) is the family drudge—overworked, ridiculed, unappreciated. Her lout of a stepbrother gets all the breaks. Edie collapses from sunstroke and slips out of this life under the sadistic hell-brandishing of a country preacher (a Mudsock with a call).

As a story, the piece was not much. But it gave a detailed description of the house, bare and shadeless on the prairie, with its cracked-earth yard swarming with geese, chickens, and pigs. The parlor had haircloth chairs and sofa, a plaster-of-Paris cat and a fruit basket of the same material, a what-not, a picture album with pressed flowers and ceremonial views of friends and relations. The exact center of each wall bore a colored lithograph ("The Defenders of Our Country"—soldiers charging a hill, with officer waving a sword—and such as that). The family library was inventoried: "History of Woodford County; Romanism Exposed, or the Practices of the Convent Revealed; Thrilling Adventures Among the Early Settlers; One Hundred Reasons why Immersion is the Only Mode of Baptism; Watts on the Mind; Baxter's Saint's Rest; Pilgrim's Progress; The Horse and his Diseases, or Every Man his Own Veterinary; The Mother's Own Book, or Daily Food for Daily Helps."

The feeling behind the sketch was simple indignation at stupidity and provincial meanness. All that its author deemed intelligent and sensitive got ground into the mud by ignorance and bigotry. The sketch showed something of what Hubbard felt about his boyhood environment after he had gotten away from it, and it had some of the emotional essence of the "Revolt from the Village" that was to pervade much later American writing.

Hubbard had another book in mind at this time, but the only record of it is in another letter to his mother, dated January 5, 1893:

. . . On Monday I leave for Cambridge. . . . Some time ago I began writing a sociological history of the United States, and this plan has taken hold of me to a degree I can not describe. You hear of men taking up a plan, but in this case the plan has taken up me, and you need not fear I will sigh for the soap factory. . . . When the chicken is ready to leave the shell it has to go or *die,* and that is the kind of Plymouth Rock I am.

As to the History, . . . what we call History . . . concerns itself with the nobility who manage the affairs of state, not the common people—when the real fact is the people are the state, not the nobles; so I am writing a record of the events that have influenced the popular mind. In our day, Vincent [one of the founders of the Chautauqua movement] has moved the people more than Cleveland—Edison more than Blaine—Frances Willard more than Harrison. So you see, it is the *thinkers,* not the politicians, who change mankind.

Just what Hubbard expected to find at Harvard, and how he would use it in his new life, is not clear. The evidence suggests that he rushed into it with very little preparation or realistic anticipation. College education seems to have been, for him at that time, a symbol of that wide-ranging life of the mind which he craved, and a ticket of entry to the world of literature. And Harvard represented the best of college education.

In spite of his thirty-six years, his money in the bank, his family, and his successful business career, Elbert Hubbard arriving at Harvard in 1893 was really a very vulnerable country boy. Harvard is a place heavy with tradition, and impervious to upstart individuals with their own ideas of what is important. Scions of the New England aristocracy were there in force, as were the second generation of the newly rich. And Harvard, in the 1890's, was not exempt from what Mencken was later to call "the dull, hollow dignity of the pedants, who . . . were anaesthetic to the new literature coming to flower all around them." There was a phenomenon known as "Harvard indifference," and Jacob Riis quoted a recent graduate replying to a former teacher inquiring as to his plans, "Oh [yawn] really, do you know, Professor,

it does not seem to me that there is anything much that is worth while."
There was nothing indifferent about Hubbard's approach to the higher
learning, but he had all the background gaps and the lopsided enthusiasms
of the self-educated maverick, as well as the desperately touchy pride.

Quite probably, the leap in the dark that he was taking made him less
brash than at any other time of his life. His first letter to his mother from
Cambridge showed more gratitude for not having been hooted from the
Yard than any other emotion. "I meet and mix with the best here on a
perfect equality; at once I am at home and among my friends and brothers,
for who is my brother save him who thinks as I do? If there is any such
thing as taking advantage of a tenderfoot here, I have not seen it. On the
contrary . . . committees to greet all newcomers and assist them . . . one
of the questions they asked me was, 'What subject are you insane on?' Which
being interpreted means that if I happen to be a crank on Temperance,
Socialism, Religion, or any peculiar phase of thought, they would introduce
me to others similarly afflicted. . . . There are men among the students
fifty years old and over, so I am simply classed as one of the boys."

But his feeling of belonging was brief. Harvard found his preparation
inadequate, and declined to admit him. There is a small mystery here, only
partly explained by Alice Moore's being in Boston. Hubbard's family and
his biographers have taken his letters at face value and assumed that his
work at Harvard began in January of 1893 and ended when he decided
that the place had nothing to offer him. On February 20th he wrote his
sister Daisy a long letter: "Harvard is a great place, dear. I haven't joined
the football team yet, but if you see me in a few weeks wearing a very
stubby growth of No. 9 whiskers you will know that I passed 98 in my
Biology." He went on to a lot of foolery about the Harvard students being
made up of the Grinds, the Sports, and the Boys. ("The Grind is a queer
'un, wears fur cap winter and summer, glasses—pants to his shoe tops—
seedy black clothes—yellow and bony—he reads a book as he walks the
street, and when he bumps into you always apologizes in Attic Greek. The
Grind never smokes, never swears, never smiles—he has all the facts but
he loses a pile of fun. The Sport is the antipodes of the Grind. He has a
rich Pa, and loud check trousers . . .") And so on. But after a great deal in
this vein, the letter abruptly switched from its academic glow to this: "Yet,
Daisy, we will shed no tears for those who have missed a college training.
We overestimate the thing. Like wealth, how many use it wisely? 'A mon's a
mon for a' that.' 'How far will that project the soul on its lone way?'" And
in the middle of March he was back in East Aurora.

It has always been assumed that this was the end of Hubbard's Harvard

career. But in 1941, an inquisitive Harvard student dug into the records
and found that Elbert Hubbard entered the College as a special student
in September 1893 and withdrew in December 1893. Which gives us to
wonder about all this talk of being "one of the boys" the previous January.
Presumably, he hung around the campus until his impasse with the academic
bureaucracy became unarguable. The fascinating thing is that he felt he
had to keep up the pretense of being a student for the folks back home. That
he came back in September and enrolled seems to show the strength of his
original desire for a Harvard education. He was not typically a man who
took rebuffs and came back for more.

When he did return (taking English courses and an introductory course
in philosophy), he may have been spoiling for a fight. For the rest of his
life he was periodically to flare up with bitterness on the subject of college
education. Exactly what happened to him that fall is open to speculation,
but the general pattern seems clear from things that turn up in his writing.
The first of these was an essay in the *Philistine* for May 1896, called "By
Rule of Three." It was directed at Professors Barrett Wendell and Adams
Sherman Hill of the Harvard English Literature Department (especially
Wendell, who was a formidable figure in the world of letters). The title
came from Wendell's celebrated prescription of "clearness, force, and elegance" for the production of good writing. Hubbard's general complaint was
that, in Harvard's English teaching, "sympathy is made a weakling and
imagination rendered wingless. I have examined many compositions written
by Harvard students, and they average up about like the epistles of little
girls to Santa Claus. The students are all right but the conditions under
which they work are such that they are robbed of all spontaneity when they
attempt to express themselves."

And as for the "Rule of Three": "Clearness is never found in literature
of the first class. The great writer is only clear to himself or those as great
as he. The masterpieces of art are all cloud-capped. In all great literature
there is this large, airy impersonal independence. The Mountain does not
go to you. Ecclesiastes offers no premium to readers, Shakespeare makes no
appeal to club raisers, Emerson puts forth no hot endeavor for a million
subscribers; all these can do without you. All Holy Writ from Moses to
Whitman is mystical. I would have each man who feels that he has something to say express himself in his own way, without let, hindrance or
injunction from writers on rhetoric. . . . Clearness should be left to the
makers of directories, force to the auctioneer, and elegance to the young
man who presides at the button counter."

Later, the specific incident which lay behind all this was discussed in a piece called "Please Be Seated." Rather, the incident was reenacted in fantasy. "Some years ago one Prof. Jarrett Bendell of Harvard did himself the honor of reading one of my daily themes. . . . on being ushered into the Presence I stood first on one foot then on t'other, and rolled my hat in a vain hope of giving an impression of the humility which I did not feel. Finally the ass opened its mouth and spake: I was told that my work was totally lacking in *tout ensemble* . . . that I would never make a writer."

To which Hubbard replied, "I do not take my literary aspirations seriously—nor yours—it is just an attempt at expression, for all life is expression. So I pray you waive the advice . . . and criticize my theme. Prof. Dumbell was so shocked at my temerity that . . . his cheroot . . . slid down his shirt bosom, inside his vest. In an instant the Professor was dancing dervish steps all over the room. . . . I asked him if I should turn in an alarm, and he told me to go to hell. . . . At last the professor asked me to be seated . . . and we had a real nice little chat about this and that."

This seems clearly of the "what I should have told the bastard" type of daydream. But it probably shows substantially what happened to Hubbard at Harvard—he felt he was being patronized and belittled, and the mainspring of his ego distempered. But he had Emerson's "One of the benefits of a college education is to show the boy its little avail" to console himself with (and he used it, in multiple variations, over and over). More than this, he had come upon a new Great Idea during his first brief weeks in Cambridge, and it was one that gave him something of an agenda for some time to come. In February he had visited Concord, with a letter of introduction to the Misses Hosmer, and they had feasted him on reminiscences from the great days of transcendentalism. Emerson, Thoreau, Hawthorne, and the Alcotts had all been old friends and neighbors, and Hubbard was quite overcome by this close brush with greatness. He wrote of it to Daisy, enclosing "a sprig from the tall pine that rocks to and fro in the breeze over the grave of Emerson, whose resting place is marked only by a huge boulder on which the chisel has never left its mark. Nearby are the graves of Hawthorne and Thoreau."

The big new thing that he found in Concord was the idea for the *Little Journeys.* He would visit the stamping grounds of the great, browse around the scenes of their grandeur, and write essays. He could discuss their lives and their work; he could tell funny stories about his visit; he could simply set down what went through his mind as he stood at the tomb or sat in the historic chair in the coffeehouse. The form was a natural for Hubbard, and he was to write 170 of them before they trailed off into business-house plugs. All his life Hubbard rebounded quickly from his major frustrations into new, driving enterprises. It was one of his strengths, but it also left residues of fury and blindness that sometimes caught up with him later.

There were other projects simmering in his mind, and in March he wrote Daisy from East Aurora: "Have got the literary eczema in a mild way—it is a humor in the blood you know, and the external manifestation is only a token of a spiritual or inward state, as the prayer book would say. Have partitioned off a room in the attic and am trying to work off the ailment." The opus in process in the attic was called *Forbes of Harvard*. Its plot was so absurd that one wonders if Hubbard was deliberately parodying the dime novels. The first part of the book showed the extent to which he had committed his vulnerable self in his pilgrimage to Cambridge. This was apparent too in his later hatred of the academic world, but *Forbes* showed the raw hurt, and showed it in typical daydream form. The story is told in letters, and as it begins, Forbes has left Harvard and is making his broken, penniless way westward. He has galloping consumption, and he bravely makes light of his condition as he writes back East (though slipping in stiff-upper-lip references to his hemorrhages). His near-mortal illness, we soon learn, is the result of a collision during a boat race—Forbes having single-handedly rescued both crews from the icy Charles River. Other facts about his Harvard life make their modest entries. He has been financial and intellectual godfather to his whole dormitory (winning a thesis prize for another student who was too upset by his mother's death to write his own thesis), and he could floor any man in the dormitory "collar and elbow" (and do as much for the Professor of Psychology). Forbes was, incidentally, the tallest man at Harvard (six foot three).

There is a dear old hymn-singing mother in the background, worrying whether her boy will keep his faith in the infidelic atmosphere of the university. And there is a maiden aunt; a truly formidable character, who invades the sacred Harvard chapel, routs all opposition with her umbrella, and takes up a collection to succor the nobly perishing Forbes. With Aunt Marie pulling strings, Forbes gets to St. Louis and sets off for the life-renewing ruggedness of the Rockies (accompanied by "Gooseberry Jake" and "Rattlesnake Pete"). There is another burst of plot to conclude the book, but it is a composite of dime-novel tricks, and the personal reference is limited to its flavor (there can be few more noble, more put-upon, or more improbably triumphant characters in American fiction, including the dime novels). The pattern of the Harvard experience is padded out by references (in Fond Remembrance, alumni-reunion style) to professorial eccentricity.

One such is part of a plea for women at Harvard to raise the tone, and it describes a lecturer as "resting one foot in a seat; and in the pause that marked the exit of one thought and the coming of another, instead of scratching his head for inspiration as some of us do, he would scratch various portions of his anatomy as the notion struck him, and we would lay bets as to what part he would scratch next."

But the whole center section of the book consists of the love letters Forbes is writing to Miss Honor Harold back East. The heroine of *Forbes of Harvard* is younger and more toothsome than the heroine of *The Man,* but otherwise the resemblance to Aspasia Hobbs, and to Alice Moore, is close. For all of her embattled feminism, Alice Moore was an upright person, with a puritan background, and Forbes-Hubbard had a considerable selling job to do. For one thing, it seems clear that Alice insisted from the very beginning of her relationship with Elbert that Alice Moore and Feminism-as-a-capital-letter-Cause were one and inseparable. Neither she nor her Cause would tolerate much of the playful and patronizing treatment that Elbert had been accustomed to giving his sisters. One of the early chapters in *Forbes* reports a great campus debate on "Woman's Sphere"—full of biblical citations, many of them downright nasty aspersions on womanhood in its entirety. This, we may assume, didn't go over at all, and that spring Elbert was asking Daisy (married now, and a professional representative of the Women's Christian Temperance Union), "Can you refer me to anything valuable published on the subject of Equal Rights—is there anything worth the having printed on the subject, similar to what Funk and Wagnalls have on Temperance?"

Elbert never did come all the way over to Alice's feminism, but he seems to have come far enough to make the *Forbes* letters to Miss Honor Harold possible. Their message is clear enough.

We have been told that certain of our inclinations are base and allied to the animal, but all of our powers have their earthly and their spiritual expression. Where one begins and the other ends, I will not attempt to say; but it is very true that it is needful a man should be a good animal. . . .

Allow a pause for a reply, and then this:

Of course my creed says, "Happiness is not dependent on outward events," but bless you, child, my creed is not the thing I believe! I only hold it theoretically. My happiness cometh from Concord, dear—no matter what the theory says.

Another reply, perhaps, and another letter:

We must be loyal to what we now see is right, unmindful of all the vows taken in days gone by.

And this:

Most men live lives of blind drudgery, without deliberate aims. . . . Few live to know truth, enjoy beauty, and reach up to the Infinite by loving one, in order that this love of one may increase the capacity to love all. Let us do this, my lady, and we will make this love a stepping-stone to the higher life.

And finally:

With you, my dear one, I claim my inheritance and come into possession of my birthright. The only shadow that ever saddens me, is the thought that we may be separated. . . . Without you I am lost—lost.

There was something like frenzy in Hubbard's comings and goings in 1893 and 1894. Harvard in January, East Aurora in March, Boston again at the end of March, Chicago (where the World's Fair was going on, and Mary Hubbard Heath was living) in both May and June. Harvard again in September, East Aurora in November, Boston after that. Somewhere along here he worked for B. O. Flower's Arena Publishing Company in Boston. Arena published both *One Day* and *Forbes of Harvard,* and two essays by Hubbard appeared in the *Arena* (the magazine edited by Flower that later became a leader in the Bryan presidential campaign and the muckraking movement.) Hubbard's job here was in circulation-building, and his stay was brief. In the spring of 1894 he was back in East Aurora. But not for long; his project of a series of *Little Journeys* fitted in with an old urge to go abroad, and he was planning a trip to Ireland and England. In effect, Hubbard was a man with two wives at this time, and the situation contributed mightily to his restlessness. When he came to write a *Little Journey* on Henry Ward Beecher (1903), he remarked: "The worst about a double life is not its immorality—it is that the relationship makes the man a liar. The universe is not planned for duplicity—all the energy we have is needed in our business, and he who starts out on the pathway of untruth, finds himself treading upon brambles and nettles which close behind him and make return impossible."

He talked of paying for his European trip by writing his "impressions" for a syndicate of newspapers. But either the arrangement fell through or was never anything but a hope, and no more is heard of it. Before sailing from New York, he made the rounds of the book and magazine publishers, trying to find a sponsor for the *Little Journeys*. No one seems to have been even slightly interested.

In England, he traveled and hiked indefatigably and he crossed and recrossed the trails of the Wordsworths, Coleridge, De Quincy, Scott, George Eliot, Ruskin, Turner, Gladstone (he had a brief audience, along with other American tourists), Carlyle, and Dickens. He took a walking tour through Ireland. But the major event of the trip was unplanned—a visit to William Morris's establishment at Hammersmith and a meeting with the Old Man himself. Like many of Hubbard's face-to-face encounters with important people, the exchange with Morris seems to have been perfunctory. But Hubbard came away from the visit with ideas about fine book publishing, arts and crafts in home furnishing, and benevolent paternalism in industry that were to kick up a lot of dust.

Back once more in East Aurora, he was busy writing up the first *Little Journeys,* teaching salesmanship in a Buffalo night school, and working on a novel titled *No Enemy (but Himself).* As the title suggests, there was a theme of self-destruction in it. Along with much else. The central character is a bachelor of strong character and independent means who becomes a tramp for kicks. A homeless boy joins him in his wanderings. The boy, being loaded with virtue, wants to get a job and pay his way, but "His Whiskers" has to show him all the tricks of the hobo trade first. When this vein is played out, they go to New York, where the boy gets his job and exhibits all the destiny-drunk qualities of an Alger-book hero. Himself takes to the road again. Events get more and more scrambled and fantastic, but there is a difference from the love-will-triumph pattern of *Forbes of Harvard.* Things go badly. His Whiskers loses a leg in a railroad wreck. It develops that his dastardly lawyer has stolen all his money. He takes to drink. Jimmy, the noble boy, is suddenly revealed to have been an even nobler girl all along. She has troubles too; she goes blind. And finally, when she is about to marry the young preacher she has come to love, the hero walks the girl and himself off a dock and they sink without a trace.

There were a new ease and fluency in some of Hubbard's writing in this book (some of the dialogue was plausibly conversational, for instance). But the interesting thing was the note of catastrophe. Neither virtue nor money triumphed, and out of love came destruction. There is no need to strain for significance; the record shows that in this year Elbert Hubbard became the father of two daughters—Katherine, born to Bertha; Miriam, born to Alice—in September of 1894.

Every Knock is a Boost

Elbert Hubbard at the time
(around 1893, about age thirty-
seven) that he decided to sell out
his Larkin partnership. (Compare
this with the photograph below,
which was taken six years later.)

Hubbard about 1899,
age forty-three

6

Growing Pains

BY JANUARY of 1895, Elbert Hubbard had been free of his "commercial skin" for two years. Not very much had gone according to plan. The door to college had been slammed. Probably he had been too eager, too much in a hurry to prove himself as a literary man, too vulnerable to the raised eyebrows of Barrett Wendell and, above all, too defiantly on his own to submit to tutelage. But was college his only access to "the realm of thought"? Obviously, he didn't think so, and in the cultural climate of the time there was little reason to. A great shaking and stirring of the American mind was under way, but little of it centered in the colleges. And a man could still get a working grasp of the outlines of human knowledge by his own efforts.

He *had* become a published writer, and this was a large credit on the accounting of his two years of freedom. True, the publications had been marginal and their impact on the reading public nearly invisible, but his words and his name had been set in real type and repeatedly squeezed against real paper. And new ideas and words were crowding his mind faster than he could write them down. So much, at least, of his dream was taking shape. He was a writer—for whom and to what effect could work itself out.

It is doubtful whether Hubbard took the time or had the peace of mind to draw up any such balance sheet as is here suggested. If he had, the ledger page for his personal life would have been little more than a blotted mess. There is some evidence that he experimented with a variety of judgments on himself (including conventional *mea culpas,* as in *No Enemy:* "Once there was a splendid woman who loved me. . . . I was unworthy of her . . . I trod on her heart and wiped my feet on her honor"). But these seem to have been passing moods, and his momentum carried him through them.

53

He got more than a little help from Alice. Feminine and vulnerable as she had been, there was also steel in her makeup. She arranged for her baby to live with relatives and she gathered herself together and found a teaching position in Denver. There is no evidence of demands or reproaches. In the context of his time and his family background, Elbert Hubbard had become a sinner beyond mortal forgiving. He had to live with this knowledge. But, thanks to Alice, it was to be several years before he had to live with other people who shared this knowledge.

These years were to be active and eventful ones—so much so that the freedoms of his breakout from soap were soon to contract into new routines and obligations. He had had another fruitless spell of "cooling my heels in the outer offices of most of the famous editors of the time" when he returned from Europe. After he was back in East Aurora and had drafted the *Little Journeys* on George Eliot and John Ruskin, he had them printed up as pamphlets by the local Pendennis Press. Before he started marketing them, G. P. Putnam's Sons accepted *No Enemy,* and invited the author to pay them a visit. While he was there, he suggested that Mr. Putnam take a look at the newly printed pamphlets (though this house had previously rejected them in manuscript). The result was that Putnam undertook to publish twelve of the booklets—one a month for a year. The first one came out in the fall of 1894.

This contract with Putnam was Hubbard's first real acceptance by the world of polite letters. (His early novels had dropped into the void and been mercifully ignored.) The *Little Journeys* formula gave him a flexible, continuing program of reaching a large audience, and a form that was admirably suited to his talents. With this as a start, he might have moved into the main current of thought and writing (which, after all, had been the idea in the first place). But this is hindsight. Hubbard was still smarting over all that time he had spent "cooling his heels." And he had been repeatedly in and out of Cambridge and Boston, where revolt was forming up against the literary establishment. Ingalls Kimball and Herbert S. Stone were at Harvard, planning the first issue of the *Chap-Book,* which was to be the most prestigious of the little magazines. Walter Blackburn Harte, who was soon to join Hubbard in a short-lived business association, was one of the group around the *Arena.* Harte was to issue a little magazine, too: *The Fly Leaf,* "A Pamphlet Periodical of the New—The new man, new woman, new ideas, whimseys and things." A lot more was simmering in the 1890's than the literary establishment was interested in publishing. The little magazines were to relieve some of this frustration and, in their personal and iconoclastic way, to build audiences for all that urgent newness. The movement was called "a revolt against the commonplace, it aimed to overthrow the staid respectability of the larger magazines and to open to younger writers opportunities to be heard." Hubbard may have felt that this rebel group was where he belonged; they had rejection by the establishment in common, at least.

In any case, in June of 1895, the Pendennis Press rolled out 2,500 copies of Volume One, Number 1 of the *Philistine*. There were several other contributors, but the tone of the magazine came overwhelmingly from Hubbard's pieces. And he was out to do some mighty nose-thumbing and to settle accounts with the literary gatekeepers. "It is because we cannot say what we would in the periodicals," he announced, "we have made this book." And the scatterguns open up:

I shudder for Richard Watson Gilder, John Brisben Walker, E. Bok, and others of the Mutual Admiration Society style of periodical makers if they are to be believed to keep the company or read the lucubrations of the contributors to the dreary masses of illustrated inanities they edit.

Mr. Gilder dishes up monthly beautifully printed articles which nobody cares about, but which everybody buys, because *The Century* looks well on the library table.

Mr. Howells maunders weekly in a column called Life and Letters in Harper's journal of civilization. This Life and Letters reminds me of the Peterkins' famous picnic at Strawberry Nook. There weren't any strawberries and there wasn't any nook but there was a good place to tie the horses.

Mark Twain says he is writing Joan of Arc anonymously in *Harper's* because he is convinced if he signed it the people would insist the stuff was funny. Mr. Twain is worried unnecessarily. It has been a long time since any one insisted the matter he turns out so voluminously was or is funny.

When I see the little things men strive and cavil over and the great ones they disregard or ignore I know that the kingdom of Liliput was . . . a lesson from real life. And when I consider how they swarm like waterbugs and quarrel over the pronunciation of words and bicker with their neighbor . . . I think sensible people might be excused for weeping or even swearing. Little people these, say I, and I would wager a dollar to nothing that William Dean Howells is their prophet and that they venerate all his works.

And there was a sneer at one of the forerunners of what we now call "adult education." This one was ironic, since many people were soon to say much the same things about Hubbard. ". . . summer announcements of the Cattaraugus Reservation have been made. The shrewd Armenians who

run this concern know the public they have so successfully buncoed for so
many years. . . . They offer culture at so much a pound and sell tons of it.
Silly women and sillier men rush to their summer schools and listen to
lectures on topics they do not understand given by men who have but very
faint ideas of what they are talking about, and rush home again with their
brains utterly befogged. . . . Purveying culture by the gross ton is as sure
a way of becoming wealthy as is belonging to the Standard Oil Company."

Those first *Philistines* set one pattern that lasted a long time. Counterparts of a sort were abundant in the twenties and thirties in college-student
publications of the lampoon variety. If we subtract the art and the sex, the
campus cutup had the same flavor, same heavy-handed humor, same showoff
needling of the respectable and of duly constituted authority. Even the sex
had a pale preview in the *Philistine*—Hubbard strictures on several European novels (moral indignation with a built-in leer). In the *Philistine* for
February 1898, Hubbard quoted an alleged contemporary who did take
the *Phil* to be a student publication. ". . . a peculiar little periodical . . . As
a specimen of amateur journalism the *P* is quite interesting, showing a zeal
that is very commendable in the young. It is published at Aurora, New York,
by the students of Wells College, although this fact is not stated . . . as the
college authorities probably do not care to stand sponsor for it . . . wavers
between optimism and pessimism with all the crudeness of exuberant youth
. . . too lively to last long . . . editor shows . . . budding genius that rightly
directed should make his name known for good ere he is forty . . . may be
only the precocity that ripens early and rots . . . while it lasts is highly
amusing."

Hubbard himself said later of this first issue: "the success of the plan
[the monthly *Little Journeys*] suggested printing a pamphlet . . . telling
what we thought about things in general, and publishers and magazine
editors in particular. There was no intention at first of issuing more than one
number . . . but to get it through the mails at magazine rates we made up a
little subscription list and . . . the postmaster adjusted his brass-rimmed
spectacles, read the pamphlet, and decided it was surely second-class matter.
. . . We called it the Philistine because we were going after the Chosen
People in literature . . . The Smug and Snugly Ensconced denizens of Union
Square called me a Philistine, and I said, 'Yes, I am one if a Philistine is
something different from you!'"

So, although the publication of the *Little Journeys* was a first taste
of success in the larger literary world, it seems to have led Hubbard to
declare himself uncompromisingly on the outside of that world. Notably,

though, he didn't simply shrug and go his own way. He had been hovering on the edge, waiting to be welcomed in. When he was kept hovering too long, he asserted his kinship and dealt himself out in one large explosion of intimate hatred. The intimacy may have been strictly imaginary, but Hubbard's performance took place from a stance that appears to be in the very center of the group he was reviling. This was to be a typical Hubbard pattern, but it was not unique with him, then or now.

The second issue continued the pattern, with much playing with names. "Rock and Bumball, Gallbert Faker, *Ladies' Fireside Fudge* and its gifted editor Mr. E. W. Sock. Mr. Poultry Bighead, W. Dean Howl." The humor became even heavier in a series of phony classified ads, one of which is enough:

> H_2 BOYESSEN, Literary Analyst.
> Ibsen interpreted while you wait
> Columbia College, N. Y.

By its fifth issue (October 1895), the *Philistine* was defining its book-review policy: "Offenders only are to be deemed worthy of Reviews . . . our column of Reviews exists, not to aid struggling authors but as the Pillory . . . to the end that others may be warned to desist." And Hubbard was responding to a patronizing comment in a little magazine from Philadelphia: "I'd rather be a good honest wild ass of the desert with long fuzzy ears than a poor imitation bird-of-paradise."

The interesting thing is that this very personal journal, born out of resentment and arrogance, settled down and became (at its best) assured, witty, and sometimes almost profound. Once Hubbard got the bile out of his system, he seems to have relaxed and breathed more easily. By the beginning of Volume 5 (June 1897), he said (in summing up "the only magazine ever started that has been self-supporting from its first appearance"): "The individuals I have jibed and jeered have often been personal friends: malice has never entered. Few there be who make greater demands on their friends for charity than I; and few indeed have been more generously treated." And the issue for March 1898 carried a piece of self-analysis that not only explained much about the success of the *Philistine,* but was a fair summary of the early phases of Hubbard's public life: "The Philistine Magazine seems to stand alone in being read by people who do not necessarily accept the editor's point of view. Its list includes every denomination, party, profession, occupation. And although I never endeavor to fit any man's mood or please any one but myself . . . very rare that a subscription is cancelled. The magazine which makes the reader think is really doing a greater service than is the one that does the thinking for him."

And it met a need. People everywhere who were groping for new ways of seeing their country and their separate selves found that Hubbard was talking directly to them. Accurate circulation figures are not to be had, but it can be safely said that the response to the first issue of 2,500 copies was substantial enough to show Hubbard that he had something worth continuing and that copies per issue exceeded 10,000 very soon. By the third year, the print order was 20,000, and by 1900 (before the *Message to Garcia* had its impact), it was 52,000. These figures can be contrasted with the *Chap-Book,* which was a literary-elitist journal from its beginning, and seems never to have gone over 16,500.

Nearly fifteen years later, Hubbard was reminiscing about the launching of the *Philistine,* and showed more frankness about his motives than he had previously: "The magazinelet was gotten out more as a joke than anything else, being a sort of take-off on the popular periodicals. It might also be said that the popular periodicals aforesaid had politely refused to accept the manuscript that had been sent them from time to time by the editor. . . . So THE PHILISTINE was issued as a sort of self-defense. But the editor had hypnotized himself into the belief that he was getting out the magazinelet just for the fun of the thing. Viewed over the miles, I fear me that there was a trace of aqua fortis in his motive."

Besides the *Philistine,* another project was under way at this time. Soon after Hubbard returned from England, he bought a hand press, type and accessories, and the Roycroft Shop took its first shape in Hubbard's barn. The name for the new enterprise came from Samuel and Thomas Roycroft, seventeenth-century English bookbinders. William Morris's Kelmscott Press was fresh in Hubbard's mind, and he set to work on a hand-wrought edition of *The Song of Songs.* There may have been a covert glee in the choice (Look what's in your Bible, you dried-up Puritans!). Hubbard wrote a rather woolly Introduction about woman, love, and things in general; Bertha contributed an amateurish hand-lettered title page. The paper was handmade, and the binding rough and arty.

This first Roycroft book set another pattern that was to go on and on. William Morris was printing books that were beautiful as books—books to be looked at at least as much as to be read. As Morris did it, this meant going back to premachine sources for all the materials, skills, and techniques that went into the product: paper, inks, type design, punch cutting, type-casting, decoration, and illustration. The culminating transfer of ink to paper was a personal, muscular operation, with a minimum of mechanical assistance. The whole approach became a mystique—at its best, an integrated art form and an affirmation of a personal integrity-in-relation-to-*things* that seemed to be mortally threatened by industrialism. This William Morris protest-and-affirmation is still echoing today (in bookmaking, it has had an enormous effect on the quality of the machine product, and it still survives as pure mystique). Hubbard caught much of this from Morris. But he went into it in his barn at the same sort of blind, headlong gallop that had carried him into the fringes of literature. The mystique, with its tight inner integrity, soon faded into the marketable gimmick. Art moved hastily on to Glory.

Perhaps symbolic of the whole operation, the note at the end of *The Song of Songs* read: "And here, then, is finished this noble book being a study and reprint of the Song of Songs: which is Solomon's, taken from the Holy Bible. Printed after the manner of the Venetians with no power save that of the Human Muscle, at the Roycroft Printing Shop, that is in East Aurora, New York. Begun on September, the third day, 1895, and finished—thank God!—on January, the twentieth day, 1896." This slap-happy eclecticism, which Frederick Lewis Allen later called "the limp leather style," became a Hubbard trademark. Designers, pressmen, and binders were saluted in colophons ("Honest Roycrofters all"). Volumes were "bound Roycroftie," and they never merely reached The End—they jolted to a stop with something like "So here, then, endeth that goodly book. . . ."

But the point, which we can easily miss today, is that Hubbard brought the book as an art object into the American consciousness. And he stirred up and activated the scattering of type men, fine printers, and designers who were to carry on the mystique of the beautiful book. As a boy in Snohomish, Washington, Will Ransom came under the influence of the Hubbard publications. His special susceptibility was typography and graphic design, and in those barren years the Roycroft output was clear and present evidence that the thing could be done (and done better). Like many others, Ransom pointed like a bird dog toward East Aurora. He never reached it, but he made a start, and he got as far as Chicago, where he joined forces with Frederic Goudy to found the Village Press. Today, few people would include Hubbard in the constellation of those who brought excellence into American type design and bookmaking (W. A. Dwiggins, Oswald Cooper, Bruce Rogers, Victor Hammer, Porter Garnett, James Hendrickson, and others, as well as Ransom and Goudy). In fact, many of those who came a little later into this field found it difficult to contemplate Hubbard without violent emotions. As, Carl Purington Rollins in the *Saturday Review of Literature* for September 29, 1934:

As different from Morris . . . as the Larkin Soap factory was different from Merton Abbey . . . this American barker who reminds one of P. T. Barnum was, strange and ridiculous and awful as the fact is, the advertiser of William Morris to the American people from 1895 to 1915. . . . Hubbard's printing was unbelievably bad . . . As a follower of the Arts and Crafts movement he was beneath contempt, both artistically and ethically . . . the mountebank of East Aurora!

In 1895, the proprietors of the Pendennis Press offered Hubbard their printshop, complete, for a thousand dollars. At that price it couldn't have been much of a shop, but it was more than a hand press, and he bought it. The *Philistine* was now a sizable monthly production job. (Volume 1, Number 5, had a Hubbard joke that is a double-take classic: "When the *Philistine* was started six months ago I had no idea that it would now have half a million subscribers.") *The Songs of Songs* was followed in the next five years by about thirty volumes, mostly in editions of less than a thousand copies, including *Ecclesiastes* and *Job,* an essay by Bernard Shaw—who was infuriated when Hubbard did a little unauthorized editing—*The Rubáiyát,* Shakespeare's *Sonnets,* and contemporary ephemera. In addition to Shaw's outrage, Hubbard incurred a lawsuit by Rudyard Kipling because Hubbard thought "The Dipsy Chanty" would make a better title for the poem he was publishing than the one its author had given it. But since this was only one of twenty-three suits that Kipling then had in process against American publishers and booksellers, there may be room for argument as to who was most cantankerous.

Hubbard's new freedom had brought changes in his appearance as well as his work. Leaving the soap business ended his "devotion to fashion." When he visited Chicago in May of 1893, his moustache was gone, he wore a cape overcoat, and he was letting his "curling locks" grow. The new ensemble impressed Mary as giving him "just a bit of a theatrical air." It rapidly became more than just a bit. In his visit to England, he found two special kinds of dress eccentricity. The first was the *fin-de-siècle* foppishness of the Oscar Wilde group (Richard Le Gallienne, who later spent two summers at Roycroft, was representative of this school). Both the flowing hair and the voluminous cravat seem to have been taken over from this group; both must have been highly unfunctional nuisances for an outdoor man and a printer. The other influence on the external Hubbard was

William Morris, whom he described as "big, bold and shaggy." Hubbard's flannel shirts, baggy pants, and heavy shoes apparently derived from Morris, and the contract between the two elements never seems to have bothered him. (He added still another item—a western-style Stetson.) But the differentness and the implied superiority symbolized by his getup were things he referred to often: ". . . the good old advice about getting my hair cut. I have gotten where I feel strange if this is not called after me in throaty falsetto by the mouth-breathers. 'Get your hair cut!' Certainly, that is why I don't. I would miss the ripe ribaldry to which . . . my ears have become accustomed."

As his public career grew—with its dependence on self-advertising— his appearance became a sort of trademark. And what had been a symbol of rebellion eventually came close to being a substitute for it. So long as he kept his costume and his hairdo, he could tell himself that: ". . . the strong man knows that progress is only obtainable by the exercise of individuality. He thinks as he pleases, writes as he feels, expresses himself in his own way, and confronts ossified social smugness by letting his hair grow long, when society's edict has ordered it short. Further than this he glorifies his dome of thought by covering it with a peculiar hat. . . . To wear a hat that is long out of fashion, or one devised by your own genius, is to throw down the gauntlet to the bourgeoisie, and say, 'Behold! As I now cover my thinkery with a hat different from the one you prescribe, so do I think thoughts that are to you impossible.' "

There was some question, during the first years of the *Philistine,* whether it was to be a magazine of many authors and of more than one editor. The first issues listed an East Aurora man named Henry Taber as the editor, Hubbard as the business manager. This arrangement soon ended in a quarrel. In February of 1896, Hubbard wrote to Walter Blackburn Harte and proposed that they join forces. Harte was the Boston literary man who had started the *Fly Leaf* in December of 1895. He and Hubbard had met during one of Hubbard's stays in the Boston area, and Harte had suggested that they form a partnership and start a magazine; this was just after the first *Chap-Book* appeared. Nothing had come of this, and both had gone ahead on their own. The *Fly Leaf* had a good reception; the Philadelphia *North American* called it "the only one of the lot, including the 'Chap-Book,' 'Philistine,' etc. which knows what it is driving at. . . . the editor of the 'Philistine' curses and swears, and devastates the atmosphere . . ."

Hubbard seemed to be proposing a full partnership when he wrote

Harte in February: "If we would consolidate the *Fly Leaf* and the *Philistine* and you come on here . . . we could, by hard work, make a life work of the thing, and thus do a John Ruskin–William Morris work, or better. . . . Get a constituency—and you have and I have—and then cultivate this constituency. Issuing our manifestos to the world direct, we will stand or fall on our merits."

Hubbard wanted a three-month trial period before negotiating a formal partnership contract. Harte insisted that they must have a solid agreement. According to Harte, Hubbard repeated that he thought a trial period was a good idea so they could get better acquainted before they signed a formal partnership but that he wouldn't be proposing any collaboration at all if he didn't think it would work out; that they "could do much better fighting the world together than apart." This, to his undoing, was enough for Harte. He closed up the *Fly Leaf* and moved to East Aurora and "started to work to build up the business. . . ." When Hubbard gave his version of the affair later, he said that "Walter Blackhart Burn came down upon me . . . remained in East Aurora two weeks (lacking one day) & didn't do a thing while he was here but tie firecrackers to my coat-tail. He then towseled his hair like a boofay artist, curst in falsetto, and rushed into 'Footlights' and another sheet like it, called 'The Critic,' telling why East Aurora was no place for a man of genius, and declaring I was a big What-D'ye-Call-It." The show-down had come when Hubbard changed his mind on the partnership and offered Harte a salaried job. This pattern of attraction-repulsion-explosion in Hubbard's relation with partners, or with employees approximating a policy-making level, was to be repeated in a few years with Michael Monahan.

In the summer of this same year, Hubbard made another trip to Europe for more *Little Journeys* material. His oldest boy, now thirteen (Elbert II, "Bert" from now on), went with him. They covered a lot of ground, much of it on foot: Glasgow, the Lakes Region, Edinburgh, Liverpool, London, Antwerp, Brussels. They tried to see William Morris, but he was in his last illness. Bert wasn't much impressed with the plant— where the Kelmscott Chaucer was being completed. Hubbard admired the Chaucer but balked at spending five pounds for a copy.

Bert kept a "log" of his trip, and his father, for some reason, interpolated a few entries. One of these reads, "Forty years old this day, God help us!" Another is a fancy credited to a meditative pause in Carlyle's old house. Hubbard imagined that he heard "a sepulchral voice say: 'Thy future life! Thy fate is it indeed. Whilst thou makest that thy chief question, thy life to me and to thyself and to thy God is worthless!' The wind still howled." The voice spoke Carlyle's own words and Hubbard found them close to home. He used them again in the first issue of a later magazine (the *Fra*).

In spite of Hubbard's difficulties with co-editors, the *Philistine* and the *Little Journeys* were getting new subscribers every week, the books were selling, and the Roycroft enterprises were in rapid expansion. In addition to the books and magazines, a variety of artsy-crafty products were being turned out and boomed in the *Philistine*. Items that were eventually to bear the Roycroft name included: pottery, hammered copper, wrought-iron and-irons and hinges, tooled leather goods, rugs, baskets, furniture, stained-glass lamps and windows, preserves, maple-sugar candy, painting, and music. The printing and binding operations outgrew several successive arrangements and finally came to rest in a large stone and half-timbered building. Both natives and pilgrims were put on the payroll when they proved able and willing to work—and to adapt. And being on the Roycroft payroll was never a simple matter of hours for dollars. It meant joining something, and it often meant becoming a different person in the process of belonging.

Some of the pilgrims were of a special sort. At this time, the tramp—the hobo, the bindle stiff—was a common figure wherever the railroads ran. Being on the road became a way of life, with its own mores, legends, songs, and heroes. (Judging by *No Enemy* and one of his articles in the *Arena*, Hubbard had sampled tramp life himself long enough to pick up a smattering of the lore.) Some of these hoboes were young, literate, and searching for ideas or movements that would give them a sense of direction and a reason for moving back into settled society. Others were simply out to see the country and prove their hardihood. Some were skilled workers—the tramp printer was a common variety—with itchy feet. As the word spread, many of these wanderers took to dropping off at East Aurora to see what was going on. Some stayed to become Roycroft functionaries. Others turned up regularly to work a few months for a stake and then shove off for more travels or a warmer climate.

In the early days, the Hubbards had offered to accommodate all comers by straight hospitality. In 1896, the magazine carried this rather fantastic general invitation: "all good Philistines . . . welcome to seats at the table and a place to sleep—of course without charge. All men and women, however, who remain over one night are expected to work for the public good at least two hours a day. There is type setting, proof reading, copying and addressing wrappers to do, besides taking care of the Roycroft Baby (limited

edition—de luxe copy), cooking, washing, and then there is a good big
wood pile."

It was soon apparent that this was no way to run either a household
or a business, and an Inn was improvised from earlier buildings. The principal guest rooms were not numbered but named: Socrates, George Eliot,
Beethoven, Edison, William Morris, and Susan B. Anthony. (Frederick
Lewis Allen later commented, "An odd team, that.") In the camaraderie
among Roycrofters and visitors, a newcomer was often called by the name
of his room. And there were jokes—as of the native who said they had
gone "plumb crazy up at the art works," carving George Eliot's name on
his door; "What are they gonna do if the son-of-a-gun don't show up?"
The source of the fieldstones for the new buildings was another of those
Hubbard touches that made good copy and added to the legend. He let it
be known that he would pay a dollar a wagonload ("Bulling the market
for boulders"). This was rolling, heavily glaciated country, and the cash-
poor farmers decided the man was obviously crazy but they would get in a
good thing before he went bankrupt. Estimates of the loads delivered run
from eighteen hundred to four thousand.

The *Philistine* was picking up advertisers as well as subscribers. Those
early ads show something about the times, and the sorts of people who were
reading the magazine. The "safety bicycle" had recently touched off the
"bike" craze. Two makes (selling for around $100) were advertised, also
spring-seat posts and lamps; three health foods and one sanatorium; two
railroads; The Columbia Bar-Lock Typewriter; two magazines: *Humanity,*
A Monthly Magazine of Social Ethics, Kansas City, Missouri; *Intelligence,*
monthly magazine of Literature—Scientific, Philosophical, Psychic and
Occult, Leander Whipple, ed., New York City; the Emerson College of
Oratory; the books of Richard Le Gallienne; and the Robinson Thermal
Bath Cabinet, Made in Toledo.

The quasi-communal nature of the Roycroft group was taking shape
too—these early years were probably the time of its greatest liveliness,
though even as late as 1908, Felix Shay's first impression was "one-third
business establishment, one-third university, and one-third horse ranch, with
just a touch of the monastic." Harry Kemp, a tramp poet, dropped off a
freight one day and later recalled "an atmosphere of good-natured greeting
and raillery, that sped from table to table. And when [Hubbard] strode in,
with his bold, swinging gait (it seemed that he had just returned from a
lecture in a distant city early that afternoon), there was cheering and clap-
ping. Guests and workers joined together in the same dining hall, with no
distinctive division."

Kemp found a place on the payroll "smearing glue on the backs of unbound books. My wage was three dollars a week and found. Not much but what did it matter? There was a fine library . . . liberal and revolutionary books . . . many people, who, if extremely eccentric, were nevertheless, alive and alert and interested. . . . Derelicts, freaks, nuts with poses that outnumbered the silver eyes in the peacock's tail and yet a sincerity, a fineness, and a genuine feeling for humanity that regular folks never achieve."

Like other groups with a feeling of being chosen and special, the Roycrofters evolved their own language and legends. The nominal orientation to the medievalism of William Morris (plus a sort of masquerade monasticism that went both with hand-illuminated books and with Hubbard's preachments) led to such conceits as Hubbard signing himself "Fra Elbertus," and sculptor-in-residence Jerome Connor being known as "St. Jerome." (Hubbard's image of himself as a sort of make-believe priest runs all through this period.) One visitor around the turn of the century was so bemused by all this flummery, and the Gothic-plus-Tudor buildings, that she wrote up the colony in a straight-faced presentation along pious lines, and her article was printed in *Catholic World.*

In inner Roycroft circles, Hubbard was addressed as "John," and this went back to an incident that became part of the legend. An upperclass visitor arrived in his stylish carriage while the Fra, in his work clothes, was toiling at the woodpile. "Here, John! Hold my horses," called the big man, and "John" did so while the visitor went inside to inquire about the availability of Mr. Hubbard. Another Roycroft specialty was "Ali Baba." This name was attached by Hubbard and staff artist W. W. Denslow to Anson A. Blackman, a native who had been the Hubbards' hired man and horse trainer since their move to East Aurora. He was whiskered, grizzled, and red-faced. In the *Philistine,* Hubbard built a completely synthetic personality of earthy humor and cracker-barrel philosophy around Ali Baba, while Denslow made him what amounted to a cartoon-comic. (Denslow would later become famous as the illustrator of the *Oz* books.) Hubbard described him as a pilferer of tobacco, a "corner-grocery infidel," and a ribald coiner of epigrams. "Two in a bush are the root of all evil" was credited to Ali Baba; so were "Every man is a damn fool for at least five minutes every day," and "If the Devil finds you idle he will set you to work as sure as Hell." Ali Baba's lecture series on "Art as I know It" was hilariously reported: "Build your Art horse-high, pig-tight, and bull-strong," and "Art is largely a matter of hair-cut."

The man Blackman was actually faithful, simple, and humorless. He used neither tobacco nor profanity and was a regular churchgoer. One of

the joys of initiated Roycrofters was to watch bemused visitors seeking out
the inarticulate Blackman for an exchange of philosophical small talk. He
may have enjoyed the attention, as Felix Shay asserts, but he also obviously
thought of himself as one sane man in a place full of the "cracked." This
performance by Hubbard—putting an alien personality, willy-nilly, onto
a real person—was also characteristic of the way he treated many of his
friends in the *Philistine*. It was not one of his more endearing traits, but
it should be noted that his public career was, in a very similar way, beginning to clamp a make-believe nature on Hubbard himself. He may have
felt the need for company.

When the summer visitors had gone and the northern winter closed
in on East Aurora, the Roycroft community carried on a considerable cultural life of its own. There were musical programs, debates, games, and
programs in which home folks were called upon to recite original poems,
stories, or essays. When Hubbard was at home, he conducted a regular
Sunday-evening meeting in the "Chapel." Many of his *Philistine* squibs and
Little Journeys drafts were tried out on this semicaptive audience before
being printed. This year-round lyceum was a lively thing.

The success of the *Philistine* had given Hubbard something he badly
needed, an audience. He had Alice ("I know a man who became fairly
wise and not absurdly great, thru writing, for several years, to a Woman
of Brains.") But, though Alice continued to be important, there were now
all those people sending in money and writing to the editor. That first sense
of holding the end of a charged wire branching out to unknown human
reactors can be quite an experience. In addition to this constituency on the
far side of the post office, there was the Roycroft community. This was an
audience in the flesh, not only for his words on paper but for his total performance. These various people carried out his ideas, brought in ideas of
their own, played roles as he directed, and required much of him, as he of
them. Always with the knowledge on both sides that they, but not he, could
be replaced.

It took several years, however, for the Roycroft group to shake down
from the "genius of chaos" that characterized its beginnings. The ground
rules got established by trial and error, often painful, and the Number One
rule was simply that Elbert Hubbard was the boss. No partners and no
competitors could be tolerated. It was, after all, his property, his money,
and his management that made the whole thing possible. Hubbard seems
to have thought of Roycroft as a sort of culture farm: artists, writers, and
thinkers would flower under his benevolent nurture, and their creative out-

put would be his to package and market. And this is pretty much the way it came to work, except that large talents and/or large egos did not flourish in such a program, and either seceded or were cast out.

The January 1899 *Philistine* lead was entitled "A Manifesto!" and seems to have marked the end of Hubbard's patience with large talents and large egos. ". . . All of these men I have fed, clothed and lodged for two years. To be sure . . . they have slept three in a bed, but I have fed them well, and given them every encouragement to persevere . . . and make men of themselves." By his account, he had been sponged on by quite a roster of minor celebrities. "Marco Morrow & Bliss Carman then came. Neither one proved facile or felicitous in handling a pitch-fork, and Ignorance (which is Bliss) was so bright that he would not get up until noon, as he said he wished to give the Dawn a chance. Richard Hovey, whom I carried thru two hard winters, showed his total unfitness for communal life by refusing to churn; & Tudor Jenks wrote no more poetry after the cider barrel was empty. So I trun 'em both out." Collaborators, he announced, "form too heavy a tail on the kite." He was through with "working for the good of all," and especially with "these batty poets, who soar high and dive deep, and never pay cash. . . . All parties are notified not to hitch their wagons to this Star."

In this same Manifesto he gave his versions of the quarrels with Taber and Harte. This latter blowup was a serious business—for Harte, and for Hubbard's reputation in literary circles. Blaming Hubbard for all that later happened to Harte, as many people did, was hardly fair. But Hubbard's reference to the matter goes a long way toward explaining the hatred some people had for him. "Five years ago a man ridiculed, reviled and denounced me in various periodicals. He was a brilliant writer, and so his tale of woe and fancied wrong found credence with those who should have known better. His railings soon became maudlin, then general. Ere long the iron gates of Bloomingdale closed upon him, and then death . . . when he was adjudged a lunatic, part of the evidence was that he had a violent antipathy toward me. The poetic unities seem to justify me in assuming that those who oppose me are mentally irresponsible."

In the early days of the *Philistine,* many of the literary rebels and young hopefuls had thought of Hubbard as one of themselves. But these successive quarrels (and the literary-circle gossip that followed them) alienated him from this group almost as completely as his sneers at the Brahmins had alienated the established editors and publishers. Hubbard may have been making an oblique apology for all the public vindictiveness clustered around himself when he wrote that "Literary men do not quarrel more than other men—it only seems as if they did. This is because your writer uses his kazoo in getting even with his supposed enemy—he flings the rhetorical stink-pot with precision, and his grievances come into a prominence all out of keeping with their importance." But so many of the literati came to see Hubbard as a highbinder that they tended to think the worst of him. Most of the biographers of Stephen Crane have treated Hubbard as a blatant idiot, whose relationship to Crane was exploitive and brutal. The evidence is meager, but it doesn't support such a reconstruction.

Several of Crane's poems and prose sketches appeared in the early *Philistines*. There is a legend that Hubbard bought two articles from Crane and lost them on a train. But the date given is June 1894, a full year before the *Philistine*, when Hubbard was probably in England. And a letter of Crane's sounds as if he had not met Hubbard before late 1895. One of Hubbard's early schemes for his following was an annual dinner of the Society of Philistines—which meant, roughly, any of his subscribers who cared to come. The first such dinner was held in a Buffalo hotel in December 1895, with Crane as guest of honor. This was before the American triumph of *The Red Badge of Courage,* and Crane was still relatively unknown.

Harry Taber presided at the meeting, and it was a raucous affair, with all the speakers being "guyed and ragged" by the participants—many of whom were Buffalo newspapermen and visiting literati, mostly roaring drunk. There are two reminiscences of that dinner in print. Frank W. Noxon shows the feeling about Hubbard common among Crane admirers: "Crane was one of the series who were driven from Elbert Hubbard by what they believed was Hubbard's abuse of them." He found the dinner a boorish affair, though he didn't blame Hubbard so much as Taber. Claude Bragdon, who had to be assured it was all in fun when he tried to walk out on the dinner, found it "still a distressing memory" in 1929. "I do not impeach Hubbard's sincerity; he admired Crane's talent . . . but that dinner . . . like the sight of a young ox, led to the slaughter." But apparently Crane didn't mind. He stayed over in East Aurora for four days, admired and dickered over a price for one of Hubbard's horses—named "Peanuts"—and that spring he wrote to Hubbard:

My Dear Hub:

I've been a rampant wild ass of the desert with my feet never twice in the same place but at last I am settled down finally & feel that my first occupation should be the writing of a profound apology for my curious silence. I expect to be in East Aurora in about 2 weeks—at least if I am still at liberty to purchase that noble horse? At that time we will chew the rag at great length and finally decide all these contested points.

Yours always,

S. C.

And, in a later letter, Crane said, "When I think of you I rejoice that there is one man in the world who can keep up a small independent monthly howler without either dying, going broke, or becoming an ass."

Hubbard's appreciation of Crane's writing was certainly not grudging: "charged with meaning like a storage battery . . . if he never produces another thing, he has done enough to save the fag-end of the century from literary disgrace." And in another place, he said Crane was ". . . an artist in his ability to convey the meaning by just the right word, or a word misplaced, like a lady's dress in disarray, or a hat askew. This daring quality marks everything he wrote. The recognition that language is fluid and at best only an expedient flavors all his work. . . . All is packed with color and charged with feeling, yet the work is usually quiet in quality and modest in manner."

Crane went on to fame, to England, and to his premature death. His brief, and early, visits and his contributions to the *Philistine* were to be Hubbard's closest approach to active association with a major talent. Of lesser talents, there would be a continuous coming and going. Few of these would leave as quite the same people who had come, and many would leave feeling that they had a score to settle with Elbert Hubbard. As often happened, Hubbard may have summed up much of this early pattern of his Roycroft proprietorship in writing about someone else. In this case, the nominal subject was Benvenuto Cellini (1902): "The final proof that he was human and his name frailty lies in the fact that he was a busybody. As he worked he always knew what others around him were doing. If they were poor workmen, he encouraged them in a friendly way; if they were beyond him and out of his class . . . he was subservient; but if they were on his plane he hated them with a hatred that was passing speech."

East Aurora was becoming an important center on the cultural map— a haven for few, but an unpredictable transfer point for many. And as its physical plant, its payroll, and its going-concern momentum came to bulk larger and larger, Elbert Hubbard's options for his "future life" began to narrow.

THE VAUDEVILLE NUMBER

THE FRA

NOT·FOR·MVMMIES

:·A·JOVRNAL·OF·

:·AFFIRMATION·:

Vol. V   JUNE, 1910   No. 3

PVBLISHED·MONTHLY·BY·ELBERT·HVBBARD
EAST·AVRORA·ERIE·COVNTY·N·Y
25·CENTS·A·COPY·2·DOLLARS·A·YEAR

A·Confession·by·Elbert·Hubb..

The cover of the June, 1910, issue of *The FRA,* founded in 1908.
The actual size of the magazine was about 9" x 13½".
The cover design and illustration varied from issue to issue.

7

Fra Elbertus

DURING THESE YEARS, in addition to presiding over all that activity at East Aurora, Hubbard was writing steadily. Each month a *Little Journey,* work on more books, and at least enough miscellaneous copy to put the *Philistine* to bed. His "universe within" was getting a lot of exploration, and his scheme of things was becoming a matter of public record.

It was a pretty scrappy and impressionistic scheme of things, but this was a time when change was outrunning understanding by a very wide margin, all over the country. The outpouring of energy was prodigious as new products, new factories, new cities, and new ways of getting rich multiplied. And with all this burgeoning power and wealth came unprecedented troubles. The mushrooming cities spawned epidemics, devastating fires, child labor, slums, crime, degradation, and corruption. In the countryside, as the old self-sufficiencies faded, the railroads and the banks assumed economic life-and-death powers over people and towns. And above the old and understandable levels of individual power and ownership, new and mysterious figures organized corporations and trusts, manipulated investment funds, freight rates, markets, and public officials. A remote shuffling of paper could bring great wealth, and could bring ruin to ordinary people.

There were no established patterns for controlling these new forces or dealing with these evils. Nor was there any common agreement on what was going on or what it meant or what could be done about it—or if it was either right or possible to do *anything* about it. Drought and deflation on the prairies could breed Populism and free silver, and William Jennings Bryan might frighten the East out of its wits in 1896. But a few bumper crops made the difference, and when Bryan proclaimed, in 1899, "I stand just where I stood four years ago," the New York *Press* could reply, "Sit down, Mr. Bryan. You must be awfully tired, too."

There was a lively labor movement, and talk about socialism and anarchism. Strikes, riots and repressive violence had punctuated the hard times of the nineties. The pitched battle of Homestead had been fought in 1892; martial law in Idaho had stopped a capital-labor war in the silver-mine country the same year; and President Cleveland had sent troops into Illinois in 1894 and mobilized the Federal courts to defeat the Pullman strike. Eugene Debs went to jail for defying an injunction, and the leisure time speeded up his conversion to socialism. But none of these upheavals led to any widely accepted doctrine or massive march to power. When it came to theory and strategy, the radicals were as obsessive a bunch of "argufyers" as the amateur theologians of Hubbard's youth. From the gut politics of the Wobblies to the superior detachment of the philosophical anarchists, rebellion against the excesses of economic individualism was fragmented by its own kinds of individualism.

The geographical frontier had largely disappeared, but there was still a lot of moving around: to the West, to the cities, through Ellis Island, up the ladders of advancement. Though there were misery, discontent, and sporadic revolt, the dominant note was change and expansion, with no limits in sight. As the old certainties about God's will and man's duty became thin and windy, and as the family, the church, and the village were no longer necessarily all of life, there was a great raising of sights. A man might not only become rich but could build a personal empire across the country. Women, some of them decided, did not have to live in bondage to biology and dependence on men. Even the reform and revolutionary visions of the time looked beyond any visible horizons—to nothing less than total victory over poverty, injustice, ignorance, disease, and coercion. As far as anyone could say for certain, whatever men could conceive of they could achieve.

In the middle of all this welter, great numbers of people faced new situations in their daily lives. Farm boys were working in factories and tinkering in off hours with the inventions that were, hopefully, to make them rich; a few people were already making more money than they knew what to do with; immigrants were finding their way in a wholly new world; corporations were replacing knowable persons as bossman, buyer and seller, corrupter of government; small-town folk were moving into city tenements; middle-class women were having difficulty filling up the daytime hours. There were no precedents in common experience for many of these situations. People needed some sort of new guidance system in the mind so they could cope. The wisdom of the elders was not much use. Someone who was himself adrift in newness had to say: Here is where you are on the map; this is what is happening, here is what you do, what it all means, and how you can feel about it.

This prophetic role was one that Elbert Hubbard has been practicing for since his early letters home. His departure from soap had cleared the ground, and the establishment of his personal community and his audience were completing the building of his pulpit. From seeking a world where he belonged, he was turning to building his own world, and permitting others, for a consideration, to tour its public areas.

One thing that became clear very early was that Hubbard's personal community was in, but by no means the same as, the village of East Aurora. It had been all very well, when he was a Buffalo commuter, to be welcomed by the nice people who came calling while he was setting up his cookstove. Now the whole intricate switchboard of his ayes and nayes, his comings and goings, and his allegiances had been rewired without consultation with his neighbors. Many of them resented it. And with his wider audience to play to, he gave his neighbors more and more to resent. At best, he was patronizing: "No man can live in a village and illuminate it by his genius. His fellow-townsmen and neighbors are not to be influenced by his eloquence except in a very limited way. His presence creates an opposition, for the 'personal touch' repels as well as attracts." More typically, he was scornful, and provincial culture was one of his favorite targets: "Perhaps you would like to know something about our Woman's Club . . . Mrs. Grubbins is President, and when she has on her other black dress and talks of the rise and fall of the Irish Empire, we are all very proud of her."

Occasionally he commented directly on affairs in East Aurora. One such piece in the *Philistine* discussed the troubles of the local pastors—good fellows, terribly underpaid, and constantly plotted against by some of the old women in their flocks. In the next issue he remarked that he had "always thought that the Philistine was not read in East Aurora. I find, however . . . something in the March number has displeased some of my good neighbors. . . . two anonymous letters in which the innocent little Magazine is pronounced 'infidelic.' One writer prays I will cease its publication, and the other says I must. Then, three times in the night season have defunct felines been placed on my front steps. And on my barn the other morning I found chalked in large letters the word RASCAL; evidently some gentleman had called, and having forgotten his card case, left his name." And a year later, he reported that "when the late town election was held in East Aurora I

was a candidate for the office of Poor Master. I was defeated . . . by as villain-
ous a combine as ever guzzled free beer! . . . There is small satisfaction in
being Overseer of the Poor, de facto, as I have been for ten years, while
the honors of the office (and the salary) go to the pimpled knave who is
Overseer, de jure."

In those early years of pontificating, there was little direction or consistency in Hubbard's output. He took what came to hand—current events,
books and ideas that were being talked about, his *Little Journeys* subjects—
and what he gave out was always "filtered through himself." Sometimes the
filtering allowed very little besides the Hubbard self to come through. And
he was experimenting with a variety of guidelines for that self. At first, there
was a strong urge toward purity and unworldliness. "Success," he observed
in 1895, "lies not so much in having one's name a commonplace among this
great American public, which falls down to worship mediocrity if it is well
advertised, as in doing one's day's work honestly and sincerely." During this
period, he made many references to "the artistic conscience," the "Inmost
Self," the "Other Self," or "the God within" as the only proper arbiter of
performance, "your compass in times when the sun is darkened." And he
seems to have had no intention, then, of spreading himself thin. "What is
the use of writing many volumes when one small book often has power
to hold us like hoops of steel? . . . Thinking comes before writing, and no
man thinks who writes so much. . . . What human genius could keep pace
with the modern Publishing System; what reputation would it not leave a
mock and a byword?"

But a few years brought changes, and by 1898 he was finding that
"the difference in our estimate of men lies in the fact that one man is able
to get his goods in the show window and the other is not aware that he has
either show window or goods." His own show window was getting bigger
and brighter by the month then, and he was experiencing the "fine intoxication" that "comes to every brain-worker when the world acknowledges with
tangible remittances that the product of his mind has a value on the Rialto."
He was also becoming involved in a dialogue—perhaps with that Other
Self—which kept echoing in his writing and his life from then on. "John
Milton was a bit of a poseur, as Schopenhauer declares all great men are
and ever have been. With the masterly mind goes a touch of the faker." A
year later, this thought had been elaborated into: "Any man who caters
to the public is to a great degree spoiled by the public. Actors act off the
stage as well as on, falling victims to their trade. . . . The man of talent
who is much before the public poses because his audience wishes him to;

one step more and the pose becomes natural—he cannot divest himself of it."

He still occasionally tried to write in the grand manner (with the help of Shakespeare), especially in his novels: "Before sunrise, even as jocund day stood tiptoe on the mountain top, the camp was astir." But these attempts to be traditionally literary were fading into a hearty vernacular vulgarity. A couple of years after he celebrated "jocund day . . . tiptoe on the mountain top," he quoted the youthful John Milton as writing home from Cambridge to his mother: "I am penetrating into the inmost recesses of the Muses; climbing high Olympus, visiting the green pastures of Parnassus and drinking deep from Pierian Springs." "This," said Hubbard, "is terrible language for a boy of fourteen. A boy who would talk like that now would be a proper and fit target for cabbages." And he sometimes sounded a little like a Professor of English himself:

A good Philistine is known by his never saying "as it were, so to speak, red letter day, seldom if ever, all along the line, signs of the times, the blush of shame, we are pained to learn, will not soon be forgotten, if I may be allowed the expression."

The railroad reporter of the Buffalo *Express* is a lightning calculator. He figured out the time made by the Empire State Express on its famous run the other day and said, "This is at the rate of less than a mile a minute." Father has an old cow out in the pasture, and when she gets real scared she can run less than a mile a minute and she doesn't seem to be going so fast either.

They call 'em a pair of trousers; why a pair, that's what I want to know. A coat has two sleeves but we do not call it a pair of coats. If a man wore no pants, society would call it singular, but to me it is singular that pants are plural.

A young reporter writes: "Would you use 'suicided'?" Well, if I owned a paper and one of my reporters used that word, I should feel compelled to resignation him.

In *Munsey's* (circulation seven million) for July . . . : "that terrible foe of the aborigine—the demon familiarly personified as John Barleycorn," Oh, oh, oh! This passion for saying something else, when you wish to say a thing, is the terrible foe of the inkling aborigine—familiarly personified as Munsey's Monkey.

Hubbard's partly buried personal life was still breaking into his public pronouncements. By all the evidence, his informal polygamy had settled into an uneasy stability. Little messages to Alice kept popping into his printed remarks. "Some day, you know, I am to write a beautiful thing that shall link my name with that of the Great Ones gone, but I'm sure I can never do it without you are in the next room at the piano." But there were also indications that he was groping for peaceful co-existence at home.

In his book on John Brown, he remarked, ". . . in that most unhappy of all unhappy things, an unhappy marriage, the grewsomeness of the condition slinks away when bravely fronted. . . . he could not have entered into pattypan emotions, and his aspirations could neither be kept from her nor explained. As it was now, he lived within himself, and no one was hurt." And the *Philistines* for July 1897 and January 1898 carried an apparently related pair of items: "Marriage is only a way station. Trains may stop for two minutes or twenty minutes for lunch. The place may be an ugly little crossroads, or it may be a beautiful village. Possibly it's the end of a division, but egad, dearie, it's not the end of the journey!" "When we were married, dearie, this day a thousand years, we expected certain things. We were quite sure of Ecstatic Bliss, but we didn't find it, dearie; no, we didn't find it! Yet we found something else which was probably better for us. So it is all through life; we work for one thing and reap another." (I find no evidence that Hubbard ever saluted Alice as "dearie.")

But as the century ran out, so apparently did the remaining viability of the Hubbard marriage. The opening sentence of Hubbard's last attempt at a novel was: "Great men often marry commonplace women," and the theme kept recurring. In the *Little Journey to the Home of John Milton,* he gave it full-dress treatment.

Read the lives of the Great Men who have lived during the past three thousand years, and listen closely and you will hear the wild wail of neglected and un-appreciated wives. A woman can forgive a beating, but to be forgotten—never. She hates, by instinct, an austere and self-contained character. Dignity & pride repel her; preoccupation keeps her aloof; concentration on an idea is unforgive-able.

The wife of Tolstoy asking to have her husband adjudged insane is not a rare instance in the lives of thinkers. To think thoughts that are different from the thoughts one's neighbors think is surely good reason why the man should be looked after. . . .

Thought is a torture, and requires such a concentration of energy that there is nothing left for the soft courtesies. The day is fleeting, and the night cometh when no man can work. The hot impulse to grasp and materialize the dream ere it fades is strong upon the man.

Of course he is selfish—he sacrifices everything . . . his wife and society, and himself, too, to get the work done. Four o'clocks, mealtime, bedtime, and all the household systems as to pink teas, calls and etiquette, stand for naught. And down the corridors of Time comes to us the shrill wail of neglected wives, and the crash of broken hearts echoes like the sound of a painter falling through a skylight.

And, for a less lofty perspective, Hubbard's description of marital incompatibility is adequate:

When a man and a woman become absolutely irksome to each other—when their heads are in a different stratum and they breathe a different atmosphere, and have no common ends or ambitions; when they cannot sit in silence with each other without positive discomfort; when they grope pathetically for a topic of conversation and never find it; when the deeds of the darkness are remembered with shame in the daylight . . .

In addition to her inability to appreciate greatness, Bertha seems to have been just too much elemental female for her husband to cope with. His Introduction to *The Song of Songs* showed a definite trepidation about physical sex. It remarked that "while woman has a sure and delicate insight into many things, in this particular she is singularly ignorant and wilful." And he went on to quote "the profound Dr. Charcot" as having "known many men who endeavored to put their marital relations on a gentle, chivalric basis, but in nearly every case the wife imposed a tearful, beseeching veto, or else she filed a hot accusation of growing coldness that could only be disproved in one way!" In dealing with Robert Burns (1900), he noted:

Very, very rare is the couple that have the sense and poise to allow passion just enough mulberry leaves, so it will spin a beautiful silken thread, out of which a Jacob's ladder can be constructed, reaching to the Infinite. Most lovers in the end wear love to a fringe, and there remains no ladder with angels ascending and descending—not even a dream of a ladder. Instead . . . there is usually a dark, dank road to nowhere . . .

The trouble with Burns was that he never "knew anything of the beauty and excellence of a high and holy friendship between a thinking man and a thinking woman . . . the marriage of the mind is the only compact that endures." This, of course, meant Alice. And later, when Alice also had an audience for her writing, she handled the subject of marriage with a very firm hand: "Propinquity is dangerous unless one lives with his ideals all of the time and does not descend to live in his lower nature. . . . Be yourself? Only your best self!" There was something unalterably detached from the world and the flesh about Alice. Though not robust, she sustained an inner combustion that carried her far beyond normal accomplishment. It was a quality she seems to have had in common with many other, more famous, crusading women—Frances Willard, Clara Barton, Olive Schreiner, Mary Baker Eddy, Susan B. Anthony, Jane Addams. It was also a quality that frightened Hubbard sometimes. One of the love letters in *Forbes* said, "Many women have a peculiar fatal power not given to men—namely, an ability to concentrate in one short effort an amount of vital force which should carry them through a long life; but, having once brought this force to bear, they are undone, and the poise of health is, forever after, a thing to them unknown. Beware, my proud and thoughtful Minerva, of this over-intensity. Dullness saves me, and most souls, from the danger I have named; not so, you."

Some of the suffrage pioneers were of a different type—strong, executive personalities, logical, legalistic, with a tendency to boom. There were many of these among the British Suffragists. Many had had childhood backgrounds similar to Mrs. Elizabeth Cady Stanton's: trying to prove to a grieving father that she could substitute for a lost son. In an essay on Mrs. Stanton, Alice was later to say that "several women have at last abandoned effeminate methods—gentle words, soft persuasions, caresses, tears, prayers . . . and have adopted masculine manners . . . to impress upon man's mind that justice is due woman." She found this "a serious criticism on a few men."

There were also crusaders for feminism who were not typical of anyone but themselves but who made such an impression on the public that they typified the whole movement to many people. There was Emma Goldman and her brawls with the police, her shock-technique assaults on the bourgeois home, morality, church and state, her headlong overflowing motherly heart, and her disorderly person and brain. There was Victoria C. Woodhull: beautiful, poised, ambitious, a natural actress and poseur with no brain at all. (After an early life of carefree and semipublic promiscuity, she married into a rich and respectable English family and·spent several frenzied years fighting the "persecutors" who remembered her past.) Both of these, in their different ways, were identified with the anarchist movement—which treated the woman question as only one aspect of the fight for total and absolute freedom. The temperance branch of feminism had its fringe elements too, such as Carrie Nation: "When the Lord tells me to smash, I smash."

Hubbard's attitude toward the woman question during those years was skittish and cute—when he wasn't backsliding on the whole thing. A passage in his book on John Brown sounded as if it might have been a direct retort to Alice:

And right here, let us nail to the barn door of obliquity the pelt of that flaunting falsehood that women sell themselves for a home. . . . the fact that he is willing to make her his wife is proof of his love, and further is sufficient reason why she should love him, and she does. . . . A woman must be clothed and fed, and what more natural than that she should love the man who promises as much?

But usually he was playful, as when the April 1896 *Philistine* remarked (appropos of nothing visible), "I observe that the New Woman still sharpens her lead pencil with the scissors." And when a lady novelist of great popularity was having domestic troubles, Hubbard noted "a somewhat guarded statement by Dr. Swan M. Burnett denying that he and his wife have separated. . . . The doctor's friends say . . . that he is tired of being referred to as Mrs. Frances Hodgson Burnett's husband. I should think more likely he objects to being identified . . . as the father of Little Lord Fauntleroy."

That matter of whether it was to become Jill and Jack bothered him often. In his *Little Journey* on Samuel Johnson, he related that when he was walking with a friend on Market Street in St. Louis, the friend told him to look quick—there went the husband of Mrs. Lease of Kansas, the Populist leader who had exhorted the farmers to "raise less corn and more hell." And Hubbard replied "God help him!" ("Not but that Mrs. Lease is a most excellent and amiable lady, but the idea of a man, made in the image of his Maker, being reduced to the social status of a drone bee is most depressing.") Alice undoubtedly pointed out that this proposition could work both ways, and the following pronouncement by Hubbard, from 1902, had a little of the purely verbal conviction of the last communiqué issued before unconditional surrender. "Even the proudest of women are willing to accept orders when the time is ripe; and I am fully convinced that to be domineered over by the right man is a thing all good women warmly desire."

Overshadowing all this struggle with flesh-and-blood women and with ideas about women, of course, was the reality of his dual domesticity. He must have known that the situation was not likely to go on indefinitely as his and Alice's secret. But neither was there any clear way for him to resolve it. And there were probably definite advantages, to him, in the way things were. An idealized Alice could function nicely as his pole star, while actual meetings could be managed to fit his convenience. If the arrangement was manifestly unfair to Alice, and to Miriam, they were all in God's keeping, and Hubbard had a great capacity to be philosophical about other peoples' troubles. Benjamin Franklin, as a *Little Journeys* subject (1898), probably came close to home:

Time is the great avenger as well as educator; only the education is usually deferred until it no longer avails in this incarnation, and is valuable only for advice—and nobody wants advice. Death-bed repentances may be legal-tender for salvation in another world, but for this they are below par, and regeneration that is postponed until the man has no further capacity to sin is little better. For sin is only perverted power, and the man without capacity to sin neither has ability to do good—isn't that so?

But if he couldn't resolve his personal life, he could shape his personal community. In fact, he had to, constantly. Although he had cut loose the more flamboyant tail from the kite, a goodly portion remained. Competitors and parasites could be sent on their way, but worshipful disciples were another matter. And, as the Roycroft enterprises expanded, he came to depend heavily on key individuals (today we would call them shop foremen and junior executives.). Keeping all these people reasonably happy and harmonious was something of a job. In the early years, Roycroft had much in common with the utopian communities that had dotted the country earlier in the century. Not economically, since the property was Hubbard's. But Roycroft had common meals, meetings, sports, studies, and a library. Cash wages were small, but there wasn't much need or opportunity to spend money. The work was still work, but there was an effort to make it humanly satisfying. There was a real—if informal and basically paternalistic—feeling of shared values, adventure, and responsibility.

To join any close-living group is to trade a certain amount of individual freedom and identity for the security and fulfillment of belonging, and sometimes for a larger identity. For many of the Roycrofters, this seems to have been a highly satisfactory transaction. For others, less so. Writing after his father's death, Bert said that he "was a severe taskmaster and at times very unreasonable. Some particularly disturbing element would start him on a tour of the whole shops. The word would fly ahead: John's on the warpath —look out!" And at such times ". . . to argue the case was usually disastrous." But Bert also said that "the severe side of his nature was about one to ten of the other. . . . You always had a chance to state your case if you attempted it when conditions were right." That Hubbard had a wry self-knowledge of his traits as a boss may be indicated by some of the definitions in the *Roycroft Dictionary:*

> *Co-operation:* Doing what I tell you to do, and doing it quick.
> *Righteous Indignation:* Your own wrath as opposed to the shocking bad temper of others.
> *Self-reliance:* The name we give to the egotism of the man who succeeds.

Hubbard had read up on the utopian communities. He wrote that "Mennonite, Dunkard, Shaker, Oneida Communist, Mormon, and Quaker are all one people . . . Come-outers. . . . If jeered and hooted and finally oppressed, these protesters will form a clan or sect and adopt a distinctive garb or speech. If persecuted, they will hold together, as cattle on the prairies huddle against the storm. But if left alone, the Law of Reversion to Type catches the second generation." He also called them "this divine principle in humanity" and said that they were "the true and literal Saviours of mankind." But in another place he remarked that "Brook Farm disbanded because the man at the head of it had no head for business. . . ."

It was partly his head for business that made Hubbard strikingly different from little-magazine contemporaries. Many of them were better educated and often much more subtle and elegant in their thinking and writing. But they also tended to think of themselves as an elite, with special proprietary claims on literature and the arts. Their revolt against the pressures they felt from the Going Concern of their America—its puritanism, its practicality, its optimism and vulgarity—led many of them to equate most of the popular culture of the time, and most especially anything involving business, with The Enemy.

Hubbard had done some revolting, too, but only after he had made his modest fortune without the help of formal learning, inherited money, or social position. And if his knowledge was thin and his wisdom capricious, his range was wide. Neither professors nor critics nor aesthetes were going to fence him out of whatever pastures he took a notion to browse in. He made an asset out of his limitations, and proclaimed that "To live in a big city . . . to meet the learned and the powerful, and hear their sermons and lectures; to view the unending shelves of vast libraries is to be discouraged at the start. And thus we find that genius is essentially rural—a country product. Salons, soirees, theatres, concerts, lectures, libraries, produce a fine mediocrity that smiles at the right time and bows when 'tis proper." He was to reuse this formulation many times. When he did acknowledge a relationship to a common stock of thought, he was grudging, if not contemptuous: "to think for yourself you ought to know what others are thinking and have thought. We work by elimination—and every wise man is familiar with all foolish schemes of philosophy." In a reference to the English Congregational preacher Joseph Parker, Hubbard quoted a Cambridge clergyman as saying "he is not a University man, and having small knowledge of what others have said and done, he is amazingly original at times—in fact he has no conception of how ridiculous he is." This reminded

Hubbard of Lincoln's wanting to send Grant's brand of whiskey to his other generals. In the Jane Austen *Little Journey* (1897), he followed this intellectual outsiderdom even further. A nation will decay in its own smug traditions, he said, "save as it is jolted out of its notions by men with either a sublime ignorance of, or an indifference to what has been done and said. . . . Do I then plead the cause of ignorance? Well, yes, rather so. A little ignorance is not a dangerous thing. A man who reads too much—who accumulates too many facts—gets his mind filled to the point of saturation. . . . In his soul there is no guest chamber."

Hubbard was a real hero for a common type of newspaperman—the would-be intellectual, or would-be writer, covering the police beat and the lectures at the women's clubs, and dreaming of escape. In 1901, Hubbard lectured in his birthplace of Bloomington. His audience was small, but he fetched the reporter from the *Pantagraph* in a way that must have had many echoes. This hometown boy found "vital suggestions on many a living question, couched in language which drove its way home in the understanding and will live long in memory." The performance "sparkled with homely humor," and the reporter concluded defiantly that "many people may believe just as does Mr. Hubbard, but not many have the courage to say so." Hubbard's appeal was also great to the brighter adolescents of his time. A friend who grew up in a small town in Pennsylvania during Hubbard's heyday has told me of making trips to the county seat for the *Philistine*. His mother burned any that she found in the house, and they were not available in the town. But a fruit-stand man in the county seat smuggled in a supply of each issue beneath a bunch of bananas, and did a brisk undercover business while they lasted.

Some of Hubbard's best advertising came from men of God denouncing him publicly. "When some of these little, narrow-minded, East Aurora type of vaudeville artists try to tell you that the Bible amounts to nothing and that Christ was the illegitimate child of a peasant girl, you'd better take their "Little Journeys" and chuck them into Hell through the sewer and put such men down as unprincipled asses." Thus a clergyman addressing a YMCA meeting. A similar clerical attack referred to Hubbard as "among the chief opponents of revealed religion" whose "publication is a disgrace to the civilization in which we live. From its literary merits it has great influence, but in fact it is poison in sugar-coated pills."

Self-improvement is an American specialty, but that of the late-nineteenth and early-twentieth centuries was particularly a part of the open-ended feeling of the time. In 1897, editor John Brisben Walker announced a home study course for subscribers to *Cosmopolitan*. He tried to hire Dr. Elisha B. Andrews, who had just been fired from the presidency of Brown University for advocating the free coinage of silver, to head the venture. There were twelve thousand enrollees within ten weeks. Even the hasty imposition of a fee of five dollars a quarter didn't slow up the inpouring applications, and *Cosmopolitan* had to give up the attempt as too big to handle. There was probably a higher content of serious inquiry in this demand than in the later business-and-social-climbing kind of home study. It showed the widespread need for something to replace the fading biblical certainties.

Other than Hubbard, most of the little-magazine editors wanted no part of this massive craving for enlightenment. The *Chap-Book* called the *Cosmopolitan* venture "cheap and easy culture," and sneered that "if we cannot have fiat money, we can at least have fiat scholars and free coinage of . . . diplomas. There is a fine flavor of cynicism in this scheme . . . that calculates the number of asses that are in the world and then sets to work to provide these asses with what their asininity demands."

The *Little Journeys* were well suited for that large audience of the semisubmerged. They were sketchy, romanticized, humorous, and apt to veer off into preachments or speculations about anything at all. The one typical thing they did for their nominal subjects was to pick some aspect of the man, his time, or his greatness and put it into lively familiar context for the reader, who may not have had any more formal education than Hubbard. In dealing with Socrates, of whom he observed that to most Athenians he was the town fool, he found a blessing for all mankind in Xanthippe's shrewishness. Otherwise:

Suppose Xanthippe and Socrates had settled down and lived in a cottage with a vine growing over the portico, and two rows of hollyhocks leading from the front gate to the door; a pathway of coal ashes lined off with broken crockery, and inside the house all sweet, clean and tidy; Socrates earning six drachma a day carving marble, with double pay for overtime, and he handing the pay envelope over to her each Saturday night, keeping out just enough for tobacco, and she putting a tidy sum in the Aegean Savings Bank every month—why what then? Well, that would have been an end to Socrates.

Here is the Emperor Claudius: "He was then fifty years old, a grass-widower —twice over—and on the lookout for a wife. He was neither wise nor great, nor was he very bad; he was kind—after dinner—and generous when rightly approached." And here Claudius's successor to the throne:

A close study of the youth of Nero reveals the same traits that outcrop in one-half the students at Harvard—traits ill-becoming to grown-up men, but not at all alarming in youth. Nero was self-willed and occasionally had tantrums—but a tantrum is only a little whirlwind of misdirected energy. . . . his mother lavished on him her maudlin love, and allowed the fallacy to grow in his mind concerning the divinity that doth hedge a king. In fact, when he asked his mother about his real father, she led him to believe his paternal parent was a god, and his birth miraculous. Now let such an idea get into the head of the average freshman and what will be the result? A woman can tell a full-grown man that he is the greatest thing that ever happened, and it does no special harm, for the man knows better than to go out on the street and proclaim it, but you tell a boy of eighteen such pleasing fallacies, and then have fawning courtiers back them up, and at the same time give the youth free access to the strong box, and it surely would be a miracle if he is not doubly damned, and quickly too . . .

When Socrates put the chesty Alcibiades three points down, and jumped on his stomach with his knees, the youth had a month in bed, and after he got around again he possessed a most wholesome regard for his teacher. If Burrus and Seneca had applied Brockway methods to Agrippina and her saucy son, as they easily might, it would have made Rome howl with delight, and saved the state as well as the individual.

Here is a comment on the marriage of a philosopher: "Comte had associated but very little with women—he had theories about them. Small men, with midget minds, know femininity much better than the great ones. Travelling salesmen, with checked vests, gauge women as Herbert Spencer never could."

All this was certainly not scholarship, but was it a bad thing to suggest to a druggist in Cedar Rapids that Plato or Savonarola or Voltaire were just such human beings as he saw in his store every day? Plainly, the Brahmins of Hubbard's time thought it a bad thing. And such a contemporary Brahmin as Joseph Wood Krutch felt much the same way about Hubbard: ". . . is a master of that semi-literary jauntiness so vastly impressive to the unlettered." (It could also be noted that our all-time master of semiliterary jauntiness was a man named Clemens.) William Marion Reedy was more generous on the same issue. "It has been said, by myself and others, that Hubbard's appeal is to the half-baked. It is true, for the greater part. But we are all half-baked for that matter. Culture is relative. People who follow Hubbard do not stay half-baked. They come out of it. He makes lovers of books out of people who never knew books before."

Sometimes Hubbard's breezy nonscholarship verged on the unforgivable. In 1902 he did a *Little Journey* on Edward Abbey, an American artist
living in England. The printed pamphlet came across the desk of George
Haven Putnam. Putnam was no longer publishing the series; they had
become pure Roycroft in 1900, but he may have felt some responsibility,
as well as a lingering—and illusory—authority. He found "a detailed and
dramatic account of [Hubbard's] visit to the country house in Gloucester-
shire . . . the charming hospitality of Mrs. Abbey, and the grace and attrac-
tiveness of the family group comprising as he remembered it seven or eight
children. . . ." Mr. Putnam was disturbed. As he remembered it, the Abbeys
had no children. He sent off the booklet to Abbey (at his club). And, sure
enough, he shortly had an agitated reply. Abbey "had never seen the man
Hubbard," and there were no children. Moreover, "the desire for children
had been the passion of his wife and . . . this description of a family that
never existed might bring her into a state of nervous prostration." He im-
plored Mr. Putnam "to do whatever might be practicable to suppress the
booklet and prevent this fake . . . being reprinted in book form."

Mr. Putnam went into action, "brought pressure on Hubbard and
secured the cancellation of the chapter in the proposed book." Hubbard
was not at all abashed, though he admitted "that he had never made the
visit and had . . . never seen Abbey. He had secured some description of
Abbey's country home and he thought that the beautiful English lawn
would look 'kind of empty' without children." Mr. Putnam was further
outraged by Hubbard's saying, "A man ought not get annoyed at a little
thing like that; particularly when I took such pains to crack up his art."
Mr. Putnam was premature in his satisfaction at "having secured the cancellation of the chapter," however. The "goodly brood of little Abbeys—I
dare not say how many. I believe it was nine a year ago, with an addition
since" is still there. Through all the subsequent editions, they "run wild and
free along the hedgerows."

More admirable than Hubbard's facility in filling up empty lawns with
imaginary children was the flavor of his prose. At a time when, for ordinary
people and literary pundits alike, writing worthy of appearance in print
meant formality, classical allusions, and pomposity, Hubbard was developing
that rollicking vernacular style which startled and often delighted. It helped
bring him an audience but it shut him out of the world of the purists forever.
("'Who ever heard anything like that before?' ask the literary and philosophical hill tribes in fierce indignation.") No gentleman, no scholar, could
be so barbarous. As he had said about Whitman, when Hubbard "wanted

a word of fourty-four caliber, and there was nothing in stock but boys' sizes, he grabbed his quill and scratched one into shape."

He repaid the purists for their scorn many times over. "The person educated to write," he said, "never writes anything worth reading." His recipe for having something worth writing about" was "a knowledge of humanity and of the relationship of one thing to another." ("Doesn't rhetoric and a knowledge of the classics enter? In the language of George Ade, 'Not a tall, not a tall.'") He was always happy to belabor the "Learned Ones who consider any endeavor to change language, so it will be a better vehicle for the conveyance of thought, as rude, crude, ribald and in bad form. One who uses words in new senses, or invents a new word, is an uncultured person, unfit for polite society. Belay there—you goggle-eyed, pedantic pedagogues!" As for language mechanics: "To write well you must possess a goodly grain of indifference to grammar. Contempt will not do—just indifference—because when you hate a thing you imitate it. Educated people write Johnsonese and Samuel Johnson lives for us not in his own written words, but for his undress talk in the presence of an indiscreet barbarian."

Finally, the other special element that set Hubbard off from the literati was the fascination he found in doing things—tangible, practical things, from chopping firewood to running a business. Though he thought he had renounced the commercial world, what he had renounced was only the matter of grubbing for someone else's business and by someone else's rules. As the Roycroft enterprise took form, he found a vast creative satisfaction in all of it. And it was his celebration of the burden and the glory of his kind of business proprietorship that led to his most famous piece of writing. *A Message to Garcia* was a workaday Hubbard preachment, tossed off in one sitting in the aftermath of the Spanish-American War, and dropped into the March 1899 *Philistine* without a heading. It set off a fair-sized tidal wave that was still eating into remote beaches after Hubbard's death and that was to wash Hubbard himself a considerable distance off the course he thought he was sailing.

8

Messages

WHEN A RISING FLURRY of orders began to come in for the March *Philis-tine,* Hubbard was puzzled as to what the fuss was about. According to his own account, he asked an assistant "which article it was that had stirred things up," and was told it seemed to be "that stuff about Garcia."

There were about fifteen hundred words in the piece, beginning: "In all this Cuban business there is one man stands out on the horizon of my memory like Mars at perihelion." It proceeded, in mildly fractured history, to relate that early in the war, a "fellow named Rowan" had carried an urgent communication to General Garcia of the Cuban revolutionaries, going alone from the beach at night, through the jungles, into the mountains. He found his man and he delivered his message. The story itself needed only a few sentences; the rest was the preachment. "The point I wish to make is this: McKinley gave Rowan a letter to be delivered to Garcia; Rowan took the letter and did not ask, 'Where is he at?' By the Eternal! There is a man whose form should be cast in deathless bronze and the statue placed in every college of the land. It is not book-learning young men need, nor instruction about this and that, but a stiffening of the vertebrae which will cause them to be loyal to a trust, to act promptly, concentrate their energies: do the thing—'Carry a message to Garcia.'"

There were three main points in what followed. One was the "im-becility of the average man":

Slipshod assistance, foolish inattention, dowdy indifference, and half-hearted work seem the rule . . .

You, reader, put this matter to a test: You are sitting now in your office—

six clerks are within call. Summon any one and make this request: "Please look in the encyclopedia and make a brief memorandum for me concerning the life of Correggio."

Will the clerk quietly say, "yes, sir," and go do the task? On your life he will not. He will look at you out of a fishy eye and ask one or more of the following questions:

Who was he?

Which encyclopedia? Where is this encyclopedia?

Was I hired for that?

Don't you mean Bismark?

What's the matter with Charlie doing it?

Is he dead?

Is there any hurry?

Shan't I bring you the book and let you look it up for yourself?

And so on concerning "this incapacity for independent action, this moral stupidity, this infirmity of the will, this unwillingness to cheerfully catch hold and lift . . ." All from the perspective of the "man who has endeavored to carry out an enterprise where many hands are needed." This led to the second point, sympathy for "the employer who grows old before his time in a vain attempt to get frowzy ne'er-do-wells to do intelligent work; and his long, patient striving after 'help' that does nothing but loaf when his back is turned. . . . the men who are striving to carry on a great enterprise, whose working hours are not limited by the whistle, and whose hair is fast turning white through the struggle to hold in line dowdy indifference, slipshod imbecility, and the heartless ingratitude which, but for their enterprise, would be both hungry and homeless."

The third point, of course, was that message-carriers are rewarded. Success comes to "the man who does his work when the 'boss' is away, as well as when he is at home. And the man who, when given a letter for Garcia, quietly takes the missive, without any idiotic questions, and with no lurking intention of chucking it into the nearest sewer, or of doing aught else but deliver it, never gets 'laid off,' nor has to go on a strike for higher wages. Civilization is one long, anxious search for just such individuals . . . he is wanted . . . he is needed and needed badly—the man who can 'Carry a Message to Garcia.'" And, sprinkled throughout, was the alternative: "out and forever out the incompetent and unworthy go."

The mass distribution of the *Message* was begun by George H. Daniels of the New York Central. Other corporations joined in. Judges read it aloud from the bench. Generals ordered it distributed among their troops. Governments passed it out to their civil servants. As Stewart Holbrook has commented, "All sorts of societies except labor unions took up the demand." With the rise of mass production and nationwide corporations, the boss was not only away a lot, he was often an impersonal legal entity like a holding company. Something was needed to replace the old master-servant (or master-journeyman-apprentice) relationship—something to keep the corporate help on its toes. (It was not small business proprietors who accounted for the millions of reprints.) Also, many ordinary people whose self-respect required of them an honest day's work for a day's pay must have welcomed this chance to identify themselves with a hero. And there were the Eager Beavers, alert for a pathway to the top. Success was very much in the foreground of the American Dream then, and the *Message* became one of the showpieces in the onward-and-upward literature of the time. And, as textbook publishers looked for current material to replace the pastoral homilies of the McGuffey *Readers,* the *Message* took on a widespread secondary life in the schools.

It should be noted, too, that the dream-hero of the *Message* has two special characteristics. First, he has no human ties to his fellows (they are lounging around asking "What's the matter with Charlie doing it?"). The message-carrier rises, alone and untouched, out of the rabble of incompetents. The second thing is that he doesn't rise too far. There is no indication that he is on his way toward supplanting his boss. He is wanted, needed, and will be rewarded, but he goes on carrying messages, with no back talk. He isn't really a person at all, but a genie summoned by rubbing a cash register. (This particular dream is not at all dated, as any number of today's private secretaries can testify.)

Even in the business community, there was some dissent to the chorus of acclaim. Another railroad man—George H. Heafford of the Milwaukee & St. Paul—found it "a gratuitous insult even to the lowest average of intelligence and ability," and he wrote to Daniels, protesting this "outrage upon civilized humanity which should be resented by everyone." And to political radicals and many literary men, the *Message* was simply proof of what they had suspected all along—that Elbert Hubbard was a mercenary tool of the Interests, or a fake and a barbarian.

There wasn't much middle ground in the reception of the "stuff about Garcia," but that was not the fault of William Marion Reedy. He provided a typically friendly but firm corrective to Hubbard's extravagances. "The article has had quite a vogue, as it deserves," he began, "if only as a good specimen of Mr. Hubbard's easy and fascinating style." But that was about as far as he could go in praise. "The idea that whatsoever lies before a man to do, that he shall do with all his might, is part of the practical religion of civilization. . . . all great institutions in this country are largely 'run' by the subordinates of the men who draw the big salaries. The imbecility of the average man is *not* appalling. Inability and unwillingness to concentrate upon a thing and do it are *not* the rules of life. On the contrary, the astonishing thing about American business life is the amount of ability developed therein, the readiness of all employees to do their best and the unique adaptability of the average workman."

Hubbard himself was startled by the uproar over the *Message,* and not happy that his principal claim to fame should rest on it. "I do not consider it by any means my best piece of writing; but it was opportune—the time was ripe. . . . The combination of theme, condition of the country, and method of circulation was so favorable that their conjunction will probably never occur again." In 1900 he had the original manuscript bound for presentation to the Buffalo Public Library. His covering letter was a mixture of diffidence ("may be of some slight value") and a cockiness so great that it ran over into fantasy: "Within ten months it has been reprinted over nine million times. I grant you that this alone is no proof of literary excellence; but the fact may be of value to the Zulu who shall sit on the broken buttress of Niagara Bridge, in shedding light on the mental qualities of those who lived in the year Eighteen Hundred & Ninety Nine."

There is some mythology about the genesis of the *Message.* Hubbard said, "The thing leaped hot from my heart, written after a trying day, when I had been endeavoring to train some rather delinquent villagers to abjure the comatose state and get radioactive." (A later version reads "to train some rather delinquent helpers in the way they should go." He did have to live with the villagers.) And Hubbard credited his son Bert, then sixteen, with having suggested the key idea—that Rowan was the real hero of the war—while the Hubbard family sat around the dinner table. ("The boy is right!") Later, Bert told a different story: that he had "goofed" on a responsibility and that the *Message* was a paternal lecture directed straight at him and that everyone at Roycroft knew it. When the New York Central ordered a million copies, said Bert, "I got chesty. If anyone mentioned my late act of 'imprudence,' I came right back with—'Well, you think you are so smart, let's see you inspire another world-beater.'"

But, when all the nonsense has been peeled away from the *Message* and its reception, there remains a residue of meaning not to be laughed off. The imperative of meeting a need with action, of being alive and responsive, and of getting the needful thing wrapped up is neither trivial nor dated. This drive—with its inner tension and its focus on outer reality—is not universal or overabundant, or easily evoked when lacking. (The Peace Corps is probably learning a lot about this.) In Hubbard's time—as Reedy pointed out—there was a lot of this "practical religion," but most of it was at the service of the rampant individualism that was building the country (to be sure), and was also building into the country many of the problems we are now floundering with.

For Hubbard, the Gospel of Work was one of the few items in his philosophy not subject to change and ambivalence. Work was salvation and destiny. "Work stops bickering, strife and . . . waste. It makes for health and strength. The reward of work is not immunity from toil, but more work—and increased capacity for effort." The principal Hubbard pronouncement still alive in collected familiar quotations is this one: "If you work for a man, in heaven's name work for him! If he pays you wages that supply you your bread and butter, work for him—speak well of him, think well of him, stand by him and stand by the institution he represents." (An expanded version of this is framed and displayed today in FBI offices.) But his prescription for the man in the wrong job was equally forceful: "When you revolt, why revolt—climb, hike, get out, defy—tell everybody and everything to go to hades! That disposes of the case." Hubbard had made his own work pattern and it suited him fine. When he said "Blessed is the man who has found his work," he was talking about himself. The others were another matter, and had better find a proper master to give them messages to carry. This switching between admonishment and introspection is blatantly obvious in successive issues of the *Philistine* in 1905. In November he gives advice: "If I worked for a big man and wanted to get his place, I'd cultivate the spirit of obedience and not the spirit of initiative . . . when in doubt, do as you are told!" So much for lesser breeds. In December comes this: "To be subject to the will of others, with volition eradicated is perdition, and I know of none other."

In the same year as the *Message,* another literary sensation illuminated a darker side of the American Dream of 1899. Edwin Markham's "The Man with the Hoe" appeared in the San Francisco *Examiner* and went on to international fame. Thousands of people identified, most of them vicariously, with the "slave of the wheel of labor" who was "humanity betrayed, plundered, profaned and disinherited" by "masters, lords, and rulers." Benjamin De Casseres called the poem "the battle cry of the next thousand years." It spoke for the widespread unease about social injustice, and it looked to the coming revolution from below, "when the dumb Terror shall rise to judge the world." At the turn of the century there *was* some reason to expect a rising of dumb terror in the future of this country. Monopoly capitalism often seemed beyond the reach of any control by democratic processes, and a fog of demonology was spreading. The "Interests," the "Trusts," the "System," the "Invisible Government," and (always) "Wall Street" were symbolizing the sources of frustration, misery, and hatred for the underdog.

This situation was soon to pass what Hubbard would have called a "pivotal point." It wasn't clear at the time, and it is arguable now, but in 1904 the Supreme Court, in effect, sustained the authority of public government (represented by President Theodore Roosevelt) over private government (represented by J. P. Morgan). This got the situation off dead center and set in motion the process that has been called "countervailing power." From here on, industry, commerce, labor, farmers, legislators, reformers, voters, judges, and government executives were to mix it up in a bruising melee that worked, mostly, because it went on changing with the country.

None of this hindsight perspective was available to Hubbard when the *Message* made him famous. What he saw were such immediate and gratifying developments as the doubling of the circulations of the *Philistine* and the *Little Journeys* within a year. By late 1900, the *Philistine* claimed 90,000 and the *Little Journeys* 32,000; by 1902, the *Philistine* figure was 110,000. Tufts College gave him an honorary Master of Arts. Railroad executives sent him free passes, and a big-business stratum new to his experience sought him out for luncheon. The demand for his lecturing moved into the upper brackets, and Major Pond—the leading impresario of talking celebrities—took over his bookings. His parents passed their golden-wedding anniversary and retired to East Aurora. Perhaps most fateful of all for Hubbard's future was that the Roycroft shops expanded and tooled up to handle a much greater volume of printing and publishing.

From all indications, Hubbard took eagerly to all this celebrity and good fortune. Though he had complained that public figures were forced into posing by the expectations of their audiences, he devised several performance-acts of his own that do not seem to have been altogether necessary. When Major Pond booked him into New York City for his first big-time appearance, he turned up at the Waldorf to register, with Ali Baba close beside him (the Waldorf was also the site for the lecture). The room clerk looked at the pair of them—whiskers, weatherbeaten faces, flowing hair and neckties, hickory shirts, baggy pants, and outlandish hats—and decided the hotel was full. Reporters were gleefully taking the bait ("Apostle of

Simplicity Refused Admission to Waldorf-Astoria") before the hotel manager could retrieve the situation.

There was also something contrived in the whole flavor of his lectures. His audiences in those years were typically people who had read his printed output but never seen him. They came expecting a ribald and profane performance by an outlandish egotist. What they found was a quiet, modest exposition by a man whose diffidence seemed often to require the audience's active support to keep him from shrinking into nothing. His first biographer, Albert Lane, found it so hard to "understand how the *Philistine*'s 'Heart-to-Heart Talks' and the smooth, clean, strong and sympathetic words of the lecture, could emanate from the same mind," that he went to East Aurora to figure it out. (He emerged with pretty much the image of the Fra and his work that Hubbard wanted him to have.) This platform manner was a deliberate tactic—"The audience is the female element, the orator the male," and the thing was to bring out maternal compassion. "Usually the great orator is on the losing side. And this excites the feminine attribute of pity, and pity fused with admiration gives us love." (All this diffidence, and being on the losing side, could play perceptive tricks. Miriam Allen de Ford, who heard him once, remembers him as a "wispy little man.")

The subject matter of his lectures was also calculated to disarm. Mostly he talked about "Roycroft Ideals" or "Home Folks at Roycroft." He drew a picture of an enterprise totally dedicated to beauty, truth, and natural goodness. Its primary purpose seemed to be to educate and train the local young people as it paid them wages (giving them the abundant life right at home, and saving them from the wicked and heartless cities). And all bathed in a light of gentleness and benevolence. He made a very special thing of Roycroft as a sort of rescue-and-reform agency. Ne'er-do-well boys (just misdirected energy and no one to believe in them) were made into solid citizens. Local girls who had gone wrong were salvaged from the road to hell and gently molded into Good Women. One of Hubbard's executives had served a penitentiary term for forgery, and his rehabilitation echoed through dozens of lecture halls and was related many times in print. Hubbard's own part in all this was only implied. He was the modest shepherd of this community, greatly privileged to be able to serve. And, to the everlasting fury of his detractors, not one of these claims was totally and demonstrably false, though back home in East Aurora, some of the elements of this public image were not appreciated. When visitors inquired about the location of the reformatory, or invited confidences from one of the cornfed virgins on the staff as to how it felt to be saved from a life of sin, there might be resentment. But this sort of thing could always be brushed off in a preachment on the ingratitude of the common man and the betrayal of saviors. By and large, as Reedy said, "All things work together for righteousness and profit at Hubbard's happy home."

Emerson may have provided the formula for Hubbard's public self in those years: "It is easy in the world to live after the world's opinion; it is easy in solitude to live after our own; but the great man is he who in the midst of the crowd keeps with perfect sweetness the independence of solitude." After a season on the road with Hubbard, Major Pond said: "Everywhere he went he had something nice to say to the porters, baggagemen, hackmen, conductors, waiters. He seemed incapable of hurting any one's feelings. Everybody was in love with him." But there was a strain involved in this, and at home and in the shops it sometimes showed. As Bert said, "Elbert had nerves." Mostly, though, it was in his writing that he found release for the emotions that didn't go with "perfect sweetness." The rest of the Pond quotation is: "But when he gets set down by himself with that caustic pen of his, whom he loveth he chasteneth!"

Reedy noticed this, too. "The contrast between the brashness of some of his writing and his personal diffidence is startling. He talks with a queer combination of horse sense and the moving of the spirit. His personality is hypnotic—more especially upon women." A little later, Reedy amplified this: "There has always been a suspicion of pose about Elbert Hubbard. The man, upon closer acquaintance, dispels the suspicion. He believes in his work. He believes in humanity. He believes in himself. The jocose Hubbard is the most superficial. The true man is earnest, almost solemn . . . there is much of the seer about him. He is strangely of the vulgar, and frustratively transcendental, brutally strong and softly feminine."

Reedy seems to have been one of the few contemporaries whom Hubbard allowed to see that "true man" over a period of years. As a result, Reedy's comments—almost alone among the many judgments in the Elbert Hubbard record—are negotiable at par. The son of an Irish policeman, Reedy came to be a sort of Midwest anchor man in the revolt from the cultural domination of New England. He had much of the freshness and generosity associated with the American West, though he was also a relay point for the literature and ideas filtering in from Europe. His personal life had been even more mixed up than Hubbard's. As a young newspaperman, he was nearly done in by irregular hours and the sporting life of St. Louis. His first wife (a former madam) spent all her savings seeing him through the Keeley Cure. In 1896 he became sole owner of the weekly

Mirror, soon to be *Reedy's Mirror,* and his influence as an essayist and a publisher of new writers began to spread.

Like Hubbard, Reedy had a direct, vernacular style and a lively, unorthodox mind. He referred to his own taste as "a mixture of that of the highbrow and the journalist." Unlike Hubbard, he had little itch for personal glory. The most spectacular find of his publishing career was Masters' *Spoon River Anthology,* but he published, criticized, and encouraged a very large sampling of European and American talent. He seems to have first met Hubbard shortly before the *Message* appeared. The acquaintance continued throughout Hubbard's life, with "gentle joshes," practical jokes, admonishments, and laudatory plugs floating back and forth between them in the *Philistine* and the *Mirror.*

During all the public attention and activity that followed the *Message,* the personal judgment day that had been hanging over Hubbard for six or seven years began to close down. The *Philistine* was carrying such admonishments as "When in doubt, mind your own business," and the March 1901 issue contained an overwrought denunciation of gossip and slander which added up to ". . . speak ill of no one, not even as a matter of truth." And his readers may have wondered why he kept coming back to such pronouncements as ". . . it is not seldom that love-children possess a very superior mental and moral stamina. . . . I might name a dozen or more of the strongest among all the sons of earth . . . who were born outside the pale of the marriage contract. The expression we use to distinguish such is a wrong one . . . but I am glad it now takes the place of its much coarser synonym." The secret was getting around. A period in his marriage had arrived that he was probably describing when he wrote, in the *Philistine* for June 1903: "She is losing her husband. . . . She begins a system of espionage —letters are opened. . . . And her punishment consists in finding her suspicions true. . . . And now the heart . . . becomes an abyss of cruelty and revenge. She is willing, aye, anxious to disgrace, destroy and damn to lowest hell."

The March 1901 *Little Journey* was to be on Mozart. When it appeared, it told the following story. Hubbard had taken his nearly finished manuscript along on a lecture trip to Wisconsin, to revise it on the train and have it ready for the printers when he got back. With the train approaching Chicago on the return trip, the porter tidied up the car while Hubbard was out of it, and he chucked the messy-looking sheaf of scribbling out into the prairie winds. What to do? "To reproduce the matter was impossible, for I have no verbal memory—something must be written, though. I decided to leave Chicago in an hour by the Lake Shore . . . and have the copy ready for the Roycroft boys when I reached home." This preliminary explanation took care of three pages. Each succeeding section was headed, "Chicago," "Laporte," "South Bend," "Elkhart," etc.

Chicago was a sort of tuning-up. It ran through several standard themes: that artistic temperament is nonsense unjustified by any amount of talent; that men are as whimsical as women; that "the artist is the voluptuary of labor, and his fantastic tricks often seem to be only Nature's way of equalizing matters, and showing the world that he is very common clay, after all. To be modest and gentle and kind, as we can all be, is just as much to God as to be learned and talented, and yet a cad."

At Laporte, Mozart came onstage—an instance of "great talent and becoming modesty. . . . He had humor. Ah! That is it—he knew values— had a sense of proportion." There followed a couple of pages about the young Mozart. South Bend brought a diversion: "We take an interest in the lives of others because we always, when we think of another, imagine our relationship to him. . . . biography . . . to a degree . . . is a repetition of our own life. There are certain things that happen to everyone, and the rest we think might have happened to us, and may yet. So as we read, we unconsciously slip into the life of the other man and confuse our identity with his." Elkhart came back to Mozart: ". . . I would have liked to have Mozart for a friend and companion. . . . Genius needs a keeper, once said Mr. I. Zangwill, probably with himself in mind. Yes, Mozart needed me to plan his tours and market his wares."

Reminiscences about the young Hubbard's skill with horses led to Mozart burning himself out at thirty-five, and: "At the age which Mozart died I had seen all I wanted to of business life . . . being the only man in America who had all the money he wanted, and so just turned about and went to college." With a few remarks about college, this section went back to Mozart needing a friend, and too bad Hubbard hadn't been there. And then, at Waterloo, something quite violent came forth:

Friendship is better than love for a steady diet. Suspicion, jealousy, prejudice and strife follow in the wake of love; and disgrace, murder, and suicide lurk just around the corner. Love makes demands, asks for proofs. But friendship only hopes to serve, and it grows by giving. Do not say, please, that this applies also to love. Love bestows only that it may receive, and a one-sided passion turns to hate in a night, and then demands vengeance as its right and portion. . . .

Friendship means calm, sweet sleep, clear brain and a strong hold on sanity. Love I am told is only friendship, plus something else. But that something else is a great disturber of the peace, not to say digestion. It sometimes racks the brain until the world reels. Love is such a tax on the emotions that this way madness lies. Friendship never yet led to suicide.

Toledo brought a momentary calm and told us that "just at the age when Mozart composed and played his 'Requiem,' getting ready to die, I was going to school and incidentally falling in love. I was thirty four and shaved clean because there were gray hairs coming in my beard. Love has its advantages, of course, and the benefits of passionate love consist in scarifying one's sensibilities until they are raw, thus making one able to sympathize with those who suffer. . . . Love is mad, raging unrest and a vain reaching out for nobody-knows-what. Of course the kind which I am talking about is the Grand Passion, not the sort of sentiment that one entertains toward his grandmother." The rest of the trip was standard *Little Journeys* copy, and Mozart was carried to his pauper's grave approximately from the East Aurora station.

Hubbard had reason for being disturbed. At about this time, Bertha left him, taking Ralph and Katherine. And his national audience soon had this personal debacle dramatized for them. Miriam had lived with Alice's married sister in Buffalo while her mother taught in Denver. In 1900, Alice found a new teaching position in Concord, and took Miriam to live with her. This ended the arrangement with her sister's family, or so it seemed. But her sister's husband was a lawyer, and more than a year and a half after Alice and Miriam had moved to Concord, he sued Hubbard, in Alice's name, for nonsupport of the child. (Hubbard referred to the suit as blackmail.) Though the case was settled out of court, the story had been carried by the wire services, and Elbert Hubbard had been nationally advertised not only as seducer and adulterer but also as a man who refused to support his child.

Along with everything else, Michael Monahan—who had come to Roycroft ten months before as an editorial helper—chose this time to stage a very public quarrel with his boss. He hired the East Aurora Opera House and papered the town with handbills inviting one and all to come and hear his grievances. A large audience heard him pour out his outraged discipleship: "I refused to allow myself to be bribed or driven away. Both attempts were made. . . . I care not how clever a man may be, how shrewd an advertiser, how plausible an impostor, if you please, let him cut loose from honor and faith and truth, and his end is foredoomed. . . ." He urged the Roycroft workers to repudiate "the hateful slander, offspring of an evil mind," that they were a lot of "women of lost virtue, and men of lost honesty" reformed by the nonexistent reformatory. "I warn the man . . . that if he persists in his insane course, both public and private, within two years the owls and bats will take possession of his gothic tower."

Shock at the marital scandal seemed to be uppermost in Monahan's overwrought mind. "He would be a great man . . . and supply a new moral code . . . the first article of which should be that a man ought to hate his own wife and love his neighbor's—or somebody else. . . ." But all through his denunciation ran the frustration and hatred of a man who feels he has been used by someone inferior to himself. "Poor little man! How woefully he has deceived himself with his pert repetition of commonplaces, his ridiculous assumption of a message, his flash ignorance and irreverence, his absurd personal fakery, his degenerate female following, and the indiscriminate worship of the half-baked." Monahan announced that he, Monahan, deserved much of the credit for Hubbard's success as a writer. (He was probably the man Reedy quoted as replying—when Reedy asked what was wrong between him and Hubbard—"Bill, he takes me out and walks me over those roads and talks to me and I go home and go to bed, and two days afterwards the *Philistine* appears and everything in it is mine! Mine, but mutilated!")

The Buffalo *Express,* in printing Monahan's Opera House speech, noted that "Mr. Hubbard left town this afternoon for a Western lecture trip. He will not return for several weeks."

The Fra DeLuxe

Art is largely a matter of hair-cut.
—*Ali Baba*

9

How Can Sin
Be Sin?

ALL OVER the country, the clergy and the more righteous editorial writers jumped at the chance to settle accounts with this infidel upstart. Those who had been manning the dikes against modernism and insisting that doubt led straight to hell had their proof, and they used it. The more secular commentators said things like "We are glad to know that our prophesies concerning this all-around rogue are being fulfilled." One of the more genial comments came from the New York *Sun:* ". . . out of each squabble he escapes unscathed, credits the advertising account a thousand dollars, puts a little extra coin in the ginger jar and goes peacefully on his way. It is said that like Faust he has sold his soul to the devil."

Hubbard himself seems to have been unprepared for the storm of abuse. Almost at the time the roof fell in, he had blandly observed that whereas "the fanged dogs of war" had once been "turned loose upon the man who dared to think," nowadays there was "only a fat and harmless poodle, known as Social Ostracism. This poodle is old, toothless, and given over to introspection; it has to be fed on pap; its only exercise is to exploit the horse blocks, doze in milady's lap, and dream of a long lost canine paradise." But after a few months of attention from this toothless poodle, he noted that "it is a satisfaction to a vast number of people to hear of the downfall of others. . . . If joy comes to you the news will go unheralded, but should great grief, woe, disgrace . . . be your portion, the wires will flash the news . . . and flaming headlines will tell the tale to people who never before heard of you."

What may have hurt more than the public disgrace was the bitterness of onetime disciples. There were many of these. One of them worked up his disillusionment into a *Little Journey to the Home of Elbert Hubbard*, neatly printed in Roycroft style. Its author—Paul W. Mavity, of Indiana— had "believed that [Hubbard] has a great mission . . . trusted that his professed ideal of kindness would save him from a breach of duty or honor, when, therefore, we awoke . . . to find that he had long ago fallen . . . we were sick about the heart, miserably sore and disappointed." Hubbard could rationalize this sort of thing away, if he worked at it ("If your friend reveals his humanity and the rabble forsake him . . ."), just as he could be jaunty about his standing with his neighbors. "A good many people in my own town used to point me out as I passed and touch their foreheads . . . until it came to be generally known that I had a bigger bank balance than any one in town, and then instead of explaining that I was a fool, they said I was a rogue." But his parents, his sisters, and his children were not so easy to face down.

It seems from the record that he didn't "face" his kin during this time of trouble any more then he had to—he sent them letters. To his mother, this:

MY DEAR MOTHER;
Just this word, good Mother Mine, to tell you that you need have no fears for your son. I want no apology made for me—I need no vindication—*it is the whole that counts.* My heart is right and I am in the hands of God. The foolish little fearing folk may desert me and this is well. There is no lie on my lips, and I am not a hypocrite. If I go down it will be because I deserve it, but look you, *I am not going down.*
It is a beautiful, sunshiny morning!
Your boy—Bert.

And when the storm broke in the papers, he wrote to Mary: "Never mind what they say, your brother is trying to live an honest life, and a life of usefulness." He said nothing at all about the facts in the case, and he rejected questions in advance by saying, "You need not answer this—I know I will ever have your love, and you are ever my sister." Taken by itself, this letter suggests only that he was the victim of some abominable conspiracy. And was being magnanimous about it (". . . my face is filled with lines of care! Why should we hate? Well, we will not.")

Mary was not fooled. When she came to write her reminiscences, though she said nothing about the circumstances of the scandal, she went straight to the heart of its results and she wasted no time on Elbert's pretenses:

Elbert hated suffering and shrank from giving pain, or witnessing it. In spite of great independence of character, he craved affection and sympathy to an unusual degree, yet he became the center of a cataclysm which, it seemed at the time, would break hearts, and inflict wounds that a lifetime could not heal. He was to meet averted faces that had been kind and friendly, and to see hands withdrawn that had joyfully clasped his. His own flesh and blood was to deny him, and recriminations and vituperations were to be heaped upon him. . . . Before the separation was accomplished, youth was crushed, faces were drawn and haggard with suffering, bright hair was dimmed and grayed, and bodies worn to emaciation . . .

In the record of this period, the only hint from Hubbard that he might have an indivisible responsibility for what has happened was in the letter to his mother ("If I go down it will be because I deserve it . . ."). No apologies, no regrets, no recognition of any judgments but his own. Only the matter of whether or not he was going to survive (". . . look you, *I am not going down."*) He does seem to have made some effort to level with the public—on his terms. When Bertha filed her suit for divorce, he issued a statement that he and his wife had "temperaments essentially antipathetic to each other." But he implied that Bertha was an unwifely social butterfly who left him to do all the work at Roycroft—and this infuriated her friends and supporters. Later he referred to Alice as his "affinity," and the nation's press had a merry and vindictive time with the word.

These fiascoes seem to have soured whatever impulses he may have still had toward straightforwardness. He withdrew to his inner defenses and let things blow over. ("The true solace for private troubles is to lose yourself in your work." "Disgrace consists in mentally acknowledging disgrace.") And from here on, he seldom varied from a strategy of "no comment" to personal questions and to criticism. ("Never explain; your friends do not need it and your enemies will not believe you anyway.") He had his work, and he made it his sanctuary, though the editorial asides designed to find value in his trials and rebuild his self-esteem were frequent. "Just how much discord is required in God's formula for a successful life, no one knows; but it must have a use, for it is always there." He referred to "the individual who accepts what Fate sends, and undoes Calamity by drinking all of it," and he asked, "How can sin be sin if through it I rise to spiritual heights before unguessed?" But it was not too long before the *Philistine* had moments when it sounded like old times. "It is a great man who, when he finds he has come out at the little end of the horn, simply appropriates the horn and blows it forevermore."

After things had calmed down a little, Hubbard sent a letter to his parents—both of them. After all allowances have been made for the ten-year strain of secrecy and deception, the wreckage of his personal life, and the public and private hate still surrounding him, this letter is still a remarkable document. In effect, it congratulates his parents for having proved worthy of him. Also, like many of Hubbard's more self-centered pronouncements, it touched obliquely on something profound—in this case, the human need to be accepted, as is:

MY DEAR FATHER AND MOTHER:

I am deeply gratified to know that in my hour of bitterness you have stood firm and held your peace. It is not necessary that you should endorse all that I have done; neither is it for you to exonerate me. You have simply loved me. A great opportunity has come to you—an opportunity to be great and generous and kind, and you have been all of these. I congratulate you—I am proud of you.

I was your baby boy forty-six years ago; I was your son twenty-five years ago; you have been proud of me all these days of sunshine and fair sailing. Then when calamity lowered and disgrace seemed nigh, what a humiliation if you too had deserted and denied me. "Canst thou not watch with me one hour?" It is at Gethsemane that the weak ones reveal their nature—but you have stood firm—it will go down to your eternal credit in the Book of Life.

God bless you and keep you. May you live many years to know that your son has been worthy of the love that did not desert him in his darkest hour.

The love you have given me I keep, and yet send back.

For I am ever

Your son ELBERT

During the scandal and the divorce, very little of the playful message-to-Alice sort of thing appeared in Hubbard's writing. There are parts of his outburst in the Mozart *Little Journey*—love turning to hate, and leading to insanity and suicide—that could conceivably refer to Alice as well as to Bertha. There was a passage that kept recurring during this period: "To have known a great and exalted love and have it fade from your grasp and flee as a shadow . . . is the highest good." And he referred often to standing alone.

Some of the long-lasting East Aurora legends insisted that Alice precipitated the scandal by demanding a showdown—she was determined to become visible and have her rights, according to this story—and the lawsuit was of her making. Since pride and independence were central in Alice's personality—her feminism rejected absolutely the notion of a woman, however cherished and domestically indispensable, receiving her livelihood at the whim of a man—any self-seeking demands by her seem most unlikely. But she was also a mother, and no matter how often the *Philistine* celebrated the natural superiority of love children, the situation was manifestly unfair to Miriam. It does seem possible that Alice was persuaded, at least, by her brother-in-law to go along with the lawsuit. It is also consistent with the record that there may have been a period of estrangement between Elbert and Alice during the time of the scandal and divorce. In discussing Mary Wollstonecraft and her desertion by Gilbert Imlay, Alice was later to write:

When one must question and chide, when the answers are evasive and obscure, it is the beginning of the end. Why cling to what is not yours? . . . For nearly three long years she endured all the agony a woman can suffer. . . . It would not be truth to say she was undaunted through all this, for her courage failed many times and she gladly would have died. . . . to know all of life, one must experience what Mary Wollstonecraft Imlay did when her love and her un-limited confidence were betrayed.

If Alice had done much questioning and chiding, she might have run into a brick wall. Hubbard could be very generous, but on his own terms and in his own good time. His resistance to anything he saw as coercion could be stubborn beyond the merely rational. Early in the life of the *Philistine,* Hubbard signed a contract with one Fred Gardner of Chicago. This agreement paid Hubbard a flat fee per issue for the advertising space in the magazine, and left it to Gardner to set rates, sell the space, and keep the proceeds. At first, the arrangement was a good one for Hubbard—a guaranteed income without risk or overhead. But as the circulation grew, the ninety-nine-year contract became a gold mine for Gardner. There came a time when Hubbard notified Gardner that the arrangement was no longer fair, hence void. Gardner sued him—and collected—several times for income due, plus legal costs, before Hubbard bought off the contract.

It seems entirely possible that two such extraordinarily strong-willed people as Elbert and Alice—with the emotional pandemonium of Bertha's bitterness and the public uproar crackling about them—got into an impasse of misunderstanding and pride that took considerable sorting out after Bertha got her divorce. But if so, the sorting out was finally accomplished, and on January 20, 1904, Elbert Hubbard and Alice Moore got off the train from Boston in Bridgeport, Connecticut, and inquired as to the nearest Justice of the Peace. The marriage was performed, and they took the next train for New York. Hubbard gave his occupation as "'publisher" and then changed it to "farmer."

Two of Hubbard's sons stayed with him after the divorce. Bert, the eldest, was already a stalwart Roycrofter. Sanford, the youngest, was different. Inarticulate and sometimes moody, he took little interest in words or abstract ideas. When Harry Kemp stayed at Roycroft, Sanford was either working with the lumbering gangs in the woods or sitting alone in the wigwam he had built. Books of Indian lore were the only kind of books he cared about. He was also something of a physical prodigy. By the time he was fifteen he was nearly six feet tall, broad-shouldered and handsomely muscled. His bare-torsoed photograph had appeared widely in breakfast-food ads. (The Oil City *Derrick* commented that Hubbard "brings his boys up on Grape-Nuts, but fails to provide them with shirts.") According to Kemp, the advertising stunt was strictly Hubbard's doing—Sanford didn't eat the stuff. At least once, Hubbard took Sanford along on a lecture trip— perhaps as a sort of ambulatory testimonial to the Roycroft way of life. Opie Read remarked in the Chicago *American:* ". . . what big, tall, splendid, pink-cheeked fellows these East Aurora boys are! . . . there was a little ovation for the Fra and Apollo; that is the way it is everywhere . . . he has coaling stations in every city. Yet I hear from various sources that he also has a goodly list of enemies."

Both Sanford and Bert grew up without benefit of haircuts. The summer he was fifteen, Sanford revolted and persuaded the fearful East Aurora barber to close-crop his head. That evening he received an ovation in the Roycroft dining room, but his father didn't speak to him. According to Kemp, Hubbard's only disciplinary lever with Sanford was to threaten to send him away to a high-toned prep school. Bert, on the other hand, wore his hair long until some years after his father's death. His feelings for his father combined "a most profound love for him together with a sort of fear that made me respect his word or wish without back talk . . ." He remembered two occasions in his boyhood when his father had whipped him. The second of these had been severe. ("Dad was mad. His day at the soap-factory had been a bad one and he was much off key.") and Bert had contemplated running away from home. But "in two days Dad brought me out a regular two-wheeled bicycle." This incident may have been on his father's mind when he wrote his Tennyson *Little Journey* (1900). "I have noticed that in households where a strap hangs behind the kitchen door . . . it is utilized not so much for pure discipline as to ease the feelings of the parent. They say that expression is a need of the human heart; & I am also convinced that in many hearts there is a very strong desire at times to thrash someone."

When Bert was in his teens, he and three of his friends built themselves a shack in the Roycroft woods. His father took no interest in the project until one day when he took to his horse to find Bert, who was holed up in his cabin and hadn't come home on schedule. Not long after, Hubbard took over the cabin as a writing retreat for himself. He sometimes brought along a friend or two for a weekend. Monahan was terrified by the field mice—"terrible beasts"—that ran along the rafters at night.

The *Little Journeys* often dwelt on gifted fathers and their sons—less often on gifted sons and their fathers—usually with wistfulness. This line of thought went back at least to February 1899, when the *Philistine* remarked: "It is a humiliating fact that great men are not capable of transmitting their genius to their sons . . ." As late as 1912, Reedy quoted Hubbard as complaining that "his boys are the only people who never read what he writes." This wasn't strictly true, nor would it have been a very admirable remark if it had been true, and Reedy commented with a somewhat embarrassed irony, "That is the fiercest pang that pierces the heart of genius." As often happened, Hubbard indicated elsewhere that he knew better: "no man can deceive his children—they take his exact measurement, whether others ever do or not; and the only way to win and hold the love of a child (or a grownup) is to be frank and simple and honest. I've tried both schemes."

Discipleship—whether from his sons, his employees, his readers, or his lecture audiences—was something Elbert Hubbard needed, resisted, sought, and rejected, all his adult life. When Harry Kemp first turned up at Roycroft, he got the full treatment over the woodpile.

I caught up the axe and fell to with enthusiasm. As we worked, the Master talked, talked with me as if he had known me for years—as if I, too, were Somebody. There was nothing he did not discuss, in memorable phrase and trenchant, clever epigram. For he saw that I believed in him and he gave me, in return, of his best. For the first time I saw what human language is for.

Kemp was highly sensitive to the whole cycle; he was on an extended pilgrimage in search of father-heroes—to worship briefly, to search out their weaknesses, quarrel with them, and push on to the next one. He saw Hubbard at his best in their first encounter; he stayed at Roycroft long enough to hear "the current [Roycroft] proverb, that [Hubbard] always quarrelled not long after with anyone about whose shoulders he first cast his arm." And their quarrel came after Hubbard invited him to write a sonnet to head the forthcoming *Little Journey* on Thoreau. The sonnet appeared, but with no byline. For the young Kemp, this was unforgivable, and not even Hubbard's offer to make him the Roycroft Poet could mollify him.

In his writing, Hubbard blew both hot and cold on discipleship. He knew his power with youngsters like Harry Kemp, and he often gloried in it:

It is a great thing to teach. I am never more complimented than when someone addresses me as "teacher." To give yourself in a way that will inspire others to think, to do, to become—what nobler ambition! To be a good teacher demands a high degree of altruism, for one must be willing to sink self, to die—as it were—that others may live. There is something in it very much akin to motherhood—a brooding quality.

But, over the long pull, "to sink self" was not one of his talents. He knew this, too, and he said, in the same passage:

The men of much motive power are not the best teachers—the arbitrary and imperative type that would bend all minds to match its own may build bridges, tunnel mountains, discover continents and capture cities, but it cannot teach. In the presence of such a towering personality freedom dies, spontaneity droops, and thought slinks away into a corner.

He came back to this distinction between teacher and doer several times, sometimes referring to the towering-personality type as a "willopus-wallipus." And in 1904 he tried to swear off from the hero business for good by announcing that "the man who craves disciples and wants followers is always more or less of a charlatan. The man of genuine worth and insight wants to be himself; and he wants others to be themselves, also. Discipleship is a degenerating process to all parties concerned."

But he never made it stick, anymore than he ever overcame his associated addiction to lecturing. After his post-*Message* season in the big leagues, he wrote to Major Pond: "If I get down to business here and cut off all distractions, I can make a name equal to John Ruskin's or Thomas Carlyle's. *I can do it,* but I must keep out of sight in order to succeed. To merely talk is not to succeed, and the public is only a devil that takes a man to the top of the mountain and then casts him on the stones beneath. So make no more lecture engagements for me." But he was soon making his own lecture bookings. And a little over a year later, after boasting of his "eighty-one lectures, with a net profit to myself of a little over ten thousand dollars," he said, "Lecturing is hard work; it makes prodigious demands on one's vitality; and since I am told we are going through life for the last time, I am about through with public speaking as a business." But he wasn't through with it. It seems to have met a deeper need than emulating Ruskin and Carlyle.

Part of the attraction was financial, of course. The lecture tours not only meant fees; they kept public interest simmering in Hubbard-Roycroft. He sometimes referred to his trips as "the dash for the dough." His payroll was to total over $3,000 a week by 1909. Probably there were other factors that kept him lecturing. In the early years, a lecture trip gave him a chance to see Alice, for one. And it was probably also useful as a way of getting away from storms and confrontations, like the one with Monahan. Further, these forays into the "outside world" helped keep his "thinkery" active. In his last years, when his writing output had badly outrun his ideas, he used the trips themselves as a steady source of copy.

But his earlier insight into the conflict between public performance and private creation did not die easily. It put him through some complicated broken-field running. Hubbard's writings up to around 1905 have frequent passages of this kind: ". . . it happens again and again that a man gets a surfeit of society—he is thrown with those who misunderstand him, who thwart him, who contradict his nature, who bring out the worst in his disposition; he is sapped of his strength, and then he longs for solitude. He would go alone up into the mountain. What is called the monastic impulse comes over him." And he wrote that men "of masterly talent" are "not gregarious in their natures. The 'jiner' instinct goes with a man who is a little doubtful . . ."

Then another element entered the pattern, an alternative procedure, for use when the mountains were not available: "There are two ways to guard and keep alive the sacred fires: one is to flee to convent, monastery, or mountain . . . the other is to mix and mingle with men and wear a coat of mail in way of manner." The coat of mail was ready at hand—the flowing hair, eccentric dress, and overextroverted public front. Evidently he convinced himself that a lecture tour could serve him as well as a monastery.

Alice Moore Hubbard, 1910

10

Mortgage-Burning

THERE WAS MUTTERING in East Aurora at the coming of the new Mrs. Hubbard. Many small towns of the time would have made life intolerable for the second wife after such a scandal. But the Roycroft group was a society in itself, and Alice had had years of practice in living by her own light, with or without the approval of her neighbors. Nor is a more unlikely candidate for the role of scarlet woman easily imagined. Dard Hunter—who came from Ohio as a young artist-craftsman at about this time—thought Alice "more strait-laced and puritanical than anyone I had ever known" (as well as "most likeable and agreeable").

Not that it was easy, even for Alice. The Roycrofters had their own traditions and mores, and there was resistance, especially when it became clear that Alice was to be not only Mrs. Hubbard but also something like chief executive officer of the whole enterprise. Harry Kemp came back that spring for another stay, and found "many secret complaints" floating around about the changes Alice had made—such as separating the hired help from the Inn guests in the dining room. Kemp was a little resentful, too, and described Alice as having "a sharp hatchet-face, eyes with the colour of ice in them . . . a cold, blue-grey." But he admitted her "great instinct for organization and business enterprise." And there was no question that Roycroft needed this kind of talent. It could stand some shaking-down from its "genius of chaos" without any danger of becoming stuffy.

For Hubbard, these early years of his second marriage were good ones. In 1902, the *Philistine* had remarked, "When your wife and your affinity are the same person, society has no mortgage on your soul." That particular

109

mortgage had been paid off. Other long-term obligations were to make themselves felt, but later. He wrote a series of essays of homage and gratitude to "a rich woman—one rich in love, loyalty, gentleness, insight, gratitude, appreciation." His "simple tribute of truth" declared:

Alice Hubbard, in way of mental reach, sanity, sympathy and all-around ability, out-classes any woman of history, ancient or modern, mentally, morally and spiritually. To make a better woman than Alice Hubbard one would have to take the talents and graces of many great women and omit their faults. If she is a departure in some minor respects from a perfect standard, it is probably because she lives in a faulty world, with a faulty man, and deals with faulty folks, a few of whom, doubtless will peruse this article.

Publication of these tributes, in 1907, in a little volume called *White Hyacinths,* went a long way toward restoring Hubbard's public reputation.

The New York *Times* said, "Coming at a time when the world seemed given up to . . . defamation, it marks the very high tide of appreciation." The Detroit *Press* found the book "tender and gentle and sweet." Reedy's comments were both generous and penetrating. "It is written with a sort of abandonment of self not usual in the very clever Fra. . . . it rises beyond mere gush and compliment, and presents to us a woman who is human and not an idolized doll. Mrs. Hubbard must be all he says she is, and more, or she never could have subdued the Fra himself to that tenderness and modesty and spontaneous admiration based on rational and not sentimental grounds . . . In introducing us to his wife Elbert Hubbard gives us a new light upon himself and one that glamours him even in the eyes of those of us who have been most critical of his dichotomies and dissonances as a thinker and writer."

By this time, Hubbard could use a few well-publicized kind words. True, he regularly reprinted in the *Philistine* the livelier of the drumfire of insults he was getting in the nation's press. He put them under some such heading as: "Sundry slight Acerbitations of certain Good Men and Virtuous temporarily Disgruntled with Themselves." This was part of undoing Calamity by drinking all of it, no doubt, and it made good reading. The Boston *Transcript* said that "in appearance he somewhat resembles Daniel Webster as he might have looked after a long spree, and deprived of the kind offices of a barber." The New York *Sun* observed that "Hubbard would have made Brook Farm pay big dividends—to himself." The New Orleans *Picayune* made a wisecrack that Hubbard was to take over and work hard under his Ali Baba front: "To him, art is merely a matter of neckties and hair-cut." And the Memphis *Appeal* had fun with: "That Battle Creek

Breakfast Food Prize Boy is only a sample, we hear, of a limited edition of twenty-five de-luxe copies signed and numbered by the author."

When Hubbard observed that morality was a matter of geography, editorial writers reacted on cue by inviting him to locate forthwith in "the Fiji Islands," or "east of Suez where there ain't no ten commandments and man can raise a thirst." The Syracuse *Post-Standard* said, ". . . certainly the Fra should know, for he has traveled much and tried all kinds of morals, and now gets along without any," while the Chicago *Record-Herald* observed: "So it is, but the man who attempts to set up the moral standards of Timbuctoo in Evanston, Ill., for instance, is likely to have trouble on his hands."

The Utica *Observer* ran a little story: "When Fra Elbertus was here, he went out to the Insane Asylum and made a speech to the inmates. Before he had spoken ten minutes a woman got up and in a voice that shot clear above that of the speaker, shouted, 'My God! I cannot stand any more such nonsense as this!' It was the first sign she had given of returning sanity." Hubbard used this one later as direct reminiscence: "Never did I have a more attentive audience. Of course some of them laughed in the wrong place—but that always happens. Halfway through the talk I was going strong, when a gaunt old woman stood up, flapped her arms and shrieked . . ." All this was showmanship of a brisk order—and it must have been frustrating to critics who could find little to say about Hubbard that he hadn't already said, or reprinted, about himself—but it was better showmanship when he had eulogies to print on the same page as the "Growls from the Groucherinos." (Such as: ". . . the best writer in the world, and the clearest thinker. I don't always agree. . . . I revere him because he says what sets me to thinking, and he has taught me more than any other man I ever read.") So it was good business, and doubtless personally gratifying, to be able to contrast the catcalls with Reedy saying that *White Hyacinths* was "Hubbard's one achievement in literature thus far. . . . the book reads like an abdication of pontificality and comes upon us as a breathtaking surprise."

In the relative quiet of this period, Hubbard seemed often to be groping for a more mature religious stance than the rowdy iconoclasm of his battles with orthodoxy. He seldom did much more than grope. There were too many new battles taking his attention, as when he reprinted the following "from the pen of a meek and lowly Catholic Priest . . ."

The editor of *The Philistine* is an atrocious liar. . . . this poisoner of wells . . . moral microbe . . . violates every principle of public decency and fills the

Christian soul with rage. . . . The mind of such a scoundrel is like a red light district and his conscience like a sewer. He blasphemes the Deity, thinking in his maggot soul that he is an Ajax . . . even less dignified than Ingersoll . . . a cur dog . . . spleening his tiny bark at the infinite sea. In every country, in times of decadence, these Lilliput Satans congregate just as flies gather around a putrescent carcass.

"If you imagine," noted Hubbard, "that the good old religious spirit that burned Savonarola at the stake, and caused the streets of Grenada to run ankle deep with the blood of Jews, has entirely died out, please read these gentle words. . . ."

In 1905, the *Philistine* paid its respects to revival meetings: ". . . an orgie of the soul, a spiritual debauch. . . . This hysteria of the uncurbed feelings is the only blasphemy, and if there were a personal God, He surely would be grieved to see that we have so absurd an idea of Him, as to imagine He would be pleased with our deporting the divine gift of reason into the hell-box." Hubbard was reacting here, probably, to scars of his own childhood, but he was also trying to find solid ground for present use when he went on to say: "Two things a man must do—get free from the bondage of other men; and second, free himself from the phantoms of his own mind. . . . Effervescence is not character . . ." But, in due course, he had to interrupt his groping to print a rebuttal from Billy Sunday: "I do not care whether a man lives in East Aurora, East Paradise, or East Gehenna, if he despises the word of God he has got something coming that will make him stutter at the Last Great Day. The Philistine is doing more to blight faith than any other publication in America. I have no use for self-appointed sissified long-haired prophets."

But there always remained the question of what happens after we are liberated? What is man and how should he live? Hubbard had some resistance to being pressed for this kind of answer. "To lead men out of captivity is a thankless task. They always ask when you take away their superstition, 'what are you going to give us in return?' They do not realize that superstition is a disease, and to give another disease in return is not nice, necessary or polite." But the questions remained, for Hubbard as well as his followers. He had said, and he rephrased the idea more than once, that the "so-called infidel is often a man of great gentleness of spirit, and his disbelief is not in God, but in some little man's definition of God." But there is no one place to look for Hubbard's God, or any sustained conception of life. As elsewhere, his thinking was in short takes and intuitive leaps.

Sometimes he seemed ready to grant that religion was an answer to a need rather than a tyrannical conspiracy. "Dogma has less place now in religion than ever before," he said in 1903; "many deeply religious men eschew the creed entirely. . . . That is good which serves. Religions are many and diverse, but reason and goodness are one." As for the long view, "a certain type of religion fits a certain man in a certain stage of his evolution, and so to that degree religion is necessary. An ethnologist is never a Corner Grocery Infidel." And at this time he seemed to be downgrading his own crusade when he said that "the destiny of the liberal church is not to become strong and powerful, but to make all other denominations more liberal. The Church, being a part of society, evolves as society evolves . . . very rarely are religious opinions consciously abandoned; they change and are modified into something else."

There was a strong element of mysticism and fatality in Elbert Hubbard that was apt to appear whenever he came to the end of his never too long rational tether. "Life is a paradox" was a favorite summary, and this one continued: "Every truth has its counterpart which contradicts it, and every philosopher supplies the material for his own undoing." This pursuit of paradox and this resistance to thinking too far or too closely led him into some tangled pronouncements. When he said that "superstitions are ossified metaphors and back of every religious fallacy lies a truth," a reader might see a glimmer of meaning coming through the undefined terms. And when he announced, in the *Philistine* for December 1902: "The man who lives truth does not think it worthwhile to formulate it. He knows no more of truth than the fishes of the sea," this was his Emersonian intuition riding high. But from this he went to: "It is the gyve and fetter that make a man formulate truth. Only prisoners meditate. And so does the philosopher forever meditate upon plans for escape—escape from his own limitations, and the bonds of custom, prejudice, ignorance, and pride." This bit of free association was a rare one. It conceded that human limitations are both inner and outer, and it tossed in pride as a limitation. Hubbard seldom mentioned pride on any basis other than "of course" and "so what?"

Hubbard's fatalism showed itself repeatedly in his own tactics for coping with destiny. He had a sometimes latent conviction that indirection was the best way to navigate. "Most of our best moves are accidents," says the William Morris (1900) *Little Journey,* "and every good thing begins as something else." Two years later—at the time of the scandal—he was saying that "a goodly dash of indifference is a requisite in the formula for doing a great work. Nobody knows what the Goal is—we are sailing under sealed orders." There was some mistrust of humanity in this, which became explicit in 1909: "We lose that for which we clutch. The hot attempt to secure a thing sets in motion an opposition which defeats us." The long split in his personal life probably had a lot to do with this feeling of being rudderless. One of his early remarks of this kind sounds like very personal reminiscence only slightly disguised. "On sober second thought," he remarked in 1897, "I am not sure what is a tribulation and what a blessing. I'm not positive I would know a blessing should I see it coming up the street. For as I write it comes to me that the Great Big Black Things that have loomed against the horizon of my life, threatening to devour me, simply loomed and nothing more. The things that have really made me miss my train have always been sweet, soft, pretty, pleasant things of which I was not in the least afraid."

Two of the strongest forces in Hubbard's growing up seemed to be at war in him for most of his life. One was Calvinism—not the specific doctrines, but the bred-in-the-bone conviction that man was a poor and fated thing by himself but that glory and fulfillment lay in resting in the Lord and doing His will. The other was the rampant individualism of the material world. Here, as elsewhere, Hubbard seemed to want it both ways. He launched out on his sorties after what he wanted. When this got him in trouble, he turned on his back and floated with the current and told himself that "the last word is this: Nothing matters and no difference what happens the end is well." Or, as his strength came back and his enemies were confounded, "Religion is in the heart of man and its chief quality is resignation and a grateful spirit."

Hubbard's "universe within" often heaved and shook with his conflicts. Much of his better writing reflected this inner dialectic. This endless winnowing was perhaps what his sister Mary had in mind when she wrote that "his whole life, whatever his mistakes, was a search to find God."

Alice's religion was more matter of fact. It was simply "to express the best within us in love, art, music, literature, oratory, building, sowing, plowing, reaping, and work done from the joy in one's heart." And one of the few times she touched on the possibility of human perversity concerned a hymn that had given her much "trouble and speculation" as a child:

> Prone to wander Lord, I feel it,
> Prone to leave the God I love;
> Here's my heart, Lord, take and seal it,
> Seal it for thy courts above.

"How could a man be prone to wander from what he loved?" Alice asked. She could see no sense in it; "Why must God catch this heart, take it and chain it to Him, willy nilly, if it were His already?" The back of her hand to Him, anyway; "What business had He with it if it were not His?"

During the period of Hubbard's "search for God," there was a noticeable reuniting of many of the subdivided Protestant sects. This was especially true in rural areas. As sectarian differences came to seem less important, and as population either dwindled or was replaced by Catholic immigration, there were often more churches than could be supported. In some towns the situation came to a choice between one united church or no church. Hubbard claimed to have once called the starveling East Aurora preachers into conference and proposed that they all go to work for him. Then he would support one central Temple of Man for the town—no creed, no dues, open to all. "Two were inclined to accept it, two laughed heartily and refused to take me seriously, and three flew into wrath and called me names." And, with the dilution of denominational intensities, churches began to pay more attention to life on earth. Especially in the cities, with their vast new evils, religious groups became increasingly involved in reform and welfare work.

In spite of his own part in it, Hubbard's reaction to this creeping secularism was mixed. His stubborn Puritan underpinning sometimes found the relaxing of orthodoxy not entirely admirable. "Most preachers who dole out the glad tidings of great joy—that most every one is going to hell—do not believe it for a moment," he said. "They are plain hypocrites and grafters. This is what saves their relish for chicken-pie and gives them capacity for pastoral calls." And the fact that many churches were becoming "largely social clubs" did not please him. He was often disturbed by this spreading softness, and he complained that "these Men's Clubs of the Presbyterian Church are only possible by dressing the preacher as a clown and having him dance a jig on the Sacred Book." As for higher dignitaries, "Our bishops now are a weakling lot . . . if they be Methodist bishops, who are only make-believe bishops, having slipped the cable that bound them to the past, we pound them familiarly on the back and address them as 'bish.' "

In Hubbard's groping—and that of many of his contemporaries—establishing a new conception of religion involved coming to terms with science. Darwin and his followers had shaken the authority of the Book, so it seemed logical to look to them for equivalent answers. Many people tried —some with an illusion of success—to invest science with the responsibility of confirming that God was in His heaven and all was right with the world. Revelation was suspect, but science was to prove that "the unknown cause that rules the world by unchanging laws is a movement forward toward happiness, growth, justice, peace and right. Therefore the scientist, who perceives that all is good when rightly perceived and rightly understood is really the priest and holy man. . . . The more we know of this world the better we think of it." A little piece which he reworked several times over the years showed the extent to which Hubbard thought of science as mostly a replacement in the cast of the religion of his boyhood. "Twenty-five years ago there existed a well defined cult known as the Corner Grocery Infidels . . . continually asking, 'Who did Cain marry?' and, 'If God is all-powerful, why doesn't he kill the devil?' Then the man grinned triumphantly. . . . But now the Corner Grocery Infidel is no more. You will search in vain, unless you look in the church. He is in the Amen Corner with all his pertinacity, his cold Thou-Shalt-NOT morality, his stubbornness. . . .The thing he now doubts is Science, but that which he denies is, as before, Deity. He doubts both God's mercy and intelligence."

Many Americans in Hubbard's time got their ideas about science, evolution, society, and progress from Herbert Spencer. A self-educated man, who received little recognition from academic England until he was past middle age, Spencer was hero and teacher to the public-library scholar and the small-town philosopher. Hubbard was no exception. Of his various definitions of science, the one he used most frequently came from Spencer: "Science is the classified knowledge of the common people" (sometimes rendered as "classified commonsense"). The definition alone is a fair measure of the distance from Spencer's, and Hubbard's, day to ours.

Like his formulations about religion, Hubbard's attempts to pin down a rationale of knowledge covered a wide field. He made many a brave start: "In life everything lies in the mass—materials are a mob—a man's measure is his ability to select, reject, organize." What came next? Maybe this: "to be scientific one must be able to classify and coordinate the facts that logic and reason supply." ("Facts" from logic and reason? No observation, no measurement? Any way of checking conclusions?) Plainly, this was a rough stretch of road. Facts were often a considerable nuisance to Hubbard, and he often seemed to be acting on his own reading of Emerson to "dissipate to shining ether" their "solid angularity."

When Hubbard picked the twelve men to include in his 1905 *Little Journeys to the Homes of Great Scientists,* he showed what he thought important in science and scientists. He began with Copernicus and Galileo, whose effect on their time was roughly analogous to that of Darwin on Hubbard's America. But, in his treatment, Hubbard was more concerned with their persecution by the Church than with Galileo's use of "sensible experiments and necessary demonstrations." Sir Isaac Newton was included, of course, and Darwin. The others were: Humboldt, Herschel, Haeckel, Linnaeus, Huxley, Tyndall, Wallace, and John Fiske. And of these he thought Humboldt and Haeckel the greatest. Apart from the historical giants he could not avoid, Hubbard's Great Scientists were either naturalist-explorers (describers, classifiers, catalogers) or they were men of universal knowledge—philosophical synthesizers like Haeckel or walking encyclopedias like John Fiske. The idea of science as method, or of scientist as experimenter, hardly made an appearance.

He was not alone in his confusion about the nature of science, even though this period witnessed a dramatic public demonstration that should have been revealing. Dr. Walter Reed's tracking-down of the transmission-process of yellow fever was a story that Hubbard might have found as worthy of celebration as Lieutenant Rowan's message-carrying. It had everything: the following of a hunch in the face of authoritative ignorance, working through a tangle of possibilities with controlled experiments until the answers were solid, heroism, and dramatic suspense—and the result was a great human liberation. But if science in general was a puzzle to Hubbard, medical science was a blind spot of formidable proportions. After all, Dr. Silas had been a crank and a bore on the germ theory.

This blind spot shows up in Hubbard's long fight against vaccination. In his time there were reasons for some trepidation about being vaccinated. Vaccines were sometimes contaminated; the job wasn't always carefully done; and occasionally a child died of tetanus as a result. And there were people who objected to vaccination because it was compulsory. But Hubbard's objection was a flat-footed assertion that injecting a disease into a healthy body was an abomination. "The idea that a person after having a certain disease can not again have that disease has no basis in science," he declared. "People who live rightly are well. It is right living and sanitary surroundings that have banished smallpox." The way he mowed down realities once his intuitions had spoken was blatant in one of his early pronouncements on vaccination:

Dr. Jenner's "discovery" came from the chance remark of an unthinking, unscientific country wench. To prove his case, Dr. Jenner declared that he had inoculated his cowpox friends with genuine smallpox and that there were no ill effects. It is much more likely that in his excess of zeal Dr. Jenner lied, than that he deliberately laid himself open to the charge of committing murder.

. . . a folk-lore superstition became a scientific fact. And the falsehood went

spinning down the centuries. . . . Vaccination has got to go along with black
cat salve for itch, sheep-nanny tea for mumps, and sulphur and molasses.
Syphilis, consumption and loss of eyesight and hearing are common results of
vaccination. Health is natural; disease is abnormal.

But occasionally he contradicted his own health-is-natural brand of
nature worship. "Why does Nature retain the appendada?" he asked, at a
time when this was regarded as a major intellectual problem. "My answer
is that Nature does not know it is loaded; the Dame is ignorant, wasteful,
reckless, and faulty in many ways. She is a slattern, as we who love her
know full well."

Alice seldom got involved in this sort of puzzlement. Her idea of
science was as matter of fact as her rejection of a capricious God. Scientists,
to her, were not charged with proving "that all is good when rightly perceived"; as she saw it, they "were not making natural laws, but simply stating
them, telling what they saw." Not that her faith in a beneficent universe
was less than her husband's, but she had less time or taste for doubt and
pointless speculation. She had all that activity at Roycroft to supervise, and
with Elbert often away lecturing, it was a heavy load.

And lecturing he often was. In the winter of 1905–1906, he made
fifteen lectures between December 7th and February 4th, with three weeks
off for the holidays. Before Christmas: Kingston and Patchogue, New York;
Kansas City, St. Louis; and Wichita; starting January 10th at Cleveland,
on to Cincinnati, Georgetown, Kentucky, Dayton, Philadelphia, Baltimore,
Washington, Norfolk, Boston, and Carnegie Hall in New York City. This
was a typical schedule, and he didn't seem to resist it anymore; he rather
gloried in it as an old pro, and made jokes about it.

Introductions are usually by chairmen unknown to the audience, introducing
a man the chairman does not know. I have been introduced as Fray Albertus,
Mr. Hubbell, Mr. Roycroft and as the Sage of East Philistine. And whenever
the Chair does not whisper to me in a clove voice, asking, "Where is East
Aurora?" I am depressed, slighted, undone.

He attended other public ceremonials, too, including the fifteenth anniversary
banquet of the International Correspondence Schools. Seated between Episcopal and Catholic bishops, he was introduced as one of "the three bishops
we have with us . . . the Bishop of all Outsiders."

With Hubbard's public image in better shape, and the Roycroft enterprises growing again—by 1907, the combined circulation of the *Philistine*

and *Little Journeys* was more than 200,000 per month—the flow of visitors was increasing and the Roycroft Inn was being rebuilt. The young Dard Hunter was sent to New York City to learn the making of leaded-glass windows at a firm of church architects. When he returned, his project was to make eight large windows for the dining room—tulip clusters in pink, green, purple, and blue. It took him six months to complete the windows, and they were much admired. But the more young Dard looked at their garish colors, the more unhappy he became. One cold November morning before breakfast he went to work on them with a hammer, and was smashing out the last one when his astonished employer appeared. There were explanations, and a promise to make new ones. The last word was from Elbert as Dard was leaving the scene: "Dard, if you feel inclined to smash your next set of windows, please wait until summertime."

By this period, the Roycroft Library had a good collection of European art periodicals and books, incunabula, and Kelmscott Press books. Dard Hunter became a considerable admirer of the William Morris tradition. Few indeed of the long procession of honest Roycrofters were as congenial in talent and temperament to the Morris mystique. The skills of the graphic arts came naturally to Dard Hunter, and he took to craftsmanship with unworldly absorption—and with an impatience with people that was often a part of the pattern. When word came that Morris's daughter was to lecture to a woman's club in Buffalo, it was eminently fitting that Hubbard should send Dard to attend, carrying an invitation for Miss Morris to visit Roycroft. Hubbard added his special touch to the proceedings by telling Dard what a ravishing young beauty he was going to meet.

He was the only man in the audience, and "when I saw Miss May Morris, I knew that Mr. Hubbard had been teasing me. . . . She was not very attractive, and was at least twice my age." The lecture "was sarcastic and critical of America" and its uncultured barbarians. Dard was "disturbed and resentful," but he had been given a message to deliver, and he persevered:

After the long lecture I . . . approached Miss Morris. When she unfolded the letter and saw the signature her eyes flashed. . . . "I most certainly will not go to East Aurora, nor do I have any desire to see that obnoxious imitator of my dear father." With an air of disdain she crumpled the note in her hand and gave it back to me.

It was probably characteristic of both of them that Dard did not report the results of his mission, and Hubbard did not ask.

There were other artists, designers, and craftsmen more or less permanently at Roycroft by this time. With Alice's steady hand on the controls, the place was changing from a rather unpredictable bundle of shifting enterprises into a solid going concern. And at the productive heart of it was the printing plant, with its expensive equipment and its large complement of skilled and semiskilled helpers. And all of these people on the payroll were more than so many impersonal hands. They gave Elbert Hubbard his primary audience, his social base, and a large part of his identity. Though he was The Boss, he was also Father, Prophet, and Lord of the Manor. And this carried obligations.

In addition to the special sort of leadership and quasi-pastoral duties required of him, there was the practical need to go on "giving" work and livelihood to his flock. We can add to this the financial dynamism of an expanding printing business. In his last years, Hubbard was to reminisce about this aspect:

My first intent was to print entirely by hand. But gradually we got over that idea . . . quantities that we never possibly could have turned out by hand. Then I bought a rotary press. And when you buy a rotary press and run in debt for it, you hustle like hell and buy another rotary press, to get the money to pay for the first one. Then you have to buy a power cutter and put in a monotype to pay for the second rotary press. You didn't intend to expand, but like the beaver that climbed the tree, the dogs were after you and you had to.

And there was the important fact that the Roycroft "product" was essentially what Hubbard could mine and market from his single brain and personality. Many helpers were needed, to be sure; but everything had to carry his touch.

When the *Message* made him famous, another pressure began to make itself felt. A goodly number of people might subscribe to the periodicals, buy the books and the art goods, come to the Inn, and attend the lectures. But this audience was a limited minority group, and by 1907 or thereabouts he had pretty much reached the end of its potential as a market. There remained the business corporations, large ones, that would order half a million reprints and not haggle about price.

Many of the historical judgments on Hubbard have put it simply: he was always a phony, and once he discovered that big business would pay handsomely for reactionary propaganda disguised as culture and homely philosophy, he sold out. It wasn't that simple. The *Message* appeared in 1899. Its success pretty clearly showed what kind of preachment would keep those presses clanking long and profitably. But it would be around 1910 before fronting for business became central in Hubbard's activity. In the interim, if he sensed the direction in which he was being pushed by all these converging vectors, it didn't keep him from enjoying himself.

In 1905, he wrote a *Little Journey* on Sir Isaac Newton. Newton had been one of the pioneering minds in modern science; he had also been a devoutly religious man and a writer of theology. The combination intrigued Hubbard, and he cast around for another example of what looked to him like Jekyll-Hyde behavior. He came up with a long aside about "the greatest financial exploiter in America today." This man, whom he didn't name, was "an orthodox Christian, taking an active part in missionary work and the spread of the Gospel. In his family he is gentle, kind and tender; a good neighbor, a punctillious church-goer, a leader in Sunday-school, a considerate teacher of little children." As a businessman, on the other hand, he was "cold, calculating, and if opposed, vindictive . . . Eviction, destruction, suicide and insanity have trod in his train. A picture of him makes you think of that dark and gloomy canvas where Alexander, Caesar and Napoleon ride slowly side by side through a sea of stiffening corpses. Bribery, coercion, violence and even murder have been this man's weapons. He is the richest man in America."

Hubbard's feelings about, and relations to, the Rockefeller family and the Standard Oil Company were to undergo some startling shifts in the next few years. But in 1905, six years after the *Message,* it was hard to find much of a sell-out in that near-libel he tucked into his pamphlet on Newton. About a year later he had moved a little farther along this path. He had written a piece on Standard Oil that the company proposed to reprint, and Dard Hunter was assigned to design the cover. Strictly on his own, Dard worked a very subtle stylized octopus into his drawing, and submitted it to his employer:

Mr. Hubbard studied the design for fully a minute, and then he looked up at me with a dim suggestion of a smile. I thought I detected a slight twinkle in his brown eyes. I expected to be sent back . . . to make another, and less pointed design. But, instead, his only comment was: "That's great, the officials of the oil company are so imbued with their own righteousness they'll never recognize themselves."

Thousands of copies were distributed with the octopus on the cover, and "the officials of the 'trust' never knew what quiet satisfaction we had at their expense."

Elbert Hubbard in 1904,
in his prime as Master of Roycroft,
author of *A Message to Garcia,*
and "General Inspector of the Universe"

The Roycroft podium

11

Art & Glory

DURING MICHAEL MONAHAN'S brief honeymoon period at Roycroft, he concocted the doggerel we have used at the front of this book ("Take the / train / for East / Aurory, / Where we / work / for Art / and Glory"). Art and Glory made an appropriate motto, but with special meanings. Hubbard had tramped the museums, dipped into the books, listened to the talk of the knowing, and written several volumes of *Little Journeys* more or less concerned with artists. Nothing very definite of all this, unless it was ". . . at the last the artist only reproduces himself." As the Roycroft enterprises grew, and as experience indicated what people would buy, the haphazard eclecticism of the early days settled into an output heavily weighted with the bizarre, the imitative, and the precious. The books, copper, wrought iron, furniture, and tooled leather items were seldom art, but they were most certainly arty.

This distinction has increasingly been found a sufficient reason to damn Hubbard and all his works. At the time that all this was going on, however, it wasn't quite so simple. Between the starkness of frontier utilitarianism and the ornate gentilities of new wealth, a lot of experimenting and shaking down were needed. The Roycroft art goods may look pretty silly today, but in their time they helped to bring questions of taste, design, fitness, and beauty into an enlarging public domain as matters to be taken seriously. The process was quite similar to the impact of Hubbard's writing on people who were looking for new large ideas in a world awash with change. And as the artworks became a going concern (like the publications and the lectures), showmanship became more controlling. As Hubbard told Harry Kemp: "The people expect startling things . . . and, as the winds of genius blow where they list—when they refuse to blow in the direction required, divine is the art of buncombe."

By this time, Hubbard didn't seem to be worrying about any need "to guard and keep alive the sacred fires." He had a job to do and a payroll to meet, and "art is not a thing separate and apart—art is only the beautiful way of doing things." The artist was simply the man who does his work well and "adds to it a last touch of personality." And if this was a retreat from earlier visions of greatness, it was also consistent with another persisting Hubbard vision—that life should be one and indivisible. Work, play, love, contemplation, expression should all be kept simmering in one large pot. "Preserving the unities" was Hubbard's shorthand for this quest of wholeness. He had pulled out of the soap business partly because he had found ordinary business "a jealous god." If a man "allow religion, politics, philanthropy, love of art to creep into his waking hours . . . his financial doom is sealed." Robert Owen was a Hubbard hero because "private business was to him a public trust" and he "got his education from his work, at his work and strove throughout his long life to make it possible for others to do the same." This was Hubbard's program even more than it was Owen's. The Roycroft morning and afternoon time-outs from work—anticipations of today's coffee break, though Hubbard's helpers were supposed to spend the time frolicking out of doors and breathing deeply through the nostrils—were part of this pattern. So were the concerts, lectures, games of catch, and picnics and haying parties.

Part of Hubbard's quarrel with higher education was that it *didn't* preserve the unities—it put young people into what he regarded as an artificial and parasitic world. A large part of Alice's appeal for Hubbard had been that he could share with her most of his activities and aspirations, whereas with Bertha he had to defend himself from domestic trivia and "pattypan emotions." Similarly, Hubbard's growing glorification of the business world, after he was solidly established in his own business, came from this urge to preserve the unities. "Any man who does not enjoy himself in his business should quit it for the good of the business."

But American life was moving away from the unities. The trend had two world wars to go before it became a rout, but it was perfectly visible in Hubbard's time. In this one of his directions, he was swimming against the current. And many of his doings that came to seem so tasteless or ridiculous—such as dragging scraps of classical history or philosophy into ads for chewing gum or pork sausage—resulted from his trying to keep all of life in one compartment. He saw life whole—if often unsteadily—wherever he could; when he didn't see it that way any longer, it was often because life had moved away from him rather than he from it.

The process was often more complex than this, of course. Hubbard's perceptions and his judgment were often fitful and erratic. He had all those multiple selves to make his peace with, and few stable reference points either inside or outside of his "universe within." The same evasive quality that saturated his life characterized the Roycroft art objects—they came forward boldly but wavered into eccentricity on the point of honest expression. There wasn't enough guiding philosophy or stable vision behind them —or an assured taste on the part of the public that bought them. Only a self-conscious fumbling around on both sides for the different and the picturesque.

Hubbard's art, at its best, was something else entirely: it was zest and foolery, and putting more into everyday living than going through the motions. It was a complex internal switchboard that lit up the commonplace with special meaning and sparkle. Art was putting on a good show and playing up to—and a little beyond—the expectations of others. A story told me some years ago is typical. The man who told it had visited East Aurora and stayed at the Inn during Hubbard's last years. A honeymooning couple was eating in the dining room, and the bride was watching Hubbard across the room and commenting on his appearance and manners in a high, carrying voice. As the meal came to an end, she wondered audibly if he would drink coffee out of his saucer (the coffee may well have been Postum). The Fra made an elaborate, poker-faced production out of drinking *all* of his coffee out of his saucer. Then he went over to the couple, shook each by the hand, and presented them with an autographed deluxe Roycroft volume.

This playing up to an audience went on into practical jokes. Some of these were largely for his own amusement—such as leading fashionably dressed visitors to a picnic by a route that required fording a creek, when a perfectly serviceable bridge was just around the bend. Some were real productions. One evening the guests on the Peristyle of the Inn got into a considerable debate. Did clothes make the man? Or were externals all nonsense and only spiritual essences important? The embattled guests asked Hubbard to adjudicate. He smilingly evaded, and promised to take the matter up in "the next lesson." The day following, he rounded up the male guests for a romp in the swimming hole. When they came out of the water, their clothing had vanished—all but shoes. After there had been a period of nude meditation, Ali Baba turned up with a supply of identical hickory shirts and overalls. When the party got back to the Inn, Hubbard called to the ladies on the Peristyle to "come down and pick out your husbands."

And if Hubbard's "art" was seldom pure, it was also apt to come off second best when it tangled with the Glory that was the other Roycroft specialty. Bemused disciples were part of Glory. So were reprint orders of half a million copies, entranced lecture audiences, the overloaded East Aurora post office, and five hundred happy helpers waiting for the boss to come home with the payroll. The job-in-itself was always getting confused with its by-products or its public image. To "write a beautiful thing which shall link my name with that of the Great Ones gone" was pure Glory—as was the constant concern with greatness itself.

As the market and the payroll assumed higher priorities, Hubbard began to need more helpers whose talents ran in these directions. He already had some, including a good one in Bert, but he got something special along these lines when Felix Shay came to Roycroft.

In 1907, Felix was a young man with a lively, off-trail mind, a way with words, and a steady eye for the main chance. He was doing direct-mail promotion for a small firm in New York City and living in suburban New Jersey, where, with other eager beavers, he belonged to a self-improvement reading-and-discussion circle. One of the boys had brought a copy of the *Philistine* to a meeting, and it hit them where they lived. "There was an epigram on the cover: 'Fences are made for those who cannot fly.' Only those who have lived in a community where flying is strictly against the rules can appreciate the stimulation in that thought to a group of young fellows."

Felix sent a special-delivery application for a job, personally addressed to Hubbard. He learned later that it would otherwise have been answered with a form letter and filed away. Hubbard was intrigued, and answered, "If you are half as good as you say you are, I think you had better come at once."

This was enough for Felix. "By noon I had resigned my job, collected what was due me, and was down at the railroad station. I had enough to pay my railroad fare up and back, and three days there at a reasonably priced hotel." He got into Buffalo at two in the morning, spent a wakeful five hours in a Temperance hotel until he could get a train to East Aurora, and arrived in the early light of the winter morning. Bert took him in hand, told him to register at the Inn; his father would see him later.

So began his initiation. It was to continue for some time. "After lunch I was standing in front of the fireplace chewing my under lip, when a man in a soft flannel shirt, flyaway tie, and big soft hat, with the gentlest eyes imaginable, came in and greeted me. He did not mention his name and I was only half-convinced that he was Elbert Hubbard. I hoped he was because I was drawn to him . . . made me feel comfortable and at ease." Nothing was said about a job. Felix was invited to walk to the barn with the man in the big hat, and a woman, to see the horses. On the way, there was a game of catch. "Well, *that* I could do! So maybe I did have that 'conference' on the way to the barn without knowing it . . . the last thing Hubbard wanted to hear was my well-rehearsed phrases." The horses were saddled, and away went Elbert and Alice in a flurry of kicked-up snow. Felix was left to wonder how soon his bill at the Inn would outrun his net worth.

No further notice was taken of him until after dinner, when a group of Roycrofters invited him to join a six-mile hike in a snowstorm. If this was how it was, Felix was game, and he tagged along in his thin shoes and city clothes ("I was cold, cold.") But he stuck it out, "enjoyed the company, and managed to maintain my morale until almost back in the village, when the group stopped . . . to admire and exclaim over the way the snow had drifted against the tree trunks. Then and there I said to myself, 'This is the Nut-Family Robinson; they're all crazy!' " He might have left then, but he wasn't sure he would be able to pay his bill. The next day was Saturday and ". . . nothing happened."

On Sunday, things came back in focus. Hubbard made a talk in the Chapel, and Felix began to feel that maybe this was the place for him after all. "In the afternoon there was a cross country walk . . . fifty or more people . . . played catch all the way . . . that night I had my talk with Mr. and Mrs. Hubbard. They were very pleasant and wanted to know what I could do. I told them at length. After a while Hubbard said, 'Very well! You come to work tomorrow morning at eight. We'll pay you ten dollars a week.' Crash! . . . Hadn't I just told the man I had been making thirty-five dollars a week? . . . Slowly I realized . . . this was a test." Felix survived the test, and after two weeks Elbert sent him to Alice to negotiate a permanent salary.

Felix seems to have come closer to filling Hubbard's need for a son who would be an extension of himself than either Bert or Sanford. If Hubbard was something of a calculated hero, Felix was very much a calculated hero-worshiper. He started his job with a general assignment to expedite sales and subscriptions. No one had assigned him a place to work, so he dragged a desk into Hubbard's private office and set up shop there. His next major move was to go to the Roycroft Librarian and request copies of everything Hubbard had written. This provided his evening reading for several months, and it did him no harm when word got back to the boss.

By 1908, the *Little Journeys* had covered some one hundred and fifty-seven "greats," winding up with "Great Teachers": Moses, Confucius, Pythagoras, Plato, King Alfred, Friedrich Froebel, Booker T. Washington, Thomas Arnold, Erasmus, Hypatia, St. Benedict, and Mary Baker Eddy—another "odd team." In reviewing the history of these "tabloid biographies" and describing his working methods, Hubbard said, "It is a habit now, and like Tennyson's brook, I am going on forever." For the following year's series, he announced, "the Little Journeys will be to the Homes of Great Business Men," and his announcement set the tone for considerably more than the series of pamphlets. "I have selected this theme, not simply because there is a fine heroism in business, when done in a big way, but to picture . . . the New Science of Business."

The subjects of the new series were to be: Robert Owen, James Oliver, Stephen Girard, M. A. Rothschild, Philip Armour, John Jacob Astor, Peter Cooper, Andrew Carnegie, George Peabody, A. T. Stewart, H. H. Rogers, and James T. Hill. All were treated as heroic figures, "discoverers, pioneers," men whose special genius lay in "transforming ideas into deeds." In addition to their individual greatness, they illustrated that New Science of Business which recognized "honesty, equity, beauty and brotherhood as most valuable assets" and "may yet be a religion."

In writing of Robert Owen or Peter Cooper, Hubbard might wander a long way from solid history or biography, but that was nothing new. He was still writing what was in his heart, and the values and judgments he underlined were his own. If enough readers liked it, it was a good issue. It was different when his subjects were alive, wealthy, and directing competitive corporations. He could still be as fancy as he liked in his treatment, but inevitably, the number of reprints ordered came to be an important criterion of his success. This became high comedy with the Andrew Carnegie *Little Journey.* An autographed copy of the finished job went off to the great man at Skibo Castle. During the next weeks, the inner Roycroft circles speculated happily on the astronomical reprint order or other rewards —"maybe he'll give us a new library"—they might expect. But Andrew Carnegie had not become one of the world's richest men by advertising himself. He duly acknowledged receipt, saying that he "could not help bursting into laughter many times . . . We shall, of course, want, say, one hundred copies."

Except for one other on Edison, this series was to end the *Little Journeys.* The title and the approximate form were to continue, but for fanciful plugs for business firms: "A Little Journey to the Home of Pebeco Tooth Paste" or whatever. Usually these were bound into the ad section of the

Philistine, paid for, and reprinted in quantity. Hubbard's pursuit of greatness was circling back to the present, and merging with his need to keep those presses rolling.

Over the years he had had many "moments when we think of the world's most famous ones as surely eight feet tall, and having voices like fog horns," and he had sprinkled his early *Little Journeys* with various definitions of greatness: "I never saw a genius, and really do not know what genius is, but surely there is plenty of precedent for speaking upon themes concerning which we know nothing. Goodness me!" Genius, he offered, was "the ability to act wisely without precedent—the power to do the right thing for the first time," or "a flash of the divine spirit that goes straight to the heart of things. The man simply sees—that is all."

He had always had mixed feelings about the untidy personal lives he found among history's authenticated geniuses. A certain amount of this he could go along with, even celebrate: "Hike for respectability and cuddle safely under her Paisley and it's you for a mollycoddle." "Plaster-of-Paris saints" were no heroes of his, and a certain amount of horsing-around was part of his prescription for the good life:

. . . climb a tree occasionally, and hoot like an owl and caw like a crow; stand on your head and yell like a Comanche. The man who does not relax and hoot a few hoots voluntarily, now and then, is in grave danger of hooting hoots and standing on his head for the edification of the pathologist and trained nurse, later on. The madhouse yawns for the person who always does the proper thing. Impropriety, in right proportion, relieves congestion, and thus are the unities preserved.

But there were limits, and he had little tolerance for the "voluptuary of labor" who was apt to "assume airs and declare himself exempt along the line of morals and manners." And, of course, as a proprietor and employer, he had special reason to downgrade some of the genius types who reminded him of the many Roycroft transients who "were willing to do anything but work—. . . to run things, to preach, to advise, to make love to the girls."

As Hubbard cruised on through the historic greats of the *Little Journeys,* a somewhat weary domestic perspective on greatness began cropping out: "The great man is only supremely great after he is well dead, or to the people who see him from a distance. To those who have to live with him he is at times more or less of a trial." Amplifying this in another place, he said that "life never did, nor can, consist in doing brilliant things all day long. Before breakfast most men are rogues. And even brilliant men are brilliant only two hours a day. . . . Life is life to everybody. We must eat, breathe, sleep, exercise, bathe, dress and lace our shoes. We must be decent to folks, agreeable to friends, talk when we should and be silent when we ought. To be companionable—fit to live under the same roof with good people—consists in being neither pretty nor clever."

In his years with Bertha, he had often lamented the woes of both large-minded men and their bird-brained wives. But after he was married to Alice, he came back to less personal variations on the same theme. "To center on science and devote one's thoughts to philosophy, produces a being more or less deformed. There is great danger in specialization; nature sacrifices the man in order to get the thing done. Abstract thought unfits one for domestic life; for, to a degree, it separates a man from his kind. The proper advice to a woman about to marry a philosopher would be, 'Don't!' "

As he circled back to his contemporaries, his specifications for greatness began to stabilize. First, the man must make no bones about his own superiority. "The man of masterly mind is perforce an Egoist. When he speaks he says 'Thus saith the Lord.' If he did not believe in himself, how could he make others believe? Small men are apologetic . . . not so the Great Souls—the fact that they are here is proof that God sent them. Their actions are regal, their language oracular, their manner affirmative." Second, Hubbard's heroes had to be men of action. Ideas and sensibilities were all very well, but it was making things happen that counted. He even patronized Emerson during this period: ". . . in spite of all his pretty talk about living near to Nature's heart he never ventured into the woods outside of hallooing distance from the house. He could neither ride a horse, shoot, nor sail a boat." There was a third requirement, usually: the great man was some sort of Outsider.

As Hubbard looked over twentieth-century America for this kind of hero, most of them turned out to be businessmen. They were the ones who were changing the face of the country, providing "opportunity for all to work, earn, grow and become." They were the ". . . bold men who have blazed, and are blazing a trail that civilization is to follow." The generations since have developed a different perspective, and their historians have often seen Hubbard's Great Businessmen as exploiters, despoilers, beneficiaries of special privilege. To the progressive-radical movement, big business has meant Power itself. From Hubbard's special perspective, nothing of the sort. These men were outsiders like himself—scorned by the landed aristocrats and the literati, harried and abused by demagogues like Theodore Roosevelt and journalists like the muckrakers (none of these could have earned an honest day's pay at Roycroft), and, above all, they were self-made individualists who had never been to college.

But in spite of this going overboard, Hubbard did make some distinctions. He tried to rule out the mere boomers, speculators, and corporate manipulators as a blight on the kind of big business that was "essentially a divine calling." He also kept turning up occasional heroes from other fields. When Booker T. Washington was accused of running Tuskegee as "a tyrant, a dictator, and an egotist," Hubbard came roaring to his defense. Of course, he was all these things: "the man who advances on chaos and transforms it into cosmos is perforce a dictator and an egotist. . . . A man like this is the instrument of Deity." The fire-eating Populist, Tom Watson, was a Hubbard hero. So was Cleveland's single-tax mayor, Tom L. Johnson; Hubbard tried to start a "Johnson for President" boom at a time when Johnson was in an all-out struggle with "The Interests" in Cleveland.

As the *Little Journeys* swung into their celebration of such creative heroes as James J. Hill, H. H. Rogers, and Philip Armour, another periodical was launched from East Aurora. Named the *Fra (Not for Mummies. A Journal of Affirmation)*, it was a very different affair from the pocket-size *Philistine*. The three or four thousand words in a typical *Philistine*—three or four main narratives, preachments, or editorial essays, well broken up with aphorisms and fillers—could be read complete in half an hour. The *Fra* was big: a nine-by-fourteen-inch page, with two columns of type per page. A typical issue contained over twenty thousand words. This was a library-table magazine.

The format of the *Philistine* was admirably suited to Hubbard's writing. The jokes, the aphorisms and "orphic sayings," the brief preachments, the sly cracks at his friends and enemies—all these fitted the impudent "brownie." It was also very well suited to odd-hours, scribbling-on-the-train writing. And although Hubbard did not write all of every issue after the first few years (it was often asserted that he wrote every word of every issue), the great bulk of it was his, and it showed it.

In announcing the new magazine in the March 1908 *Philistine*, Hubbard remarked: "They say I have been protesting long enough—that iconoclasm is all right, but Ecclesiastes says there is also a time to build; that I am flippant, slangy, rude and crude. . . . I'm going to keep right on with THE PHILISTINE. . . . I'm going to jump into things I do not like, stir up the animals with my feather duster, hoot when the mood is on, and sneeze when I feel like it. But certainly, I will commend men, women, and things, sometimes." The first masthead carried admonishments: "Do not stop to think about who are with you, or who are against you. It matters little at the last . . . BE YOURSELF. The first duty of every man is to himself—self protection is the first law of life. Earn your living—take care of yourself, and then out of the surplus of your earnings or your power, you can care for others."

There was a lot of space to fill in the *Fra*. From the beginning it was a magazine of many authors. The by-lines in the first issue were: The Fra, Dr. Jean Charcot, Ernest Crosby, Charles Ferguson, Luther Burbank, Leigh Mitchell Hodges, and Alice Hubbard. There was always an opening section with a boxed head: THE OPEN ROAD / AFOOT WITH THE FRA. Sometimes it was a single long essay. More often it was a rambling miscellany, often filled out by picking up bits that Hubbard had done previously in the *Philistine* or the *Little Journeys*. In some respects the *Fra* was the *Philistine* enlarged and fancied up. But the old sassy irreverence was apt to look silly on those enormous pages. The major new ingredient, in addition to the advertising, was didactic, flashy, endless prose from many hands. The format added to the scattered effect by using red or orange ink in great blobs on initial letters and filler paragraphs. The new journal was something of a printer's showpiece, with excellent register and presswork. But all this graphic virtuosity detracted from readability. There was too much material and too little focus. Insofar as the *Fra* did show an editorial personality in its first years, it came from Alice about as often as from its namesake.

As a teacher, Alice had been an admirer of Friedrich Froebel and his opening-flower approach to education. But her handling of the *Fra*'s audience had more of the recitation-conductress in it than the permissive spirit. An early feature was a series of "Roycroft Sunday School Lessons," arranged by Alice. These were usually concerned with the great man or woman whose portrait appeared on the cover. Sometimes the material was a full-scale treatment by Alice. Sometimes it combined quotations from the subject's writings with pickups from the *Little Journeys*. Some of the Lessons began with a general health thought such as "Exercise in the open air two hours each day. Breathe through the nostrils." Some of the Lessons closed with a "Golden Text," which might be almost anything, and a "Topic for Discussion," which was apt to be quite an agenda: "Can the slings and arrows of outrageous fortune overcome one who recognizes his divinity?" "How must we exercise to be saved?" or, "Individualism says, educate and refine the individual and he will make his own environment. Is this true?"

One of the reasons for launching the *Fra* was probably the inability of the pocket-sized *Philistine* to carry the volume and kind of advertising that was becoming available. As early as 1906, the *Philistine* was getting national name-brand ads—Gillette Safety Razors, Grape-Nuts and Postum, A.T.&T., Steinway Pianos, and automobiles—along with the New Thought publishers, health foods, and correspondence schools. And with the coming of Felix

Shay, Hubbard had acquired a helper who was a natural "Ad Man." Before long, Felix was selling ads, writing ads, and philosophizing about advertising with a noisy brashness that often took the play away from his boss. Hubbard's writing style was noticeably deteriorating in these later years, and Felix aped it at its worst: "The Wise Member of the Perfesh who writes into his Ads a little more than his wild desire for Cash—eventually gets the Cash. For be it known, we always get the Thing when we are Worthy." This was less than four years after the Philistine had said: "Most advertising is economic waste. . . . If there were no advertising we would get along without our daily rot, and if we got along without it for just a few months our sense of decency would forbid our ever getting it back."

Felix became quite an operator, though there is evidence that he sometimes steered a perilous course between his hero-boss and the General Superintendent. One of Felix's early concerns had been the annual Roycroft Catalog, timed for the Christmas season. "It was not especially my work (though my activities were neither prescribed nor proscribed) but because I was interested in sales volume I made it my work." One year something was wrong; the catalog wasn't visible and Christmas was looming. "On investigation, I discovered that several of Mrs. Hubbard's bright young ladies were playing around with it, and through not knowing how, they were getting nowhere, while maintaining a great dignity. . . . they called a 'conference' . . . bookbinders, artists, coppersmiths, furniture makers, designers, printers, steamfitters and plumbers present. . . . They theorized and suggested and moved and rejected till it came time . . . to adjourn. . . . I was disgusted . . . With time slipping by, another 'conference' was called for another evening—and I took my horse and went for a ride." The next morning he received a note from Hubbard—"some one had told him half a tale"—suggesting he "cultivate the co-operative attitude instead of the censorious one" and warned him, "If you start an argument and a lengthy explanation on this, I'll know I have written in vain." Felix "said nothing, as instructed. Some one else produced the catalog . . . late. . . . I did the next Roycroft catalog without assistance."

Felix might not have been at Roycroft to do that next catalog if Alice had completely accepted a clause in her husband's tributes in *White Hyacinths*. While praising her business wisdom and listing her Roycroft responsibilities, his style suddenly turned legalistic and announced that "she hires all employees and has the exclusive power to discharge." This latter power was one he would have been happy to delegate. But the evidence indicates that Alice passed this chore back to him forthwith. In an essay on "the Work of the Realist"—a very superior type, this, who was to "create and make actual the ideal world"—Alice went to some pains to insist that this Realist had "the courage and the strength . . . to eliminate from among his workers those who, while talking eloquently . . . are destroying the road he is making toward the Holy Land of Ideals." Hubbard finally worked out his own method of showing his courage and strength in these matters. When he decided to fire someone, he waited until he was about to start on a lecture trip, and then swung the ax with a written note—everything being over and forgotten by the time he returned. Felix thought this showed consideration and gentleness. "Thus were 'scenes' avoided and unkind truths made unnecessary." It was also a one-way street, as Felix came close to finding out.

The second time that Felix got into trouble with his boss, the situation was more complicated. Hubbard had worried for some time because a few of his helpers spent evenings in the East Aurora saloons and came home late and wavering. An election was coming up, and local-option prohibition was put on the ballot. Hubbard asked Felix how he would like to lead a dry parade (on horseback), and Felix was delighted with the prospect. Preparations continued, with Felix still delighted, until the day before the parade, when Hubbard posted a notice: "Everybody on the Roycroft payroll will walk in the dry parade tomorrow." There was much resentment of the notice, but only Felix objected directly. After brooding all day, he exploded about "intimidating voters" when he and Hubbard were leaving the office that night. Felix expected to be fired on the spot. He was told off, but that was all. The parade was a great success, with only Felix, "in solitary splendor," staying at his desk. Hubbard departed the next morning for a lecture, and he left a note for Felix. It catalogued the Shay shortcomings in the way of noncooperation, knocking instead of boosting, talking back, and the like. It also terminated the commissions on Roycroft sales that Hubbard had been paying him. Hubbard had paid these commissions—which amounted to considerably more than Felix's salary—out of his own bank account so as to spare other staff members from negative emotions. It was several weeks before this cloud blew over and Felix was spoken to again.

A couple of episodes during this period may have been important in strengthening Hubbard's identification with big business. About 1907, the Typographical Union put the Roycroft publications on its unfair list. This carried nothing like the economic force it would have thirty or forty years later, and apparently it didn't even come to Hubbard's attention until the proprietor of O'Sullivan's Heels, a steady advertiser and apparently something of a disciple, wrote in to say that as a good union man he would have to discontinue his *Philistine* ads. This led to several Hubbard antiunion blasts that brought in some top-brass fan mail and probably sold a lot of reprints. But there is no evidence that it shook up the Typographical Union, and Hubbard's anger soon erupted in something that seems like pointless spite. A little sleuthing brought out the fact that O'Sullivan's Heels were made on contract by a nonunion rubber manufacturer—apparently the only kind of rubber manufacturer there was at the time. This was proclaimed to the world (February 1909) in a full page of the *Fra's* advertising space.

Roycroft workers received a Christmas distribution of an extra few dollars, a ham or a turkey, sweaters or warm socks. Everyone worked on New Year's Day, because Hubbard felt that holidaying got the year started in the wrong spirit. The June 1908 *Philistine* explained the operations of one of the Roycroft fringe benefits:

Sickness is often incipient paranoia. In the Roycroft Shop we have a "Sick Benefit Fund," which provides that whenever a person is sick he shall pay a fine of a dollar a day, for every day he is absent from work, into a fund that is divided yearly among those who keep well.

To place a premium on breaking the laws of Nature is a poor scheme. Our plan keeps 'em robust!

It was that kind of place, and when Hubbard discussed another public figure who had a reputation as a benevolent employer, "Golden Rule" Jones, of Toledo, he showed what his employees were up against:

The man who attempts to better the condition of his helpers, dividing profits with them, must be very great and good, if the milk of human kindness in his soul does not turn to bonny-clabber. To help men who do not want to help themselves, and to benefit those who look with suspicion and hate on their benefactor, is the task that confronts the generous employer . . . you must do good by stealth, and be ever prepared to have your best motives traduced and vilified.

One of Hubbard's crusades over the years had been against the horrors of child labor in mines and mills. He returned to the subject often, and he put real weeping pathos into his treatment. Consequently, an incident in 1907 caused much hilarity in the nation's press. Hubbard's account of it had cold anger and considerable philosophic interest:

There is a difference between fact and truth. The fact is the actual circumstance . . . truth is the correct deduction which you draw . . .

You may see a man running down the street—that is a fact. But the reason why the man runs is truth . . . to meet his wife; or to escape his wife; or to meet another man's wife; to capture a burgler; or he may be a burglar; to catch a train; or for exercise; or he may be a lunatic running away from his keeper. If you are writing history it will be a very grave difference whether you write this man down as the keeper or the escaped lunatic. Nature gives us facts, but it is for man to distil truth from facts. All violence of direction is fatal to truth. . . .

So much for the warm up.

The Louisville "Courier-Journal," and various other people in the South are giving me the hoarse haw-haw because government detectives have found I was employing child labor. The fact was as stated.

People who are unable to understand truth, are quite sure to fumble the fact. These children come to the Roycroft Shop an hour in the morning and an hour in the afternoon. I taught them to draw, and to use water colors, and to fold papers and to keep the rooms dusted and tidy, and to run errands. . . .

Yes, I had paid the children wages . . . the same wage that I paid full grown men and women for a like service. I was warned to never let it happen again . . . and the busy penny-a-liner flashes the news that I was collared for violation of the child-labor laws! . . . The treatment I accord to the little folks of the neighborhood is the same I accord to my own children. I bring my children up to be useful.

There was nothing at Roycroft that was remotely comparable to child labor in cotton mills. But there was plenty of the "art of buncombe." When it showed up in full public view, there was justification for some of that "hoarse haw-haw." Harry Kemp had worked in that same bindery a couple of years before the child-labor inspectors visited it, and his reminiscences had both fact and truth, too:

. . . most of the illumination of the books was done by girls, even by children after school hours. The outlines of the letters and objects to be hand-illumined were printed in with the text, and the girls and children merely coloured them between the lines. . . . In each department, hidden behind gorgeous, flowing curtains, were time-clocks. . . . his musician-prodigy, a girl of eight, who worked in the afternoons in the bindery. And when a visiting party swept through that department, it was part of her job to rise as if under the impulse of inspiration, leave her work, and go to a nearby piano and play. . . .

But she was the only one who played. And she never played except when she was tipped the wink. And it was only one thing—a something of Rubenstein's which she had practiced . . . to perfection; and *that* rendered, with haughty head, like a little sibyl, she would go back to her work-bench. And if urged to play more, she would answer, lifting her great, velvet eyes in a dreamy gaze, "no, no more today. The inspiration has gone." And, awed, the visitors would depart.

This, too, was a form of Glory.

The Roycroft Shop. Hubbard's office was in the tower.

Richard Le Gallienne, Hubbard,
and Jerome Connor, about 1904

12

Because I Could

THE PUBLIC-PERFORMANCE Elbert Hubbard reached his all-time high when he did a twenty-week tour of Orpheum Circuit vaudeville in the 1909–1910 season. His act was simply a pared-down and intensified version of his typical lecture performance. It was not the sort of thing one would expect to hold its own with tumblers, trained dogs, and song-and-dance teams. "The lecturer," said Hubbard, "comes out and says, 'I am here!' On the Vaudeville Stage when the performer walks out of the wings the audience says 'Here we are!'" But the impresarios apparently counted on a claque of disciples in each audience, with the Fra's showmanship taking over and carrying through. So it proved, and there is no question but that it was compelling showmanship. There were a few incidents, such as the lady who demanded, audibly, "Is that all that man does?"; Hubbard enjoyed telling this story. And there was a Cincinnati gallery that hissed him and sent him off the stage, out of the theatre, and back to East Aurora— from where he had to be coaxed into resuming the tour; this he didn't mention.

In St. Louis, his friend Reedy perpetrated a joke that is still remembered (though Hubbard has been replaced by Oscar Wilde in some versions). Hubbard's routine included a breather for himself and the audience, during which he left the stage momentarily. When he came back on in St. Louis, Reedy, who was a local celebrity, had risen from a box in all his corpulent majesty, and was informing the audience that it was being taken in, the performer was an impostor and not the famous Fra. Hubbard picked up the cue by assuming a hangdog expression and saying, "It is true, ladies and gentlemen. I am not Elbert Hubbard . . . my name is William Marion

139

Reedy." When he worked up the incident into copy for the June 1911 *Fra,* he commented: "The point was a little too subtle; it was what you call a slow joke, but it finally got going. The box office told me afterward that there were over twenty people came and demanded their money back, as they came to see the real Fra Elbertus—not a fake. The sissy at the box office tried to pacify them by explaining that the real Fra was a fake anyway. But it wouldn't go."

This junket took a lot out of him. He reported that, while he always wrote steadily in the spare hours of his lecture tours, he was unable to write at all on this trip. As to why he took on such a job, his answer was simply, "Because I could." Which seems very much like the reason men climb mountains. And of course he enjoyed seeing his name in lights and hobnobbing with such as Harry Lauder and Eva Tanguay. One wonders what Alice thought of it all. Arthur Hopkins said that Hubbard put it up to her to decide whether he should sign the contract. Maybe she acquiesced for reasons similar to those of the wives of men who climb mountains.

A couple of years earlier, Alice had written a charming little essay of advice to women who were to entertain celebrities: ". . . the responsibility of being hostess to a Great Man is upon you. You cannot sit still under it. . . . You begin to wonder if you remembered to put everything in his room that he needs—and even if you did, great men are often peculiar, and this G. M. might want something you haven't thought of— you must not be negligent—what would he think of you? And so you knock gently at his door. . . ." Alice was probably passing the word in the hope it would spare Elbert some of the experiences he summed up in an essay of his own titled "The Horror of the Spare Room." By no means, Alice advised, should a hostess "plan enough things to last a week for any man with unlimited strength. . . . A man who is able to entertain you is able to entertain himself. Leave him to himself. He is in good company." But it doesn't appear that Alice's advice did much good. In his last years, Hubbard's lecture contract provided that he receive an additional fifty-dollar fee whenever he was entertained overnight in a private home.

There had been a time, of course, when Hubbard was ambivalent about his public front. In 1899, Amy Leslie had noted that the author of the *Message to Garcia* was "receiving many congratulations on his masterly defense of the downtrodden denizens of the brown stone fronts. In fact all the self-made men—those who have on them the loving marks of the hammer—consider it the greatest thing since Hamlet. Fra Elbertus is very smooth; free passes and free lunches are now his without asking." That

Hubbard felt a little sheepish himself was indicated by his writing that "just one man who has put on the gloves has scored a point at my expense, and that man is a woman . . ." But as his business following came to bulk larger and larger in his public, Hubbard's travel notes became increasingly full of name-dropping and of satisfaction with being Someone Important. "The conductor just came to me with a telegram [from] the General Manager. . . . 'Fra Elbertus is on your train. Please give him anything which the Hepburn Bill does not forbid.' I think the conductor must have shown that telegram to the boys . . . the chef wanted to turn himself loose, the coon says, 'Wouldn't you like the stateroom—you can have a table there.' He thinks I'm a Kentucky Cardinal, or a Kentucky Colonel, at least. . . . I was Buffalo Bill when I got on. Then I was Cap; next I was Kuhnel; then Guv'nor. Now I am addressed in a smothered Afro-American whisper, 'Aw say, Bishop!' "

He made even better copy out of the grotesqueries of celebrity. "Recently on a trip to California, eleven different men, at different times, came up, introduced themselves, shook hands and explained that they had had the pleasure of hearing my father lecture, read all he wrote, and wished to be remembered to him." And he gave the Hubbard legend a helping hand on many occasions, as in a purported conversation between a friend and a stranger on a New York City street corner. The friend claimed he had just spoken to Elbert Hubbard. "On your life, it wasn't—that is his son. Hubbard is an old, old man. He married a young wife who is the greatest business woman in the world. She sends these young bucks out and they impersonate Hubbard. There is a fellow called Felix who gives Hubbard lectures and passes as the Real Thing. It takes six men to write the Elbert Hubbard stuff, and two to give his lectures."

Alice was seldom bothered by any similar confrontations with her public image. But when this sort of thing did occur, she used it in her own way. The *Philistine* for July 1910 has such an account. "In order to keep a degree of harmony between brain and body," she began, "I take every day two hours of exercise in the open air, and this exercise is usually on horseback. . . . I ride in the natural way, and as I ride in all weathers, I wear bloomers. It is a pleasure to saddle and bridle my own horse, and so I walk to the barn from the home wearing said bloomers."

A Methodist clergyman, an evangelist, was visiting The Roycroft Shops the other day. He ate at The Roycroft Inn, and found no fault with it. There was with this divine a goodly number of other ministers and their wives.

On the day of the clerical visits I went as usual to ride. When I came out to the road to go to the barn, every man of God and all the wives stopped, stared, gesticulated, pointed at my Quaker gray clothes, very simple, wholly plain. It is very seldom that I have seen such a manifestation of curiosity unrestrained. But the rudeness was made clear when the evangelist told one of our Roycroft boys that it was strictly forbidden in the Bible for a woman to wear "pants"; that for this offense I should be arrested and sent up for ninety days. It was a disgrace and a crime against God.

This was all of the incident. But it served Alice as the text for another seven pages of the *Philistine*. First she searched out the clergyman's authority from Deuteronomy: "The woman shall not wear that which pertaineth to a man, neither shall a man put on a woman's garments: for all that do so are abomination unto the Lord." As neatly as a lawyer demolishing opposing counsel, Alice noted that "Moses was not making fashions for the Twentieth Century," and moved on to refute the charge because "no man has ever worn bloomers. They are not a man's garment." Then she went on the offensive, and inquired, "Why not reprimand all Catholic priests, . . . the Pope and all clergymen who wear robes? I am sorry to say that these are 'woman's garments.' " Her being "sorry" was as rhetorical as her going on to say, "Of course I forgave the thirty men and women their rudeness . . . because they thought they were looking at a wicked person—and they loved to see a sight so rare."

By the time she finished expressing her forgiveness, she had taken most of the hide off the whole delegation. "It is easy to understand why those wives had such difficulty in going up the five steps into the Chapel, why they carried fifty or seventy-five pounds of surplus weight, why they must ask their husbands at home if they would know anything. For these women I had no hope." Alice could flourish the Scriptures herself, and she quoted the "sublime picture of an independent woman who had a mind of her own and knew it" from Proverbs. As for the leader of this party of righteous slummers: "What I really want is for this clergyman who is so alarmingly deficient in the spirit of the Golden Rule to have a conscious reincarnation and to be compelled to wear dresses and to be his own wife."

When Hubbard was concentrating on vaudeville audiences, he seemed less apt to feud with his East Aurora neighbors. But he documented one squabble "A Tempest In a Village Teapot" (*Philistine,* October 1908), which had the old flair. The inciting incident had the look of a planned provocation. An old feminist friend, Marilla Ricker, offered—through Hubbard—to give the village library a complete set of the Works of Robert G. Ingersoll. The Board of Education, which had charge of the library, declined the offer of these "atheistical" writings on the ground that it had a duty to protect the young against subversion of "the religious faith of the American nation." Here Hubbard entered the lists. He offered to give the library a deluxe set of *his* collected works (then in process—forty volumes, to sell at ten dollars each). He referred to his position in East Aurora: largest taxpayer, principal post-office customer, only major employer, father of star public-school-pupil Miriam, guardian of village prosperity and morals. He noted that he was just as subversive a writer as Ingersoll, cited the constitutional separation of church and state, defended Ingersoll's moral purity, and asked the board if there was nothing in the Bible to "bring the blush of shame to the cheek of innocence," and concluded, "All of which I frankly explain in order that you may not act in ignorance."

The board replied with a long, stiffly dignified letter, stuck to its guns on Ingersoll, accepted Hubbard's offer of his Works, but stated its intention to safeguard its children by setting up a restricted "department of objectionable literature" into which, possibly, some of Hubbard's ten-dollar volumes might go. This gave Hubbard the opportunity to withdraw his offer ("an honor which I had not contemplated . . .") and romp all over the board, and he made the most of it. Since the board replied no further, Hubbard had to wait a few years for a chance to rub salt in its wounds. His opening came in 1911. "The gentleman who refused to allow the East Aurora School Board to accept as a gift a full set of my books has been appointed Commissioner in Lunacy. . . . Something might here be said, but I resist temptation and pass it up."

This public-performance, Glory-laden aspect of Hubbard's life was becoming a self-generating spiral. His public self was lodging in people's minds as a symbol, a signal to start laughing, an irritant, an inspiration, sometimes an abomination. The "true man" that his friend Reedy had been in touch with was increasingly hard to locate. Reedy had his share in the Glory-making too. At one time, he issued a public challenge to Hubbard to get his hair cut. The two of them tossed this back and forth in print for some weeks. A date was set for the shearing, and they both squeezed all the copy they could out of the game before Hubbard called it off.

Even Hubbard's winding "search for God" was getting more and more mixed up with Glory. The note of honest personal concern still cropped up, but it took a lot of disentangling from the background noise. For several years he had been much taken with the naturalistic monism of Ernst

Haeckel. Since Haeckel was an evolutionist and a working biologist, his credentials were untainted with orthodoxy, and Hubbard announced that monism was the thing. He boiled it down to "All is one; all is Good; and all is God," and apparently found this mystical enough to escape his distrust of the too rational: "When you place a creed in a crucible and afterwards study the particles on a slide encased in balsam, you are apt to get a residuum or something—a something that does not satisfy the heart." And Emerson's Law of Compensation fitted in nicely with this new Oneness: "This intelligence in which we are bathed rights every wrong, equalizes every injustice, balances every perversion, punishes the wrong and rewards the right. The Universe is self-lubricating and automatic."

There was probably a promise of peace and equilibrium for Hubbard in his monism. To a man with his ever-churning conflicts, there was "beauty and splendor" in "the monistic idea." It seemed to bypass all struggle and all uncertainty about right and wrong. "How mean and small become all those little, fearsome 'schemes of salvation.'" And all the perplexities of Man Alone seemed to vanish before the vision "that God is the Whole, and that every man is a necessary part of the Whole. . . . All there is for him to do is to be true to his own nature." This was a philosophy that seemed to combine "the religious emotions of awe, veneration, wonder and worship" with a pretty potent individualism. "We advance individually as we lie in the Lord's hand, and allow ourselves to be receivers and conveyers of the Divine Will."

Hubbard was still preaching this "only religion that pays compound interest to both borrower and lender" in 1908, but he had dropped the capital letter. (And perhaps he had swung back to seeing conflict and paradox as ultimate truth: "Anchorage is what most people pray for, when what we really need is God's great open sea.") Soon after, in a public series of debates with one Reverend Dr. C. C. Albertson, Hubbard went back to his old liberation-from-superstition polemics, with no indication that he recognized his opponent as an equal manifestation of the Divine Will. Then, in 1909, a public event took place that Hubbard called "the most important announcement made since Lincoln issued his Emancipation Proclamation."

Dr. Charles W. Eliot, Harvard's president emeritus, had addressed the Harvard Divinity School's summer session on "A New Religion." Nearly seventy years before, Hubbard recalled, Emerson had challenged tradition before the same institution and been quietly exiled. Now here was the great Dr. Eliot, full of years and honors, doing it again.

Dr. Eliot's New Religion was a summary of the enlightened goodwill and near-humanism of the period. It rejected the sin-and-salvation of orthodoxy and would be built around the monotheistic majesty of Judaism and the "Christian Universal Father," plus the physicist's Energy and the biologist's Vital Force. The New Religion would entail neither divine punishment nor divine justice but would approach the "whole subject of evil from another side, that of resistance and prevention." It would be a religion of service, love, hope, growth, and unity among men, "not only to be in harmony with the great secular movements of modern society—democracy, individualism, social idealism, the zeal for education, the spirit of research, the modern tendency to welcome the new, the fresh powers of preventative medicine, and the recent advances in business and industrial ethics—but also in essential agreement with the direct personal teachings of Jesus."

There was a slight edge in Hubbard's celebration of Dr. Eliot's address. He quoted Ingersoll as having told the Reverend Minot Savage, "You should be grateful to me, for my radicalism has made yours respectable," and he asserted: "Every item in the creed of what Dr. Eliot calls 'The New Religion' I have been proclaiming for twenty-five years. Many of the people who now accept Dr. Eliot's New Religion have dented my shield, and on my corduroys are the stains of their rheum. . . . I have been a scout of civilization—and I have been on the picket-line. The main army has often mistaken me for the enemy. But now the main column has come up, Dr. Eliot riding ten paces to the front. And at the head of his legion he reads the address which I have been twenty-five years in preparing."

In his comments on the other religious-philosophical movements of his time, Hubbard showed little of the identification that monism and Dr. Eliot's New Religion excited. The group that came closest to him in temperament and doctrine was probably New Thought. Still flourishing today under a variety of names, it combined faith healing, a post-Emersonian transcendentalism with additions of Eastern mysticism, and a complex rationale of "transcend your cake and eat it too" as regards worldly goods and success. New Thought conventions were held at East Aurora. *Nautilus,* the New Thought journal, was a regular *Philistine* advertiser, and many of the New Thought leaders were closely associated with Hubbard—at least in their own minds and that of the public. (Orison Swett Marden, editor of *Success* and dispenser of inspirational business-oriented uplift, was to be a speaker at the New York City Hubbard Memorial Service; so was Elizabeth Towne, the editor of *Nautilus.*) Historian Harold U. Faulkner directly identifies Hubbard with New Thought: the "most famous" of its "leaders . . . devoted . . . to pseudoscientific, pseudoreligious lectures with one eye on the door-receipts."

But Hubbard himself was not eager to be considered a part of this group. When a New Thought convention was in full cackle at Roycroft, a reporter asked Hubbard just what this New Thought was, anyway. "Blamed if I know," said the Fra, striding off to the shops—a practical man with no time for nonsense. When he wrote about New Thought in 1908, he didn't treat it as a special cult, just a manner of thinking. "There are two kinds of thought: New Thought and Second-Hand Thought. New Thought is made up of thoughts you, yourself, think. The other kind is supplied to you by jobbers." He also called it "that peculiar proclivity to explain the thing before you understand it."

Another religious outcropping to which he paid considerable attention in print was Christian Science. This had a degree of common paternity with New Thought in the faith healing of Phineas P. Quimby. The two groups also shared a less-measurable relation to Emerson. It was not, after all, such a tremendous step from the belief that the material world was of secondary importance to declaring it altogether out of bounds and nonexistent—at least not for Mary Baker Eddy. The early years of Christian Science were stormy with lawsuits, exposés, prosecutions, and public criticism; both the yellow press and the muckrakers gave it a going-over, and Mark Twain wrote a savage book about it. But things had quieted down by 1908, when Hubbard included Mrs. Eddy among his "Great Teachers." Finley Peter Dunne's Mr. Dooley—as often in those years—said the final word in the subsiding uproar: "If the Christyan Scientists had some science an' th' doctors more Christyanity, it widdn't make any diff'rence which ye called in—if ye had a good nurse."

There were some parallels between Christian Science and Hubbard's phobia about doctors. As Alice's husband, he could hardly be too critical of a New Woman who had founded and made a commercial success of one of the two American-born world religions. Mrs. Eddy's combination of prophecy and hardheaded business management came close to the Roycroft specialties. And she and Hubbard had enemies in common and had both been ridiculed and harried. (When Mrs. Eddy was over eighty, she completely routed a panel of deputies sent by a court to check on her sanity.) There was a personal pressure also; Hubbard's current staff artist, Jules Maurice Gaspard, was a devout Christian Scientist, and had outdone himself on the frontispiece portrait for this *Little Journey*. Gaspard was eagerly waiting to read the proofs. After he did read them, he stormily refused the use of his portrait. Hubbard, after some protesting—he was paying for it, after all—acquiesced.

Hubbard did his best with all these pressures. He paid tribute to Mrs.

Eddy's leadership, dignity, and strength of character. "Christian Science as a plan of life," he said, "embodying the great yet simple virtues, is beautiful." He accepted much of the psychosomatics—he had been saying the same things for years. And he saluted Mrs. Eddy as "the most successful author . . . the world has ever seen." But he couldn't stomach *Science and Health.* He found it incomprehensible that "Deity should write in a secret language, and then wait two thousand years before making the matter plain, and then to one single woman in Boston." And he drew a clear line of dissent: "There is one thing quite as valuable as health, and that is mental integrity." He noted that Mrs. Eddy's ranks were recruited almost entirely from orthodox Christianity. This explained why her second-degree revelations were accepted so totally, and why they were not for Hubbard. "You can't give a free-thinker a book with a statement of what he must find in it. He has acquired the habit of thinking for himself."

Having settled the main points at issue, he permitted himself a few jokes. " 'The plaster-Paris smile,' the one feature in Christian Science to which many good people object, is the direct legacy of Mrs. Eddy to her pupils. 'Science and Health' says nothing about it; no edict has been put forth recommending it, but all good Christian Scientists take it on—the smile that refuses to vacate the premises. And to some it is certainly very becoming." Earlier he had made a "gentle josh" at Mrs. Eddy's famous hats. "Christian Scientists are Transcendentalists whose distinguishing point is that they secrete millinery."

Probably the creedal element that was most important in Hubbard's time—and in Hubbard's own religious groping—was the place of mankind in the cosmic scheme of things. The historic core of American culture had held humanity in pretty low esteem. Hubbard's Yankee forebears had seen man as bound in his sinful nature and forever betrayed by his overweening pride. Such salvation as they permitted in their vision was God's affair, not man's, and neither faith nor works could alter the predestined judgment. In its purer forms, this culture had had strength and dignity. But as it spread over much of the country in its three-hundred-year march, it became diluted and vulgarized. Its God shrank from unknowable majesty to something rather maudlin and pettifogging—scaring children and keeping books on peccadilloes, but reasonably biddable by a shrewd operator who played his cards carefully. As the twentieth century loomed ahead, much of the idealism and intelligence in the country was focusing elsewhere. As the awefulness of God dwindled, mankind came in for a second look, as a commodity that had perhaps been sold short.

One large segment of Hubbard's gospel—and his appeal for many of his followers—grew from this new glorifying of Man. At times Hubbard sounded like a purely earthbound humanist who has chucked all transcendent nonsense "into the dust heap of oblivion, with all the priestly phantoms that have obscured the sun and blackened the sky. The gods have gone, but MAN IS HERE." Sometimes this humanity worship waxed lyrical, even fatuous, as in the lead editorial in the first issue of the *Fra:* "My heart goes out to you, O Man, because I cannot conceive of any being greater, nobler, more heroic, more tenderly loving, loyal, unselfish, and enduring than are you." Arise, rejoice, and flex your muscles, he kept saying, "That is good which serves—man is the important item, this earth is the place, and the time is now."

Much of this exuberant affirmation seems to have indicated little more than release from the constraints of the conventional and the established. From the shadow of ancestral authority, all open sky was blue and friendly. "We no longer accept the doctrine that our natures are rooted in infamy, and that the desires of the flesh are cunning traps set by Satan, with God's permission, to undo us. We believe that no one can harm us but ourselves, that sin is misdirected energy, that there is no devil but fear, and that the universe is planned for good."

This rejection of his boyhood training runs through most of his assertions on what is good. When he omitted this negative element and polished up a set of pure affirmations as a "Credo," it was apt to approach the liturgical mindlessness which he objected to in *Science and Health:*

I believe in the Motherhood of God. I believe in the blessed Trinity of Father, Mother and Child. I believe that God is here, and that we are as near Him now as ever we shall be. I do not believe He started this world a-going and went away and left it to run itself. I believe that we are all sons of God, and that it doth not yet appear what we shall be. I believe the only way we can reach the Kingdom of Heaven is to have the Kingdom of Heaven in our hearts. I believe in freedom—social, economic, domestic, mental, spiritual. I believe in sunshine, fresh air, friendship, calm sleep, beautiful thoughts. I believe in the purifying process of sorrow, and I believe that death is a manifestation of life. I believe the universe is planned for good.

Or, in the Orphic Saying or Illuminated Motto department: "The Mintage of Wisdom is to know that Rest is Rust and that real life is in Love, Laughter and Work." He was also fond of the change-of-pace variation on a quite different level. Note how he pulled the string on this one, during

his big-business infatuation: "What we want is . . . a working system that
will allow us to meet life's overhead charges, pay interest on the investment,
and have enough balance left so we can look all theological-medico-muddle
men in the eye and tell them to go to hell."

But the old dualism of flesh and spirit, sense and soul, were things he
never really escaped. "Expression is necessary to life," he wrote in 1900.
"The spirit grows through exercise. Life is expression and repression is stag-
nation—death." But then the dualism asserted itself. "Yet there is right
expression and wrong expression. If a man allows his life to run riot, and
only the animal side of his nature is allowed to express itself, he is repress-
ing his highest and best, and therefore those qualities not used atrophy and
die. Sensuality, gluttony and the life of license repress the life of the spirit,
and the soul never blossoms; and this is what it is to lose one's soul. All
adown the centuries thinking men have noted these truths, and again and
again we find individuals forsaking, in horror, the life of the senses and
devoting themselves to the life of the spirit." And in this same period, when
he was feeling newly secure in his periodical pulpit, though living with the
unresolved pressures of his personal life, his writing was full of conflict.

At this time he said that "health and prosperity are not pure blessings
—a certain amount of discontent is necessary to spur men on to a higher
life." This discontent appeared on many levels in Hubbard. Success sometimes looked like "a subtle connivance of Nature for bringing about a
man's defeat," and "anything is better than the Dead Sea of neutral nothingness, wherein a man merely avoids sin by doing nothing and being nothing."
As for religion, it was only pure in "its state of poverty and persecution;
the good things of earth are our corruptors."

Although Hubbard had rejected revelation and the supernatural, he
had no interest in the brick-by-brick building of a philosophy. Too much
rationality was a threat, and "that quality of the mind which constructs
creeds, argues fine points, and logically proves or syllogistically disposes, will
spread its own withering aridity and dry up the fountain of the soul." So
that if Man was the highest good, it was definitely not as Intellectual Man.
Nor did the other elements of Hubbard's fresh-air-and-beautiful-thoughts
affirmations stay put through the years. He could feel powerfully sorry for
himself and his fellows. "We fight on forever and fail; we are mauled to
the earth and arise; we stumble forward with feeble vision and tired feet,
and only the love that lives in lenient hearts makes life tolerable. When
mankind repudiates us and fellowship is dead, we then turn for surcease to
the welcoming waters of the lake . . ." Even the supernatural, those "priestly

phantoms," came in for an occasional wistful glance. "I cannot help believing that the spirit of man will live again somewhere in a better world than ours." And that supreme creature, Man, appeared sometimes to have come "into life without his choice and is being hurried out of it against his will, and over the evening of his dreams steals the final conclusion that he has been used by a Power, not himself, for unseen ends."

One very personal note emerged in Hubbard's writing shortly before his public self began to get out of hand. It was almost as if he had taken time out of a lecture trip for sessions with Dr. Sigmund Freud (who was coming into a rather outraged public awareness then, and was shortly to be lecturing at Clark University). In 1907, Hubbard published a vivid little daydream titled "How I Found My Brother." The story reminisced that Elbert, as a boy of eleven, with four sisters, and all the heavy chores to do, had wished for a brother with whom he could hunt and play ball, who would help him with the work and be an ally in schoolyard fights. Then came a news item in the *Weekly Pantagraph:* The agent of a children's aid society was coming to Bloomington with twenty-five orphans for adoption. Elbert persuades his mother to let him go pick out a brother. He goes to the courthouse on the day announced, and sees "in the corner a boy with towhead and freckles. He had settled down in the corner trying to hide. He was so homely he was attractive. I walked over to him, and asked, 'Can you work and play ball—I want a brother!' I did not say anything about fighting for I had suddenly noticed he was a hunchback. He just looked at me and gulped, scared like, he was that embarrassed. 'I want a brother—will you come with me and be my brother?' I asked. I omitted all qualifications this time—my heart went out to this boy—he seemed so scared and half-sick. I could work, fight and play ball for both."

So "Brudder" is taken home and then adopted. He is fifteen and a great worker and ballplayer, "alert, obedient, willing. He was grateful for everything; whereas I was a Grabheimer from Grabville." Everybody is happy, including Elbert's parents—"at first they thought it a calamity, then they got to telling the neighbors how they sent me after him." The idyll is spoiled by the appearance of "Mudsock," the childhood bogeyman who had been shared by Elbert and Mary. He is a low and brutal type, with "red bushy whiskers," from whose mistreatment Brudder had previously run away. He appears during a ball game, waving a blacksnake whip, "yelling, 'So I've found you at last!'"

Brudder fells Mudsock with a fast ball and runs away again. The story goes on to quote letters from Brudder telling of his modest success in life and he finally reappears to "root" for the contemporary Hubbard who is lecturing at the Academy of Music in Philadelphia. "With Brudder was his grown-up daughter, a beautiful girl, a head taller than he. She called me Uncle."

Hubbard once seriously referred to this story as his "best book." Bert apparently accepted the story as autobiography, and, writing after his father's death, said he had no brother "except the adopted one he so charmingly tells about . . ." On its more obvious levels, the story seems a simple expression of Elbert's reaction to the surrounding femininity of his boyhood—he wanted a brother who could work, fight, and play ball, exactly as stated. But if he needed to dream up a brother, why the re-creation of the dead Charlie, who had been his mother's favorite child? And why the contrast between the dream-Charlie and Elbert himself? "I had intended to select a boy who looked like myself—this being the highest type I could imagine. Instead I picked my opposite . . . short, and a genuine blond . . . the smallest, the sickliest, the homeliest one in the bunch. My judgment was in the ditch, and I was carried away on the back of sympathy. It was head against heart, and heart made a home run. . . . Once I heard Mother say that Brudder was just like my brother Charlie who died when he was nine years old."

Was he bringing back Charlie to comfort his mother? To demonstrate his own godlike powers? Was he assuaging his own feelings about Charlie? Brudder is said to be "very strong," but "in his books he was a bit deficient." Charlie was an invalid, but he may well have been brighter than Elbert. There was also confusion in the story as to which brother was the leader. Though Brudder was four years older (Charlie was six years older), Elbert himself was the protective big brother when he selected the scared orphan. And when Brudder asked what Elbert would do if Mudsock came after him, Elbert answered, "Kill him." But Brudder turned out to be the heavy worker and the star ballplayer, and when Mudsock did appear, it was Brudder who acted, while Elbert was paralyzed with fright.

And why this childhood fantasy at this particular time? Hubbard's parents had retired to East Aurora several years before. They had survived the scandal and the new marriage. They appear in the reminiscences of latter-day Roycrofters only as shadowy old creatures—evidences of Hubbard's protective concern for his own, and occasionally as comic agents of his foolery, as in one story of Hubbard sending Dr. Silas to dose—with a violent herb mixture intended for horses—an arrogant young transient who had fallen ill. But there is some evidence that they didn't always accept the chimney-corner role. Felix noted that Dr. Silas sometimes sat in the front row during his son's Chapel talks, commenting audibly, "I don't agree; I don't agree." And the son would "look down and smile—delighted . . . and go on with his talk as though there had been no interruption at all." This refusal to stop acting like parents may have been even more characteristic of Hubbard's mother. Hubbard once remarked blithely in the *Fra:* "My dear mother said last night at supper that my mundane advent was to her merely a diversion compared with the pain that some of my literary effusions have caused her . . . she reads everything I write." And a curious item in the March 1909 *Philistine* announced that "parenthood is not a science—it is a toss-up. Our maudlin statements that a man is not greater than his mother is Number Six twaddle." And it went on to list historical mothers who had rejected or belittled their to-be-great sons.

In the years to come, the breakaway individualist who couldn't go home again would become something of a cliché. Establishing an identity came almost to require a rejection of family, of home town, often of the whole damned country. But this had never been Hubbard's pattern. No matter how much he outraged his parents' beliefs and expectations, it was as the high-spirited family showoff—confident of winning indulgent approval after things settled down. But there appear to have been times when he just plain didn't get that approval, and this hurt.

The number of foundlings and runaways in Hubbard's fiction is interesting. Aspasia Hobbs was a foundling, as was the fated girl-child in *One Day.* The heroine of *No Enemy* first appeared as a homeless boy. And Brudder, of course, was a lorn orphan. Some of this may have been simply picking up a common literary trick of the period. Switched babies and waifs of mysterious and noble origin were standard in Shakespeare and Gilbert and Sullivan. (The ultimate parody was the duke and the king in *Huckleberry Finn*—"you ain't the only person that's been snaked down wrongfully out'n a high place. . . . You ain't the only person that's had a secret of his birth!") To say that Hubbard sometimes felt himself a rejected child would be going a little beyond what the evidence supports. But there were certainly quicksands in his security. And overcompensations. In dealing with Leonardo da Vinci (1902), he went off on quite a tangent about the "divinity" that Leonardo associated with his birth. "This idea of 'divinity' is strong in the mind of every great man. He recognizes his sonship and claims his divine parentage." And "Brudder" seems to have come straight out of his subconscious, at an unlikely age, and during a period when he was being increasingly swallowed up in his public role-playing.

13

ℭℎe New Woman

ALICE HUBBARD'S feminism became stronger, if anything, after she had emerged from obscurity to be Elbert's affinity-wife-superintendent. Considering the bleak years she had endured, it was not strange that there was overstrain in her writings on the woman question or that she saw economic independence for women as a grim absolute. "The new woman will be free. Then she will be whatever her best judgment wants her to be," she wrote. She called on each and every member of her sex to "come out from the ranks of paupers, dependents, children, and affirm her womanhood . . . become a human being independent, capable to carry the entire responsibility of one person—that one person being herself." It was a large order, but Alice did it herself and no one can say that it hasn't been done, and done with somewhat mixed results, by thousands of American women since.

When Alice turned from exhortation to picturing the New Woman in the emancipated future, she ran into difficulties. In mapping out a social system of universal independence, and yet with a place for homes and children, she seemed to be combining polar extremes of anarchism and statism. Housekeeping should be honestly paid for, of course, and mothers should be paid for being mothers. But who was to pay them? The fathers? Could a mother be truly free if she must collect a dole from one particular man? So they must be paid by the state. And what of the children of career women? She suggested that if the state were to "educate and clothe and feed the children, dependents, and pay for all the care of the children, we should soon, very soon, have no hospitals for the State to maintain, no insane-asylums, no houses of correction, no penitentiaries, and, I believe, no saloons." Wasn't this a long speculative leap? Not for Alice. She believed that "our vices come from improper physical conditions. When our children are properly nourished, properly clothed, and live naturally, which is simply, they will no longer have a desire for poisonous stimulants."

This sort of prophecy makes curious reading today. What seemed to promise a glorious future to Alice Hubbard and to many of her feminist contemporaries—"Free mothers for a generation! What a race of men and women will then be on earth, when we have conditions where this is possible!"—now sounds more like a dehumanized beehive. The only large-scale approach to anything of the sort was in Soviet Russia in the 1920's, and it was short-lived, for cause. There are few aspects of the advanced thought of the time of the Hubbards that seem so remote and unworkable today as this matter of family and children. Total victory for woman's rights seems to have collided with something else—children's rights, perhaps.

American culture before the First World War was sharply adult-centered. The whole structure of family-church-school, as it dealt with children, was geared to transform them into adults as efficiently as possible, with no nonsense. Both conventional people and social rebels took children pretty much for granted. Possibly there was a relationship between this situation and the fact that children were sent by God, in numbers and timing as His inscrutable purposes provided. Ibsen's Nora was an internationally celebrated New Woman. She broke out of her tinsel cage that she might grow up, but she left her children behind without registering a serious qualm. And at the same time that social rebels were stretching, and sometimes destroying, the traditional patterns of marriage and family, they were often also extending a dangerously exposed salient of their children's lives. The educational ideas of Pestalozzi, Montessori, and Froebel were much in favor among advanced thinkers. In effect, this movement, which grew into "progressive education," freed the child from rote learning and subservience to authority. It encouraged self-motivation, intellectual precocity, and individualism. But often it conferred these evocative blessings on children whose emotional and social stability had been badly shaken by their parents' pursuit of freedom.

There was not much more awareness of the family as a value in Hubbard's writing than in Alice's. When he did discuss it, he often saw it as a Jewish rather than a Christian characteristic, and his feelings about it were badly mixed up with his hatred of Puritan orthodoxy: "In the average Christian household, until a very few years ago, the child grew up with the feeling constantly pressed upon him that he was a usurper and an interloper. All parents quoted Solomon as to the beauties of the rod, and that all children were perverse, obstinate and stiff-necked was assumed as a fact. To break the will of a child was a very essential thing to do." Hubbard didn't think much of Christian households. In this same piece he announced that "the houses of prostitution are recruited from respectable families where the formula, Do-not-darken-that-door-again, leaps lightly to lips that read the New Testament aloud night and morning and recite the Lord's Prayer in a bishop's voice."

Hubbard went on dragging his feet on Alice's dedicated feminism. Only a year before they were married, he expressed strong objections to one of the favorite feminist gestures toward equality. "One bride out of five," he said, asked the clergyman to omit "obey" from the marriage ceremony, and Hubbard found some mystical significance in this being "the exact proportion of divorces to marriages in Indiana and Illinois." "The woman who stipulates is lost," he said. "She is serving notice that her own sweet caprice is to have precedence over the wishes of her husband." He wound up this rather confused polemic by saying that "men do not understand women nearly so well as women understand men; but often a woman's cleverness and shrewdness and secrecy are her undoing."

In 1912, Reedy gave Hubbard credit for having "made one great discovery before any one else in this country." He had "found out the terrible unrest in the breast of the American woman, the desire to be in and of the world of things doing. To her he appealed with his books and magazines . . . has been, with his wife, a great power in the woman movement." But the truly dedicated were often annoyed by a partisanship that could put the Cause in such terms as: "the fact that one-half the race puts its clothes on over its head should not debar it from the right to vote"; or, "wise men and good neither crawl to women nor use them to bat up flies." And, though The Woman Who Understands was a Hubbard need and the implicit audience of much of what he wrote, there was another large segment obviously intended for the Boys at the Brass Rail: "You can get a good woman to do anything for you if you go about it rightly. Go about it wrongly, and your cake is not only dough, but it is burnt on the bottom and sticks to the pan. Don't talk back to me, I know what I am saying!"

Hubbard never quite echoed Alice's statement that "the psychology of man and woman is the same." He always left loopholes and qualifications. "In their love affairs women are seldom wise nor men just. How should we expect them to be when but yesterday Woman was a chattel and man a slave-owner?" In his writing—especially in the *Little Journeys*—he treated men and women as distinct, and the masculine and feminine personalities as real and different. One of the major differences he saw was that while "no man ever did a great work unless backed up by a good woman," on the other hand "the women who live in history . . . were mismated, misunderstood, neglected, abused, spit on by fate, scorned. They were sometimes loved, of course, but loved by those who had no business to love them—loved by the wrong man." And "no woman is either wise or good until destiny has subdued her by grinding her fondest hopes into the dust."

Woman had to be a "thinking woman" to deserve his respect—also a working woman. As for other women: "The average human, civilized, respectable woman is a punk outfit." And toward that modern product, the Girl, he was even more severe: "She is a disappointment to her father, a humiliation to her mother, a pest to brothers and sisters, and when she finally marries, she saps the inspiration of her husband and often converts a proud and ambitious man into a weak and cowardly cur." As for that dream girl of the magazines—the Gibson Girl—Hubbard said that she "lolls, loafs, pouts, weeps, talks back, lies in wait, dreams, eats, drinks, sleeps and yawns. She rides in a coach in a red jacket, plays golf in a secondary sexual sweater, dawdles on a hotel veranda, tum-tums on a piano, but you never heard of her doing a useful thing or saying a wise one."

There are many passages that show Hubbard's fear of and aversion to the woman who trades on her sex and demands the whole world with a fence around it as her due. "The Pretty Woman," said Hubbard, "is seldom wise and hardly ever good. There is something in her beauty that has tainted her soul, and the man who wins her comes into possession of a fine crop of absurdity, selfishness, frivolity and koncrete kussedness. Women under 30 are apt to make demands that are not in the power of men to satisfy. They want attention; they want happiness. Youth demands joy as its right, and not getting it seeks revenge." There are many other passages that simply show his feelings toward women in general. "Priests are not allowed to marry, because if they did the secrets of the confessional would be called over back fences the next day." "No sane dentist will administer an anaesthetic to a woman, without a witness; not that women as a class are dangerous, but because some women cannot be trusted to distinguish between their dreams and the facts." And for outright hatred, there is a little essay titled "The Queen of the Porch" (the "Porch" was the universal encircling veranda of the summer hotel). "She has no definite ideas excepting as regards her rights. Her desire is to make trouble; her ambition is to rule the Porch. Mankind is her door-mat; the world is her slop-jar; her religion is to badger the busy. The result of her life is that she makes two cockle-burrs grow where there were none before. A bas you bicche—hike, you Queen of the Porch!"

This was pretty strong language for a crusader, much of whose public and market was female, and he tried, elsewhere, to rationalize such feelings. A woman hater, he suggested, was only a disappointed lover. "If a man is enough interested in women to hate them, note this, he is only searching for the right woman, the woman who compares favorably with the ideal woman in his own mind."

Among Hubbard's contemporaries in the little magazines, the New Woman aroused mixed feelings. In general, reformers and social dissidents tended to include woman's rights in their platforms of the "new" and the "free." The more purely literary groups were apt to be skeptical or hostile. The *Chap-Book*—which, after a brave beginning, had settled into a smug superiority of its own—was definitely skeptical. It picked up antifeminist squibs and verses from its British friends, including this one:

> To me, a man of moderate wit,
> Not handicapped with spurious culture,
> "New Women" savor of the pit,
> The Venus blended with the vulture;
> I praise the gods, I never met,
> In life, a real "revolted daughter";
> But Phyllis is a pretty pet,
> And most of what she knows, I taught her.

Michael Monahan, in his later years, was strongly antifeminist. He referred to "the weaklings who contemplate abandoning man suffrage in this country in order to turn us over to a gynarchy." And he published a feebly satirical definition of the kind Hubbard and Ambrose Bierce had popularized: "Suffragitis: A malady of the woman of temperament. Revolt of the sexually unsatisfied or deficient. The Jacquerie of the unmated Jills of America. Anything to make Man the Goat!" This kind of sneering was typical of the romantic literati who took their cues from Europe. But it wasn't universal. Reedy, for instance, showed a mixture of feelings. His admiration for Alice Hubbard has been noted, and in 1908 he wrote a sympathetic account of Emma Goldman, "The Daughter of the Dream," at a time when she was a popular stereotype of the New Woman at her worst. But Reedy was not always shockproof; at the height of the bicycle craze he gave it as his opinion that woman bike riders would wind up as nymphomaniacs.

The lowbrow masculine attitude toward rights and votes for women was heavy-handed and patronizing. There was a popular joke that women in bustles and puff sleeves could never get into voting booths anyway, so why all the fuss? The opposition of the literati often had a more fearful note. Feminism, to many of this group, carried a threat of demasculinization. Maurice Thompson, in the *Chap-Book* in 1895, touched on this feeling: "To be a very large woman's little cat might not satisfy the highest aspirations of a manly man, even among *fin-de-siècle* poets. Some uneasiness on the subject undoubtedly exists in certain male imaginations." The Oscar Wilde scandal had caused a revulsion in England from the whole burgeoning "newness" of the *Yellow Book* period. What had begun as lighthearted experimentation in art and life had ended in disaster, and there were many who felt, like Thompson, that the "unsexed woman and emasculate man" came from the same causes and "ought to be considered as outlaws."

In 1895 and 1896, the intellectuals of England and America were reading a grim and arrogant volume titled *Degeneration*. The work of Max Nordau, a German physician and writer, the book equated practically the whole turn-of-the-century cultural upheaval with insanity. Nordau had been a pupil of Cesare Lombroso, and was extending the master's typing of criminals by physical "'stigmata' or brand-marks" to artists and writers. Lombroso thought he had demonstrated that there was a criminal type recognizable on sight. Nordau went him one better. If "asymmetry" of feature, ear shapes, and irregular teeth weren't apparent in his targets, he had a supplementary arsenal of descriptive psychopathology. All "modern" artists were insane because he said so, and in technical language. His list of degenerates was a distinguished one: Wagner, Ibsen, Zola, Whitman, Nietzsche, César Franck (!), Maeterlinck, Verlaine, Mallarmé, and, of course, Oscar Wilde. The thing that was really eating at Nordau was the attrition of "traditional views of custom and morality." His book is evidence that many of the battle lines of modernism-conservatism were shaping up twenty years before the First World War. Much of his book could have served as a workbook for Hitler's Ministry of Culture. Nordau was very positive, very angry, and full of bile, but he deserved some credit as a prophet for observing, in the early 1890's, that the Western world was undergoing a "descent into flat phenomenalism . . . the end of an established order. . . . There is a sound of rending in every tradition, and it is as though the morrow would not link itself with today."

The New Woman, naturally enough, was one more symptom in Nordau's diagnosis. Hubbard referred rather noncommittally to Nordau at the time, but his insistence in later years that "your artist is headed for the monkey house" suggests he retained some of Nordau's ideas for future use. There was a lot of discussion of Nordau in 1895 and 1896, and the term "degenerate" as a label for the New in art and literature lingered on for some years. But newness could not easily be seen as a menace in that expansive American world, and many of the reactions here to Nordau were flippant. An article in the *Chap-Book* tried to sum up the whole *fin-de-siècle* literature with American reasonableness and the wholesome forward look:

Among English-speaking people, at least, it is chiefly as a reaction that decadent literature is significant . . . an attempt to get away from the mortal dullness . . . to see life anew and feel it afresh. In many cases, it is, however, mistaken not only in morals, but in method: it confuses mannerism with originality, and unconventionality with power . . . cursing has no lasting quality. . . .

Even genius will not redeem perpetual revolt . . . Revolt is inspiring if it is the prelude to a new and better order; if it falls short of this . . . only a disturbance of the peace.

The new impulse in literature, when it comes, will evidence its presence neither by indecency nor by eccentricity; but by a certain noble simplicity . . sanity . . . clearness of insight . . . depth of sympathy with that deeper life of humanity.

And somewhat the same sort of wishful long view was often trained by the *Chap-Book* on the New Woman; Maurice Thompson said that she was "a recurring decimal . . . appearing at certain intervals with a constantly shifting value to civilization . . . halfway between a grotesque gargoyle and a dainty flower-ornament . . . at all events she means to be decorative, as she has always been, and down the ages ahead of us she will doubtless continue to charm, amuse, and marry man."

Being "decorative" was, of course, fatuously irrelevant to the feminism of such crusaders as Alice Hubbard. But there was one conspicuous omission in the feminist program of the Roycroft magazines—any realistic discussion of birth control. It was true that there was little scientific knowledge of contraception at this time. It was also true that Anthony Comstock had made the subject illegal. There were some people who saw the importance of the matter—even a few who were willing to tangle with Mr. Comstock's law. In 1906, when he was seventy-five, Moses Harmon went to jail for publication of a birth-control article in his magazine *Lucifer*. Hubbard's contributions to the subject were on the smoking-room level, as:

The bride of a year entered a drugstore. The clerk approached. "Do you exchange goods?" she asked.

"Oh, certainly! if anything you buy here is not satisfactory we will exchange it."

"Well," was the reply; "here is one of those whirling-spray affairs I bought of you, and if you please, I want you to take it back and give me a bottle of Mellin's Food, instead."

And outside, the storm raged piteously, and across the moor a jay-bird called to his mate, "Cuckoo, cuckoo!"

For a large section of Protestant-American society at this time, including many of the feminists, the deliberate separation of lovemaking from the conception of children was either inconceivable or was some sort of unspeakable whore's trick. Anthony Comstock's answer for people who could not risk babies for financial or health reasons was simply that they restrain themselves and behave like children of God instead of like animals. This probably seemed a lot less outrageous to his audience than it would now.

The most pervasive guide and taste maker in the growing women's culture of the period was one of Hubbard's pet hates—Edward Bok's *Ladies' Home Journal.* Bok had made the nurturing and shaping of a journalism appealing to women his special field, and in some thirty years he built his magazine into a mass success. Though his influence was conservative—he opposed the militant feminists, and tried, with limited success, to keep extremes and flamboyance out of clothing fashions—there must have been some uneasiness in masculine hearts at even this restrained mobilization of feminine self-consciousness. Mark Sullivan said that around 1900 there were "as many Bok jokes as there came later to be Ford jokes." So that Hubbard was, in a real sense, riding a wave of antifeminism in his sneers at Bok and his "Betcher-sweet-life-I'm-a-Lady's Home Journal."

In a diluted way, Bok's influence on American home furnishing and decoration was closer to the simplicities of William Morris than anything the Roycrofters achieved. Over the years, the *Ladies' Home Journal* agitated very successfully for uncluttering the working core of the American home. Built-in storage was encouraged—that hat rack transformed into the closet. The grimy seasonal tyranny of carpeting was criticized, and bare floors, linoleum, and bright colors promoted. As water began to come in pipes instead of buckets, Bok campaigned for working-height sinks, and as families became smaller and kitchens less populated by helpers, he argued the virtues of labor- and step-saving.

Sometimes Bok crusaded in more serious and taboo-shrouded fields. In 1906, his personal department of the magazine headlined, "The time has come to turn the light on an existing condition touching the American fireside that will appall the average woman and girl." Followed then "The

Five Results," which described invalidism of women; death, blindness, disease of the newborn; stillbirths and sterility. The *Philistine* had a gay time over "this Awful Something that Brother Bok so mysteriously sidesteps and avoids mentioning." But Hubbard didn't name it either. Though he said of Bok, "Under the specious excuse of scientific truth he gives glossed pornography," Hubbard himself, in eleven pages of leering foolery and indignation, wound up with no trace of "scientific truth" himself.

This was another case—like vaccination—in which Hubbard's dislike of doctors ran away with him. He stated that venereal disease was "exceptional, and not general," that "the woman, herself, is more at fault than the male," and that young people should not hear about such things. His concluding paragraph showed more than his ordinary Bok phobia: "Colonel Bok is no longer a fit leader for the ladies' club—he should be deposed. Let an old woman be placed in his chair, who will not merely try to titillate the curiosity of the female subscriber, but who will, at times, tell the truth. Bok must go—one, two, three—out I say! hell is murky, out, damned Bok!"

This gambit by the *Ladies' Home Journal* was ahead of its time. It cost Bok seventy-five thousand cancellations. But it cracked the wall of silence, and by 1913 Eugène Brieux's *Damaged Goods,* with the subtitle, "A Study of Syphilis in Relation to Marriage," was playing to grimly attentive audiences in New York City. A feature article in *Harper's Weekly* described these audiences, which were 90 percent feminine: streetwalkers, social uplift workers, "mouse-like women . . . wives and sisters of suburban clergymen . . . hardly a face in all the crowded house that does not sooner or later take on an expression of painful reminiscent understanding." The performance played six shows in Buffalo, and this time Hubbard was impressed. After brooding on the matter for a couple of months, he came up with a solution: Let every engaged man present his fiancée with a life insurance policy on himself. This would guarantee his health without making a special issue of it.

"Why are husbands lobsters?" demanded a feminist in the September 1910 *Philistine.* Hubbard answered that it was the rigidity of marriage that made all the trouble. "Freedom in divorce is the one thing that will transform the marital boor into a gentleman . . . that will correct the propensity to nag, in both male and female." But he went around and round on the matter of divorce. When he was in the throes of his own family breakup, he exclaimed to a friend, "The Catholics are right, there should be no such thing as divorce!" Earlier he had said that "the State should take its heavy hands off and give the man and woman liberty" when they gave "no joy to each other." In 1904 he admonished "our zealous New Thought friends, who clamor to have marriage made difficult and divorce easy," that after all "the whole question has been thrashed over for three thousand years and all schemes tried," and later he adopted the New Thought formula himself.

Hubbard commented several times on the Mormon community in Utah. Mostly, he strongly approved of this persecuted group for whom "there is no closed season." He noted that "Before the Gentiles came . . . there were no paupers, no gamblers, no prostitutes, no drunkards in Salt Lake City." He was impressed by the industry and contentment of the Mormon women, and he observed that "monogamy is not necessarily the beautiful picture that the story books show, and polygamy is not the shameful thing that the W.C.T.U. of Connecticut think." But there were too many contradictions to his Alice-oriented feminism in Mormon society. He made little attempt to explain them; he let the boom swing over and take him the rest of the way on the other tack. "Polygamy does not debase nor prostitute woman. It simply prevents her evolution. In polygamy there can be no equality—women is forever an underling. In intellect she can never rise to man's estate and walk with him hand in hand. Man is her master—therein lies the curse to both."

In 1907 and 1908 a novel by Elinor Glyn, titled *Three Weeks,* was a scandalous sensation in both England and America. Hubbard's comments on it are in the *Philistine* for June 1908. "I wasted an hour on it between Willimantic and Boston," he said; "then I threw it out of the window to the great moral danger of the trackwalkers." He said that "Its sub-title should be, A Study in Lust, by a Pure Woman. I say a pure woman because a genuinely bad woman takes it out in the natural way, but a pure woman hands the public her lubricity done into a volume." He called it, accurately enough, "a woman's book, written for women. Men sin and forget it, but women live their sins in dreams and wallow in the muck of their minds. Men may be beastly in their badness, coarse, rude, crude and cruel, but they do not finger their feelings, nor refine vice, serving it with a faint filling of fromage and patchouli. . . . Three weeks is the end of the limit. Three minutes would be long enough."

The hour that Hubbard spent on the book must have been a busy one. He gave his own synopsis of the plot—which he called a "straight three weeks of barnyard." His description of an early round of the romance had Miss Glyn's heroine "plant a motherly bromide kiss upon his red, chaste lips—a smack that resounds thru the pages like the sound of a steer pulling its foot out of a buffalo wallow." Few books ever roused Hubbard to such overwrought and vivid comment. He reprinted several climactic passages verbatim; and he adopted the Glyn substitute for asterisks as a standard ending for jokes—the "whirling-spray affair" story quoted above has it. Here is one of his samples of Glyn:

Slowly she came back and bent over and over of her own accord—so low that at last she was level with his face. And slowly her red lips melted into his young lips in a long, strange kiss.

And outside the night winds sighed and soughed and lost birds called sorrowfully to their mates.

Hubbard's final punch line—after four quotations of this sort—was, "Wouldn't that give you the peewees?"

Elinor Glyn herself was hurt and bewildered by the public reaction to her book. She wrote a special introduction to the American edition in the (vain) hope of staving off a repetition of the shock and raucous laughter still echoing in England. She said that, for her, the book was "a deep study" and "beyond the ordinary laws of morality." She acknowledged that for many people—"moles, grubbing in the earth for worms"—the book would be "but a sensual record of passion." But the non-moles who "look up" would understand "the deep pure love, and the Soul in it all." (Readers like Hubbard found very little Soul in such passages as "She undulated about, creeping as a serpent over her lover.")

Hubbard was right about Miss Glyn being a "pure woman." A Scotch-Irish girl, fatherless from an early age, and a flaming redhead in a social world that considered red hair a misfortune, she grew up on the fringes of the fashionable upper classes. She married a middle-aged, indulgent, and totally unromantic Englishman, and the genesis of *Three Weeks* came during a holiday in Lucerne. It had two elements. The first was an entirely proper acquaintance with "a handsome young man . . . typical product of Eton and Oxford, endowed with splendid physique, personal charm and innate good qualities . . . but intellectually and emotionally sound asleep." Before long "I found myself wondering what such a young man might become if a really attractive woman who knew the world crossed his path."

The precipitating event came when, in the grip of what her husband called "spring fancies," she bought a huge tiger skin and arranged it, and herself, on the floor of their hotel suite. And her husband laughed at her. Years later she was able to be philosophical about it: "We had to get a special trunk for the creature, and Clayton was really furious about it, poor man . . . He said it was bad enough to have to travel with a woman who had thirty-seven new dresses, a train of antique admirers, and a maid who fell out of bed, but to have a huge tiger-skin as well was more than an Englishman could stand!" At the time, her reaction was violent, sustained, and literary. ". . . wild imaginations . . . were poured out . . . in a torrent of words which I could scarcely control. In six weeks the book was finished." And a tiger skin played a prominent part in it.

Readers like Hubbard took the tiger-skin scenes and their "undulating about" as representing a simple, almost clinical eroticism which they found a shocking and unnatural preoccupation for a woman. Miss Glyn never understood why she was so grossly misunderstood. Toward the end of her life—after a long stay in Hollywood, during which she enriched the American vocabulary with a special meaning of "It"—she saw her life as having been dominated by "the desire for *romance*." And romance was no mere physical matter: "a spiritual disguise, created by the imagination, with which to envelop material happenings and desires, and thus bring them into greater harmony with the soul."

There may have been a profound man-woman difference pointed up here, but it was not one the intellectual feminists were prepared to recognize. In a deeper sense than votes for women, *Three Weeks* might be seen as a symptom of the emerging New Woman. And, aside from the "patchouli" dalliance, one element in Miss Glyn's daydream that probably disturbed Hubbard was that it described the total domination—for his own good, of course—of a man by a woman.

Neither Hubbard's qualified feminism nor. Alice's "Man and woman will understand each other when both are free" have turned out according to plan. In the last years of the *Fra,* there were to be clear indications of some of the perplexities to come. In 1915, an article by a woman referred to "the Great American Husband . . . the Human Cash Register, and the Domestic Doormat." And a single issue in 1916 carried two articles, both by women, of sober second thought about the New Woman. One, titled "The Independent Woman," says: "I have met a great many of these women—stenographers, saleswomen, teachers and librarians—and it is the tragic truth that they are a restless and embittered class. And they know— the dullest of them—that in spite of their independence they have been cheated of a woman's normal life." The other article said flatly, "Women are emotional as the sparks fly upward." It criticized "the class of feminists who are unwilling to admit the native emotionalism of women." The article

would not have pleased Alice Hubbard. "Such women may cry *equality,
equality*—but there is no equality, in the sense in which they mean it. Instead, there is complemental unity, which is a thousand times better. . . .
when the nature and special ability of each sex is fully cognized and conceded by the other, there will be less sex-antagonism and more cooperation
between men and women." So that several years before the Nineteenth
Amendment, American women had gained a good deal of the independence
for which Alice Hubbard had crusaded, but disillusionment was already
spreading.

In the Hubbards' time, the sexes were sharply separate. Little boys had
manly chores to do, and manly sports. Little girls helped their mothers, and
when they played, they played House. There was little casual mixing and
there was considerable mystery. Puberty was clearly marked and publicly
recognized—a boy put on long pants and a girl put up her hair. Then came
well-regulated courting and marriage. But there was often also an inter-
mediate period in which respectable girls were protected from knowledge
and experience while their future husbands learned about sex from prostitutes, and sometimes the pattern continued after marriage. There is more
honesty today, and much more toleration of individual differences—and
great confusion about what a man or a woman is supposed to be and do.
And while we are most aware of the customs and perplexities of the
"modern" way of life, there is probably nowhere between the Appalachians
and the Mississippi that a fifty-mile radius will not include people living
essentially nineteenth-century lives. It is small wonder that boards of
education are battlegrounds.

Two things seem clear in the whole complex picture of woman in
Hubbard's time and now. There has been a great increase in expectancies.
Life is counted on to yield dividends of self-realization that would have
seemed damnable to our Puritan forebears, and definitely excessive to the
Hubbards. Today's symptoms of despair need to be seen in relation to this
hope and life hunger. And, in our time, we not only expect more but our
range of choice has vastly expanded. For both men and women, the available
number of more or less workable patterns of living has multiplied many
times. Much of the surface uniformity in America that so many people find
so dreary may be a compensation for an underlying pluralism so great—and
sometimes so lonely—that this dull common ground is needed for rest and
reassurance. It has been a long way from Alice Hubbard to Mary McCarthy.
And from Elbert to Hugh Hefner.

Elbert Hubbard about 1910

14

Big Business
&
More of It

IN MARCH 1910, Hubbard passed another "pivotal point" in his love affair with the business world. The lead article in the *Fra* was titled "The Standard Oil Company," and it exuded no faintest breath of criticism for its subject. It saluted the occupants of the executives as "graduates of the University of Hard Knocks. They have played the game according to regulation American rules, and they have won because they had the foresight, patience, quickness, courage, good cheer, economy, skill." As for their erstwhile competitors—five years before, he had seen them as the victims of "bribery, coercion, violence and even murder"—"the men who went down before them failed for lack of these American qualities."

On one level, the article was simply press agentry, written to sell reprints. But in the recesses of Hubbard's "thinkery," it was more on the order of an appeal to reason and justice, to save the country from ruin. As Hubbard saw it, the seven years just past—the great days of the muckrakers, and of Teddy Roosevelt and his Big Stick—had been "a cyclone of defamation, vituperation and exposure—much of it indecent." The result had been the Panic of 1907. Which was only to be expected when "you raise a cry of 'Stop thief' and turn the powerful resources of the government to harassing enterprise . . . to confiscate its property, take away its character, destroy its good-will . . ." In an argument that was to echo for several generations, Hubbard appealed to common sense to "realize that business is built on confidence, that when we destroy faith in our commercial fabric we are actually taking the roofs from homes, snatching food from children . . ."

The Standard Oil Company was incidental by the time Hubbard reached his peroration: "Shall we blast, wither and destroy with the breath of our mouths all that civilization holds dear? I think not. We can direct and regulate, but we will do it in justice and not in blindness and wrath, lest . . ." And as for Ida Tarbell, who had been one of the original muckrakers, and whose calm, factual history of Standard Oil loomed unshaken over Hubbard's intuitive preachment, there was very little he could say fairly. So he said it unfairly: she was not a liar, "she is worse than that—she is an honest, bitter, talented and prejudiced person who wrote from her own point of view . . . the ditch, where her father's wheelbarrow was landed by a Standard Oil tank-wagon." This kind of infighting came easily to Hubbard. Facts had always been more or less beside the point, and since Miss Tarbell "shot from cover and she shot to kill," he was in the fight for keeps, too. "Such literary bushwackers should be answered shot for shot."

Hubbard was a little late in getting mobilized against the muckrakers. Much of their early sniping at corruption, power, and exploitation had not been too far from some of his own crusades. The afflatus of moral indignation, the stance of embattled outsiderdom—these were qualities that Hubbard had often shared with what he called "the Tarbell-Steffens-Russell-Roosevelt-Sinclair method of inky warfare." The big difference was in how Hubbard—and the muckrakers—saw and interpreted what was happening in the country.

The overriding reality in American life at the turn of the century was the accelerating concentration of economic power. This was symbolized as The Trusts, and pictured by such cartoonists as Frederick Opper as an ever-expanding family of silk-hatted slobs labeled "Beef Trust," "Steel Trust," "Sugar Trust," and so on. These monsters were changing much more than the economic structure of the country. The old morals and values often seemed to be fading or irrelevant; the belief in America as a country of open-ended opportunity was shaken, and so was the faith in democratic government. It was this widening gap between the nation's sustaining visions and things as they actually were that the muckrakers exposed and explored. At the same time, new techniques of printing and distribution, and the growth of advertising, combined with expanding public literacy and concern with national issues to make a mass market for popular magazines. For nearly a decade, the muckrakers rode this wave in fine style and gave their public a vivid and frightening look at what was going on in their country.

For Elbert Hubbard, this was also the decade in which those converging forces in his inner and outer lives were leading him to discover, and celebrate, that New Science of Business. As for the muckrakers, well, many of them were the same crowd who had once kept him cooling his heels in outer offices and called him a philistine. As for Theodore Roosevelt, he was a long-time Hubbard hate. Perhaps they had too much in common, but the bombastic, strenuous egotism of "Teddy Rex" had been infuriating Hubbard for some years before the Roosevelt presidency: "Just a kid is our own Teddy . . . only an over-grown fighting kid, with a dirty face, buttons all off his clothes thru much 'rastling.' . . . Teddy is as high now as he will ever get." When Roosevelt opened fire on the trusts, Hubbard took his cue from such of his entrepreneuring heroes as James J. Hill, who was lamenting that "it really seems hard, when we look back on what we have done . . . in opening the country and carrying at the lowest rates, that we should be compelled to fight for our lives against the political adventurers who have never done anything but pose and draw a salary." And when Upton Sinclair gave the nation a queasy stomach with *The Jungle,* and the resulting uproar forced Roosevelt to act, Hubbard's contribution to this bit of history was:

Upton Sinclair scored two big points on Packingtown and its Boss Ogre. They were these: First, the Ogre hired men and paid them to kill animals. Second, these dead animals were distributed by the Ogre and his minions and the corpses eaten by men, women and children. It was a revolting revelation. It even shook the nerves of a President, one of the killingest men in the world, who, not finding enough things to kill in America, went to Africa to kill things.

The meat-packers were said to have distributed a million copies of the *Little Journey* on Philip D. Armour (1909), from which this gem was taken, along with a boiler-plated news story headed "Elbert Hubbard Lashes the Muckraker Crowd."

By 1911, Hubbard's fronting for his new heroes was getting a little frantic. He made a cover display for the December *Philistine* of "I am not in the business of defaming America nor using as a doormat the things that are building it up: I believe in Big Business and more of it." And when the *Titanic* went down in 1912, something like overidentification had set in, and his eulogy of the upper-crust casualties verged on the hysterical: "The Strausses, Stead, Astor, Butt, Harris, Thayer, Widener, Guggenheim, Hays— I thought I knew you, just because I had seen you, realized somewhat of your able qualities, looked into your eyes and pressed your hands, but I did not guess your greatness. You are now beyond the reach of praise—flattery touches you not—words for you are vain." One might ask who invited him to the wake, anyway.

The climax came in 1914 with the Colorado coal strike. This became open industrial warfare, sufficiently feudal and savage to authenticate the most militant Marxism. There was a mobilization of the country's radicals on the scene and in the press, a public uproar, and a Federal investigation, which placed Hubbard's role in the matter in the public domain—and indicated one of the ways in which that Roycroft payroll was being met.

Hubbard had written John D. Rockefeller, Jr.: "I have been out in Colorado and know a little about the situation there. It seems to me that your stand is eminently right, proper and logical. . . . Many of the strikers are poor, unfortunate, ignorant foreigners." They thought they were fighting for freedom but were actually being "preyed upon by social agitators." Hubbard went on to tell Rockefeller that he was "writing something on the subject a little after the style" of a recent piece of his in the *Fra.* This had been called "The Copper Country," and dealt with a somewhat similar miners' strike in upper-peninsula Michigan. "Someone should carry on a campaign of education," said Hubbard, and would Mr. Rockefeller be interested in distributing copies of the *Fra* that would contain Hubbard's article?

Rockefeller's reply was formal and chilly. About all it said was that he would be willing to see Mr. Hubbard's article on conditions in Colorado. Three weeks later Hubbard wrote again, sending the Copper-Country *Fra,* pointing out that "our friends up north have distributed a large number of these, sending the magazines out from here, duly blue-penciled. I have upwards of a million names of members of Board of Trade, Chambers of Commerce, Advertising Clubs, Rotarians, Jovians, school teachers, all judges, members of Congress, etc. It seems to me that we [we?] could well afford to circulate . . . copies of the *Fra* containing a judicious and truthful writeup of the situation in Colorado. The price of extra copies of the *Fra* is $200.00 a thousand." Then he used the needle: "Just here I cannot refrain from expressing my admiration for the advertising genius desplayed [*sic*] by those very industrious, hard working people, Bill Haywood, Charles Moyer, Mother Jones, Emma Goldman, Lincoln Steffens, and Upton Sinclair. They are continually stating their side of the controversy. I believe if we would state ours . . ."

Mr. Rockefeller was still not buying. He offered to pass on any suggestions to the mine operators in Denver, who were handling all publicity. In another week Hubbard asked for the name of the "publicity man" in Denver, and just happened to mention a "delightful game of golf with

your father on Saturday. How fine and brown and well and strong he is."
(This jolly old gentleman, of course, was the same one who had once put
Hubbard in mind of a sea of stiffening corpses.) Junior replied the very next
day: ". . . Father has spoken of your visit . . . He is indeed in the best
of health . . ." and suggested that Hubbard see the head of the Rockefeller
affiliate in Denver, a Mr. Welborn, to whom he wrote of Hubbard's expected
coming. He also passed on to Welborn the advice he had received from
Ivy Lee, his thousand-dollar-a-month public relations man, to let Hubbard
make any study he wanted to, strictly on his own, and then see what his
article looked like before making any commitments. Mr. Welborn replied
that the *Fra* reprint price looked high to him but they could see what
developed. As for Hubbard, he didn't have to go back to Colorado to write
his piece, but if it took a trip to sell the reprints, it was worth it.

Hubbard's piece in the *Fra* ("In Colorado") appeared in the January
1915 issue. It was a complete whitewash of the mine operators, painted a
rosy picture of the life of a miner, and invoked the specter of red revolution.
"The question in Colorado was not . . . wages, or conditions of labor, nor
working hours. It was a matter of changing the form of government of
the United States." This revolutionary demand, as Hubbard went on to
say, was for recognition of the union and acceptance of a closed shop. It
was perfectly true, as he asserted, that radicals from the whole country had
assembled in Colorado and that many of them were using the situation for
their own purposes. But it was also true—and this was nowhere to be
found in Hubbard's travel notes—that the coal towns were pure industrial
feudalism, with company houses, company stores, fences, and gates manned
by armed guards. And corruption, brutality, and tyranny were widespread.
Hubbard's golfing act paid off handsomely. Testimony at the hearing indicated that the mine operators bought a million copies of that *Fra*. (Hubbard's reference to the transaction was: "John D. Rockefeller said 'Great!'
and bought a dozen copies or so.")

As the hearings moved along before the Federal Commission of Industrial Relations, it became apparent that Hubbard had not only moved far
out in front of his *de facto* clients, but that they were turning off in another
direction. John D. Rockefeller, Jr., spent three days on the witness stand,
and largely reversed the popular impression that he was the villain of the
piece. He proved remarkably uninformed about the conditions of life in his
mining subsidiaries, shocked by the bloody chaos that had erupted, and
anxious to straighten things out. He invited Mother Jones to his office.

They talked for an hour and a half, and she emerged to tell reporters that she had changed her opinion of him completely: "We have been misrepresenting him terribly, and I as much as anybody else."

The younger Rockefeller also expressed his wish to meet the other union leaders "as man to man," and called them "as clean-cut fellows as you would wish to see." This honeymoon atmosphere stiffened a little the following day. Mother Jones had had time to reflect: "I've been in jail so long my head's out of gear," and Upton Sinclair had sent her a stand-fast telegram: "We are sure you will not let yourself be overcome by the sweet odor of the American Beauty Rose." She called for deeds instead of words, and denounced the proposed open-shop collective-bargaining agreement as a fraud. But she still felt that Junior was "a very pleasant young man." Hubbard tried to deal himself in on the good feeling by declaring that "a little mingling of the Rockefeller head with the Mother Jones heart will not do anybody any harm."

But it did him little good. Hubbard's part in the Colorado strike—like his earlier defense of the meat-packers—gave him a strong taste of "the disgrace that comes from talking in public about something of which he is beautifully ignorant." His correspondence with Rockefeller appeared in the published hearings. Norman Hapgood printed the whole thing in *Harper's Weekly* under the heading "Elbert Hubbard's Price." Hapgood's own comment was brief: "Mr. Hubbard's proposal, it will be seen, had two parts. 1. To sell his opinion. 2. Later on to make an 'investigation' in support of that opinion."

This was almost as unfair as Hubbard's dismissal of Ida Tarbell's factual reporting because her father had been put out of business by Standard Oil. Hubbard had been in Colorado. He wasn't planning much more of an investigation than he could make from the depths of his Morris chair. He knew what was what in Colorado and what he would write about it. Mr. Rockefeller was uncommonly stupid to be so cautious about getting in on a good thing. Hubbard's opinions weren't for sale—only reprints.

But this seems to have been the high-water mark of Hubbard's over-identification with big business. He was even bothered enough by Hapgood's contempt to violate his own maxim about never explaining. He wrote to Hapgood ("My dear Norman") a letter that mixed ingratiation ("You and I both belong to the Illini. . . . I appreciate your worthy qualities of brain; I know your kindly heart . . .") with patronizing (". . . that muckraking no longer pays, I, as a journalist, for your sake, much regret"), brushed off the *Harper's Weekly* drumbeat repetition of "Elbert Hubbard's

Price" as pure advertising and quite understandable among friends ("a chemical trace of piffle in publicity"), but undertook to deny absolutely that his opinions were for sale or that he was uninformed about matters in Colorado. Then he leaped to what he probably thought was an overwhelming offensive: "You have succumbed to the temptation of trying to place an old friend in a disgraceful light before the world, this for the transient satisfaction of some undefined personal whim . . . the love of fame and the will-to-vengeance have taken you captive . . . Nevertheless, I wish you well, and while I regret that *Harper's Weekly* has few readers, and no advertising to mention, I yet believe there is a place for your services if you can but realize that today the world needs builders and creators, not sappers and incendiaries. With all kind wishes . . ."

No reply is in the record. The best that Hubbard could manage as public rebuttal appeared in the June 1915 *Philistine:* "If any one wants to know Norman Hapgood's price, the answer will be found on the back page of *Harper's Weekly* for last week. . . . a full-page ad for cigarettes."

Over the years, since he had written a little piece titled "I Am an Anarchist," and later called himself a Fabian Socialist, Hubbard had made many attempts to come to terms with economics and politics. These were not ideal subjects for his temperament, but he did try. In the January 1902 *Philistine,* he took on the trusts:

The Trusts were made by the People, and the People can and will unmake them, should they ever prove an engine of repression. . . . The next move of Evolution will be Socialism. Socialism means the operation of all industries by the People, for the People. Socialism is cooperation instead of competition. Competition has been so general that economists mistook it for a Law of Nature, when it was only an incident. Competition is no more a law of Nature than is hate. Hate was once so thoroughly believed in that we gave it personality and called it The Devil.

The Trusts are getting things ready for Socialism.

Humanity is growing in intellect, in patience, in kindness, in love. And when the time is ripe, the People will step in and take peaceful possession of their own.

Five years later, he repeated the same bland assurance that "As to the monopolies, the trusts are getting them in shape so they can be passed over to the people, as soon as the people have reached a point where they can manage them." But this time he addressed himself to "our socialist friends," no longer including him, and bade them "take hope by remembering this: twenty-five years ago there were over one thousand distinct toll turnpikes or plank roads in America controlled by companies or individuals. Now the highways belong to the people! . . . So, ye weary sinners, fresh courage take . . ."

At about this time, Hubbard began to formulate a new vision of business as service and efficiency. He was impressed by the way retailing had moved from fraud and haggling toward tidy and impersonal mass distribution. He credited John Wanamaker with inaugurating the "one-price system" in 1865, and he called it "a saver of nerve-force beyond computation." The Owl Drug Stores, an early western chain, added brisk efficiency, standardization, courtesy, and cleanliness. Another clue came from a hardware maker who spruced up his retail outlets with window displays. (Hubbard would have loved supermarkets and drive-in shoping centers.) "The modern, sure-enough saint," he said in the December 1906 *Philistine,* "is the business man who sticks to the one-price system and tells the truth." After the Great-Business-Men *Little Journeys,* he began the process of cashing in on the name, but his choice of subjects was also a rough indicator of what he found admirable in this brave new world. From 1912 to early 1914, for instance, the *Little Journeys* visited the S. H. Knox five-and-ten chain, the Loyal Order of Moose, the Ad-Clubs, the Owl Drug Stores, John H. Patterson and National Cash Registers, the Sells-Floto Circus, the Norwell-Shapleigh Hardware Co., Steero Bouillon Cubes, White-Steel Bathroom Furniture, Eastman Kodak, White Rock Beverages, Kellogg health foods, Grinnel Sprinklers, Rotary Clubs, Wall Street, and the University of Hard Knocks.

In one of Hubbard's last published formulations on the trusts (March 1915), he finally got down to something like specifics: "The possible evil in the 'Trust' is not in its organization, nor in its bigness, nor in its success. It is three-fold: first, corruption of public officials to obtain special privileges . . . second, the consequent oppression of the competitor and the consumer; third, watering the stock and then extorting excessive profits to pay dividends." But that was about as near to a bill of particulars as he came. Most of his late pronouncements on this subject were beautifully inspirational and vague, as in this from the *Fra* for April 1908:

We mustn't go back to Primitive Christianity, or Communism, or Socialism, or Peaceful Anarchy—if these things are desirable we will reach them by going on to them. For us Utopia lies beyond, not behind. . . . Trusts are beneficent, economic factors in our evolution. You say that they do harm; yes, grant it, but they also do a vast amount of good. It is the trusts that gave us the ocean cables, the Trans-Continental Railroads, the Telephones, the Greyhounds of the Sea, and these are the things that give us our dream of a United Mankind. The age is creative, constructive, inventive—we are builders, not destroyers . . . And the wealth we are producing is being used for the most part, for the benefit of mankind. It is reinvested, not hoarded. Nature is automatic and kills the man who misuses her gifts.

As we have seen, even in his blast at the muckrakers, he had granted that "we can direct and regulate . . ." But the place where he always boggled and jumped the track was the question of *who* was to regulate, and how, and through what institutional devices—other than Nature's, and Emerson's, Law of Compensation.

This was a common enough puzzle. Industrialism *was* something new and portentous, and there was little agreement on what to do about it. Worship the new magic and bow down to its high priests? Operate it by the dark of the moon and pretend we were doing something else? Or maybe stone these wizards from the land? Those who had their hands on the controls were not apt to see that there was any problem. If pressed, they might even claim Divine Right, as in the often-quoted pronouncement of George F. Baer of the Philadelphia and Reading Railway: "The rights and interests of the laboring man will be protected and cared for—not by labor agitators, but by the Christian men to whom God in His infinite wisdom has given the control of the property interests of the country, and upon the successful Management of which so much depends."

Hubbard wouldn't have put it in quite those terms, but his persistent distrust of government—any government—worked out to very much the same end product. When he tried to define the proper sphere of government, he worried out some such statement as that "government is a sort of corporation . . . a matter of business, and related to matters of the education of the young; the care of the old, decrepit and infirm; the keeping of public records; the question of good roads, public parks, pure water and fresh air. Government gives opportunity and protects the individual in his rights." Or, in a more typical form: "The business of government is to make all government unnecessary, just as wise parents are bringing up their children to do without them."

Much of Hubbard's suspicion of government came from its long association with an established Church and with warmaking. So, in his earlier phases, he had espoused a sort of pacifism-anarchism. "People who do not readily pass under hypnotic control have been known to answer back," he wrote then, "in which case they have occasionally been arrested for contumacy and contravention by stocky men in wide-awake hats, who lead the strenuous life. Savages like to go to war; we do not. All we ask is the privilege of attending to our own business. We have work to do, and wish to work while it is called the day. But they will not . . . these demagogues, politicians and rogues . . . they will not leave us alone—these men who insist on governing us and living off our labor. They tax us, eat our substance, conscript us, draft our boys into their wars."

He also distrusted the democratic process itself—the capacity of ordinary people to govern themselves. He defined public opinion as "the judgment of the incapable many opposed to that of the discerning few." But he made comments like this one, which reverses its field at the end, although he didn't seem to notice: "All men are created free and equal. This is absolutely true leaving out all those who have hare-lip, strabismus, a lupus habit of body, legs that are not mates, wills that do not obey the throttle-valve and passions not under the control of the air-brake; also those born on the East Side and those with parents who work for the Coal Trust at eighty cents a day." Lincoln's democratic faith—"why should there not be a patient confidence in the ultimate justice of the people? Is there any better or equal hope in the world?" is not to be found in *Elbert Hubbard's Scrap Book.*

Hubbard's perspective on democracy seemed to depend on whether he was on the defensive or the attack. A few damnations from the orthodox could make him feel himself one with the martyrs of freedom, and the natural enemy of the herd. And whenever the status of his kind of Great Man was brought in question by government, reformers, or by "this inert, greasy, obese thing, a Popular Majority," he took it as a personal challenge. And, quite frequently, the only form of government that made sense to him was "Democracy as applied by the beneficent Strong Man." On the other hand, someone else's arrogance could occasionally make him a dedicated democrat. He put on his brass knuckles in dealing with a forgotten Brahmin, "a Nice Man by the name of Harry Peck. I believe he has some kind of a job working around Columbia University." Mr. Peck had been "throwing off pot-boilers on Popular Education and among other things he says, 'What a University should do is to produce a small and highly trained patriciate, a caste, an aristocracy if you will. This aristocracy should control the destiny of States, driving in harness the hewers of wood and drawers of water who constitute the vast majority and whose happiness is greater . . . when governed than when governing.' " Apparently, said Hubbard, "Mr.

Peck has small respect for the Emancipation Proclamation that was issued by a hewer of wood. What t'ell is the need of having an education at all if every one has one!" And this time he invoked the mob on his side: "The highly trained patriciate has ever tried to harness the hewers and drawers and the latter have ever had a tendency to arise and cut off the well stored heads of the patriciate. . . . Harry Peck should cease calling plain, honest folks names and fall in line and educate us—we are not so dangerous then."

Whenever Hubbard tried to get down to cases on government and business, he left a power vacuum. "Supervision of our great organizations is necessary," he acknowledged. But such supervision "must be conducted intelligently, and not as an inquisition. And it should be taken entirely out of the guiding hands of political parties." Political parties, of course, however grubby and corrupt they may have seemed in Hubbard's time (or any other time), were the basic machinery of democratic government. If supervision were taken out of their hands, what others were available? Certainly not those of organized labor; that meant "the rule of the walking delegate, who rides in a taxi and never works." About the only hands left were those of the business-industrial leaders. This would have been roughly the same operational setup as "the Christian gentlemen to whom God in His infinite wisdom has given the control . . ."

But if Hubbard never came up with an answer for this, neither—in any final sense—did the American people. The working principle that finally pulled Hubbard's generation around its critical corners was formulated, and implemented enough to make it real, by Theodore Roosevelt: ". . . every man holds his property subject to the general right of the community to regulate its use to whatever degree the public welfare may require it." But the same principle had to be reimplemented by a later Roosevelt to get the country around bigger and yet more critical corners. And there is still substantial dissent.

And if Hubbard's grasp of political economy wasn't much, he did sometimes make long-range prophecies that have stood up rather well. During his middle period he once did a little speculating on the future of radicalism:

Both Anarchists and Marxists fully believe that the present social order is to go down in ruins. The new regime, according to Emma Goldman, will be a time of individualism, when no one shall work for money, . . . and love will be supreme. According to Eugene Debs, the New Order will be a more highly systematized plan of government than we now have, where everything will be managed for the good of all. So, theoretically, anarchy and socialism are opposite poles of the same planet. But . . . dissolution without organization is anarchy; and since there are about fifty-seven varieties of Socialists, and the whole party is split into fractions as to ways and means, no sane man can see anything but anarchy ahead if Marxian Socialism should have its way. And anarchy being disorganization, means a quick return to tyranny, thru the rule of the strong man who arises in his lust for power and takes command by right of might at the psychological moment.

This was a pretty fair advance description of the Russian Revolution, as Emma Goldman was to live to find out.

According to Reedy, Hubbard had a private strategy that underlay his fronting for big business. Reedy wrote in 1912 that Hubbard felt there was much to be said for an approach to the corporate boss men that would "get next to them and liberate their good energies in other directions." Hubbard, said Reedy, "is not a sociological reformer. He isn't interested in economics particularly." And though he had no time for special privilege, "he has a theory that . . . we can spoil the big fellows who have been despoiling the many," that they are "mostly good fellows [who are] in the mill and can't get out" and that they "have been so unmercifully hammered that they are grateful for the smallest word in their favor. . . . The rich man, these days, is, to no small extent, the under dog. So Fra Elbertus regards himself as the friend of the oppressed. And he looks straight at you when he says it. Of course the oppressed subscribe for copies by the year in thousands."

In 1914, however, Hubbard may have felt that he had been badly let down by those rich underdogs. Here he—and he alone, was the frequent implication—had been defending business against the muckrakers, the radicals, the Federal government itself. He was sounding the trumpet: "History is reaching a Pivotal Point. A new deal is at the door, and as Alaric overran Rome, so is Anarchy ready to engulf us," and getting himself crucified by the likes of Norman Hapgood, while John D. Rockefeller, Jr., was off turning the charm on Mother Jones. Hubbard even had to promote a golfing match with John D., Sr. (and golf was something Hubbard despised), to get these idiots to accept his help. He told them about it, too, in a *Philistine* piece called "Publicity by Default."

The thing that lives in history is not the event. It is the written account of it. . . . The stupidity of big business in being perfectly willing to leave publicity to its enemies is almost past belief. . . . Today civilization is sitting on the crust of a crater, dangling its heels and whistling *Annie Laurie*. Big business would do well to come out of its comatose state, organize a bureau and teach the world a little economic truth.

Hubbard could also be irritated with the business world when it didn't live up to his visions for it. "When I uphold big business," he complained, "it does not for a moment mean that I justify big business in grinding its employees and the public." The tide of public opinion was running strongly toward economic reform, and Hubbard felt compelled to insist that "Big Business must be run by big men" who have "sympathetic hearts and are humanitarians as well as economists." He was obviously disturbed by the blasting he was getting from the reformers. Even his friend Reedy was ribbing him by proposing a Hubbard-for-President movement, on a platform of "STAND PAT. The world is all right, so far as we are concerned. Be kind—but get the money." He did much more defensive protesting than was his habit: "It will not do to say that men are deliberate falsifiers because they disagree with us," and more directly, "I object to the accusation that I have sold my soul to Mammon because I write what is in my heart. From a certain point of view a man sees certain things."

Hubbard's cultivated serenity was in bad shape during this period. His writing shows a considerable hardening of the spiritual arteries. Instead of the onetime blandness (in which he could wind up a polemic paragraph with a certain abashment at his own violence: "A philosopher may at times be a chucklehead, and for this the law does not provide a penalty, for to be one is punishment enough. God have mercy on us all!"), he snarled and ranted. He had a new pet hate in Louis D. Brandeis. Probably Brandeis, with his meticulous documenting of economic facts—his orderly, statistical, exhaustive, and unanswerable Briefs for the People—was an intolerable reproach to Hubbard's pontificating. And the righteousness of those "wrist-watch slummers" enraged him: "the only things that are ninety-nine per cent pure are Ivory Soap and Louis Brandeis." When he opened up on Brandeis, he could be vicious: "Business Baiter, stirrer up of strife, litigious lurer on of hate and unrest, destroyer of confidence, killer of values, commercial coyote, spoiler of pay envelopes . . . Gompers, Goldman and Gyp the Blood rolled into one, and given a degree from Harvard."

The sometimes brilliant, sometimes outlandish vernacular metaphors that he had once whipped up as he went along were used and re-used until the Hubbard prose—and the frenetic imitations turned out by his ad-writing staff—had become almost a private language. His basic stock of ideas was kept circulating in any and every context. More and more of his earlier writing, especially the *Little Journeys,* was cannibalized to fill space. A lot of his writing in this late period was dictated to a secretary, and this increased the splintered effect.

All of this conflict and frenzy were having their effects, and the June 1914 *Philistine* carried an outburst that sounded near desperation. War seemed imminent that spring. But with Mexico. And Hubbard told himself that "life turned on a choice of evils" and "better that we should make war on a foreign foe than to have war at home carried on by the demagogue and the business baiter. Sitting listlessly on park benches are two million men out of jobs, undone . . . better to be ruled by warriors and fighters than by greasy grafters and pompadour politicians . . ." But it was a great shock to Hubbard—as to most Americans—when war exploded in Europe. Less than a year before he had said, "The belief that we are enslaved by the capitalist is as foolish as the fear that Germany is going to make war on England."

ALI BABA in Original Binding.

15

Vestibule to Paradise

INTERESTINGLY ENOUGH, those years of increasing sound and fury in Hubbard's involvement with big business were also years in which his Roycroft community became most stable, productive, and delightfully evocative as a place to visit. Probably it was here (and only here) that his preeminence was not threatened. As the Master of Roycroft, his role had become established and accepted, and this gave him an unusual freedom in performance.

There are many entranced comments in the record by visitors to the Roycroft Conventions. These summer get-togethers had some things in common with the Chautauquas, of which there were more than five hundred in the early 1900's. Probably the most novel of the special Roycroft features, aside from the Hubbard personality, was the inclusion of the paying guests in the institutional chore-doing. There was no coercion in this but it was the thing to do, and making hay, cutting wood, or hoeing potatoes was both a social icebreaker and a novel experience in itself to many a heavy thinker or corporate executive. Hubbard would lead the guests into the fields, encourage them to wield hayforks or hoes or whatever, and say, "Keep it going 'til I come back"—which he had no intention of doing.

One of the several "Little Journeys to East Aurora" in the record was by Terence V. Powderly. This onetime head of the Knights of Labor found Hubbard's community "not a paradise, but would make a first-class vestibule for one." Labor leaders were not often Hubbard fans, but the same large idealism that had caused Powderly to establish workers' cooperatives and advocate industrial arbitration led him inevitably to East Aurora. (By this time the labor movement had swung away from Powderly's broad social

181

reform and into the wages-and-hours, craft unionism of Samuel Gompers.) Powderly's reactions were typical of many of the summer visitors: "There was no starch, no fuss and feathers, no ostentation, no pomp or ceremony . . . like one great family coming home to a reunion. No one feels a stranger or ill at ease . . . no place for the artificial man." He was much impressed with Hubbard, and said that he "talks less of himself than any man I know" and "radiates love of the beautiful, the artistic, and the useful." His final verdict was that "the world will write Elbert Hubbard a benefactor of the race."

In spite of a high percentage of "one-idea men" in attendance, these gatherings were informal, lighthearted, and spontaneous. There was a mild taboo on too much intellectual contentiousness—a tradition of "Get in the ball game and forget it." The Roycroft counterparts of "THINK" signs were wall mottoes admonishing "Only one person can get mad at a time." Hubbard's dislike of argument went a long way back. When he was writing the love letters of *Forbes of Harvard,* in 1893, he went into rather flowery detail: "The healthy intellect is not given to logic, controversy and syllogistic warfare. It is the intuitive soul which listens close, inclines the heart and wastes not its forces in windmill duels." His prescription then for a practicing prophet was: "Let him speak his thoughts, but answer no vain quibble. Let him write his message on the wall of time, but tarry he shall not, to explain or apologize to those who will not, or can not understand." After all, "vain are words; and called upon to prove, we stammer, beat the air, and lose the golden thread of sweet communion."

The *Philistine* ads for the summer conventions were arch and cute, but apparently they weren't too far from being accurately descriptive:

All Immortals and Subscribers . . . are especially invited to be present and join the gladsome glee.

There will be three Formal Programs a day, but not too formal—morning, afternoon and evening—when men and women of Note will speak, sing, recite, vibrate and otherwise disturb the ether!

There is always much good-fellowship at these Conventions. Introductions are tabu. Everybody knows everybody else. Good will and the laugh in which there is no bitterness prevail. Music will be a feature. There will be gentle walks afield, tramps to the Farms and Camps, and demonstrations at the Roycroft Woodpiles. As for the Ideas—everybody is welcome to all he can bring and all he can carry away. Perhaps you had better not dress too fine—flannels, corduroys, khaki, stout shoes and a Smile!

Minor and major celebrities came, some regularly. Among them: Gutzon Borglum, Eugene Debs, John Burroughs, Alfred Henry Lewis, Brand Whitlock, Margaret Sanger, Clarence Darrow, Carrie Jacobs Bond, Harry Lauder, Hall Caine, Scott Nearing, Robert Barr, Ella Wheeler Wilcox, Booker T. Washington, Ellen Terry, Judge Ben Lindsey, Henry Ford, Dr. Algernon Sidney Crapsey, Horace Fletcher, David Bispham, and William Marion Reedy. To be sure, it was more comfortable to be a paying guest than one of the extra hands hired for the season. Alexander Woollcott spent the summer of 1906—he was a freshman at Hamilton College—doing janitor work, and later called the place "a debased Oberammergau." But for many other young people, a summer job in East Aurora was a lark. College girls worked as waitresses, and there were many romances. The young Burton Rascoe was a Hubbard fan while still in high school in Oklahoma. He was also quite an operator, selling Hubbard-style advertisements to the local merchants and ghost-writing papers for the members of the ladies literary club. In due time, Rascoe visited East Aurora. Unlike many of his contemporaries—who seemed in later life to have to write their youthful Hubbard-worship out of their systems by damning Hubbard—he was generous in his reminiscences. He said that Hubbard, "whatever may have been his limitations (he was a superb showman, and all showmen have a degree of charlatanry . . .) *did* have a deep sense of the essential values of a living literature and was . . . interesting the masses in the arts . . . and in the handicrafts. . . ."

Edwin Markham, riding his overnight celebrity as the author of "The Man with the Hoe," visited East Aurora and gave Hubbard the occasion for a typical stunt. According to the story, the white-bearded "Professor" was met at the train by a group of Roycroft notables, all in overalls and carrying hoes. The party proceeded to the potato field, where they put the hoes in operation and Ali Baba gave forth with philosophy: "The hoe is all right, and all men should hoe. If all men hoed a little, no man would have to hoe all the time. To hoe all the time slants the brow. To never hoe tends to hydrocephalus and nervous prostration. Let us all hoe—a little."

It was this sort of clowning that made people look twice at Hubbard, and their second look asked a question that became a cliché: "Is he sincere?" The question annoyed him enormously and he kept ringing changes on it: "The question which is agitating Buffalo is this, 'Is Niagara Falls sincere, and isn't all that noise made for the purpose of attracting attention to itself?'" When he was asked the question directly in writing by the president of a Boston woman's club, he answered, "I certainly am sincere, altho I am not always serious." And he followed this with an answer to "Do you practice what you preach?" which is a little like a dog chasing its tail: "No man always practices what he preaches, because he preaches the ideal, the perfect, and he preaches in his best mood. . . . when it comes to life, all you can do is live your life, because you live in the midst of fools—[who] ask you, 'Are you sincere?' "

Cleveland's reform mayor, Tom L. Johnson, commented that "people who have been to the Roycroft Shops never ask that threadbare question . . ." Johnson and Frederic C. Howe "motored" to East Aurora for a visit with Hubbard and (Howe's account) "found him in the fields with his shirt open at the neck and his hair flowing to the winds. He installed us at the Inn. There was music and talk and Hubbard was an engaging host. He impressed me as a real person, courageous and honest in his personal interests, in spite of the fact that he commercializes his work. He drew to himself all kinds of people." Johnson carried a Hubbard motto card in his pocket for moments of stress. It read: "The man who is worthy of being a leader of men will never complain of the stupidity of his helpers, of the ingratitude of mankind, nor of the inappreciation of the public. These things are all a part of the great game of life, and to meet them and not go down under them in discouragement and defeat is the final proof of power."

It was quite a show he put on, and always it was a one-way process, and a mixture of the spontaneous and the calculated. Playing catch and throwing a medicine ball around were standard Roycroft recreation, for Hubbard and everyone. Horseback riding was his lifelong pleasure. But though there came to be many team sports at Roycroft, Hubbard neither played nor watched. Card-playing and dancing he tolerated for others, though he disapproved. He held forth to his Chapel audiences about anything and everything, but Shay never knew Hubbard to sit down on the Inn Peristyle for unplanned conversation. It was Hubbard's custom, in introducing a speaker at Roycroft with whom he disagreed, to inform the audience what it was going to hear, what was wrong with it, and where the real truth lay before he allowed the speaker a chance at his preshrunk listeners. (According to Felix Shay, even this didn't stop Steve Reynolds, who was making converts to Socialism before Hubbard called off further Reynolds lectures.) There had to be a preconceived pattern in Hubbard's activity—and it had to be his pattern.

Occasionally a visiting celebrity would get out of hand. Horace Fletcher was a Roycroft regular during Felix's period there. Fletcher's specialty—it put "Fletcherism" and "Fletcherize" into many dictionaries—was the doctrine that food should be chewed far beyond the point of diminishing returns; a well-Fletcherized meal took at least a couple of hours. Sometimes his resistance to ordinary eating went even beyond this, and during one of his Roycroft visits he undertook a forty-day fast. Forty days is a long time, and "the tension affected every one, and intensely annoyed and distracted Hubbard. . . . Toward the end of the self-imposed abstinence, some sort of internal decomposition set in, and actually Dr. Fletcher could almost be smelled on sight! Hubbard beseeched him to end it, and finally he did." Felix, who tells the story, decided he would try a fast, too, and after "eight days I had lost twenty pounds, my temper, and most of my friends. . . . Then The Fra issued me an ultimatum . . ." These events later supplied the impetus for a Hubbard preachment titled "Foods, Fasts and Fools."

By this time, though, Felix had pretty well learned where the invisible lines were that might not be crossed. He was a great carrier of messages, and some of the chores that came his way were not much fun. One issue of the *Fra* featured a cover portrait and feature article on Mangasarian, the liberal minister and phrasemaker who ·was having a great vogue with Chicago freethinkers. The magazine came out of the bindery when Hubbard and Shay were about to leave for Chicago, and Hubbard had the inspiration to take along a thousand copies to pass out to Mangasarian's congregation. The several hundred pounds of the *Fra* were packed into old trunks "with ragged tin edges" and put on the Chicago train.

When Hubbard, Shay, and baggage got to Chicago, Hubbard decided that the regular drayage prices were exorbitant, so he scouted around and came up with "a weazened old man with a three-legged horse and a three-wheeled wagon. This impossible combination he wished on me and then hurried off to Orchestra Hall" to present an inscribed copy to the central figure in this surprise party. Felix, in his best clothes, had to wrestle the sharp-edged trunks onto the wagon, get them to the Hall, and get them off onto the sidewalk. By this time Mangasarian had read the article, discovered that Hubbard had treated some of the facts of his life with carefree improvisation, and flown into a rage. He ordered Hubbard and his magazines off the premises. Hubbard left in a fine fury of his own, and Felix, after a meditative pause, left too. The trunks of freshly printed *Fra*s remained on the sidewalk.

In another Chicago adventure, the teetotaling Hubbard let himself be kidded into a drinking a cocktail and a glass of champagne. When he and Felix emerged into the raw January night, with two heavy grips each and a train to catch on the other side of the Loop, Hubbard would have no part of hailing a cab. "What we need, my boy, is a walk!" And walk they did, burning up the excess food and the alcohol. Hubbard never took a taxi if he could avoid it, and once in New York when Felix tried to insist that walking would make them late for an appointment, his boss took off down Fifth Avenue at a run, leaving Felix to chase him through the crowds. And though Felix had learned when to keep his opinions to himself, he was also permitted a measure of licensed impudence. Once, on returning from a trip among the "outlanders" with a lighted cigarette in his hand, he encountered Hubbard and a pair of unworldly celebrities. Hubbard gave him a quizzical look and asked, "Felix, have you ever read my essay called 'The Cigarettist'?" Felix slapped on his cap and bells, and retorted, *"Read* it? Hell—I wrote it!"

One of Dard Hunter's Roycroft assignments also became a notable conversation piece. A young widow arrived at the Inn, to stay while a one-copy edition of a memorial volume to her late husband was produced. Dard had one week to inscribe the material by hand on heavy vellum. The widow "said she would supply the binding material herself," and in due course she produced "a rolled parcel" from her trunk. The booklet went forward to the bindery, but Dard's professional curiosity was eating at him, and he "finally asked what sort of animal had produced leather of such delicate grain." He had asked and he was answered: ". . . tanned skin from the back of her late husband." The book was completed, and the widow left. Word came later that she had remarried, and the Roycrofters speculated on "what a strange feeling the second husband must have had when he saw the memorial book lying on the drawing-room table and perhaps thought of himself as Volume II."

But fun and games notwithstanding, the Roycroft operation was still a business. And, in those last years, more and more time and talent went into the production of advertising. Hubbard himself had been a little slow to commit himself. He had to insist that "I write advertising for rest and recreation," and that "I only write about the things I know have merit plus."

But there were all those pages in the *Fra* every month. It was easy enough, at first, to ramble along under the line "An Advertisement by Elbert Hubbard," with some sort of free associating that would point more or less in the direction of the product. He could start with "Robert Southey was Poet-Laureate of England. . . . Robert Southey and Samuel Coleridge married sisters . . . one fine moonlight night, captured by the cosmic urge. . . ." This was as good a narrative hook as could be found in many a short story, and could be extended for several paragraphs: "Southey and his wife were happy ever afterward; excepting when Coleridge came to visit them, which he once did and left his wife in care of her sister, and never came back." A transition was needed about here: ". . . near the foot of the waterfall . . . is an old lead pencil factory . . . in this shop, Mrs. Coleridge worked. . . ." The rest was easy. Pencils could lead to Thoreau and Emerson and on to: "Great literature is always written with lead-pencils—I always write with a lead-pencil, and before I start away on a little journey I pocket a dozen Blaisdells, and then lie in wait for ideas." This just about did it, except for a nod to the Blaisdell specialty (wrapping the lead in paper instead of encasing it in wood): "Even a woman can sharpen one!"

When cultural allusions were not handy, a straight sales talk could easily be beefed up with a little color. "Among other good things, Life-Insurance insures you against your own indiscretion when the fit is on to go after a financial wildcat, which, as Lincoln said, may be only a louse on your eyebrow." And, for Burroughs Adding Machines, he could easily go on for a full page on this theme: "How I pity the man who forces his brain to do goose-step; . . . Teach your brain to do LITTLE THINGS, routine things—over and over the same—and presently you have a LITTLE BRAIN."

But, as Felix signed up more and more contracts for twelve months of these productions, they probably came very soon to look like something other than "rest and recreation." Inevitably, other hands began doing the writing; first it was Felix, and then, as the volume kept rising, Felix "usually had in training one clever young fellow—or was it two?—who could lend a hand . . ." The operation had its own momentum, and soon became not only something beyond Hubbard's control but independent of any particular individual.

Through 1909 and well into 1910, Felix was riding high. The *Philistine* was carrying a regular signed page of his earnest counsel to his clients: "An Advertiser is a Wise Person who annually spends sums of money for the purpose of Boosting his Biz. Usually he succeeds—but he must first learn to tabu the Blue Pencil Habit. . . . When the Boy brings along Something Good, don't smother him with a scowl. . . . Don't say 'It's not practical.' It may merely be above your Thought Level. . . ." There is evidence that all this came to be a little too much for Hubbard, and the April 1910 *Fra* carried a paragraph reading: "Felix felicitates himself on being it, since THE FRA is becoming a vogue. Take a tumble, Felix; the text is secondary to advertising, of course, but people would still read THE FRA even if it carried no ads."

This must have hurt. I find no evidence that the events were directly connected, but at about this time Felix left for another job. Hubbard's own account said of Felix: "He wore his hair long, and annexed a stetson that had a wider brim than mine. He wrote just like me, only better. . . . He did me good service and when a certain Weisenheimer from Baltimore came along and offered Felix ten thousand dollars a year I lost my laddybuck." The Roycroft ad factory went on operating without a visible hitch. (Felix came back to Roycroft after a few years, and was going strong, very much as before, when the Hubbards left for their trip on the *Lusitania*. When Felix came to write his book about Hubbard, he made no direct mention of any gap in their association.)

The grip of these advertising compulsions showed no sign of relaxing after Felix left, and Hubbard was himself pretty thoroughly hooked by then. "Advertising is fast becoming a fine art," he said, "Its theme is Human Wants, and where, when and how they may be gratified. It interests, inspires, educates—sometimes amuses—informs and thereby uplifts and benefits, lubricating existence and helping the world on its way to the Celestial City of Fine Minds." By this time, advertising men were beginning to tell each other that they constituted a profession. Ad clubs were flourishing in many cities, and a good deal of young intellectual talent was finding its way into them. These Ad clubs were loaded with Hubbard admirers, and booked more and more of his lecture engagements. He repaid their homage with many a "boost": "When we want to hear really good sermons nowadays, we attend a weekly lunch of the ad club, and listen to a man who deals in ways and means and is intent upon bringing about paradise, here and now." And just as Hubbard sometimes played with the idea that life would be much simpler if the whole disputatious, troublesome mess of popular government were put in the hands of men of business, so his distrust of the people cropped out with a new twist during his last year: "There is no going back to the 'rule of the competent few.' Popular government is here. If we are ruled by the worst, we must then thru education evolve that 'worst' into the best. As a matter of self-preservation we must make the 'worst' tolerable and tolerant." And by education he meant advertising—by and for business.

This new emphasis on the Ad Man as savior brought him a lot of denunciation, of course. Some of it was expected, as in "A New Year's Greeting to the Fra" by one Reverend Elmer Willis Seal. He sounded like a onetime disciple who had given up hope, now that Hubbard's "art has been prostituted to advertising. . . . Pebeco, Jones Little-Pig Sausages, Gilette Safety Razors, and Forest Home Hams arouse the nimble wit of the Fra into get 'em quick ecstasies. He has even written a pome exploiting a

Pop-Valve. . . . simply the High Priest of Publicists and Sinners—the Fra Diavolo of Letters." Less expected, perhaps, was the storm that blew up when he published a *Little Journey* to a Great Dentist—this Great Dentist being one who advertised. And there was some dissent even among the new fraternity of Ad Men. One of them, in *Printer's Ink,* found the Hubbard advertising phenomenon hard to understand. "Hardly an ad fails to advertise Hubbard as much as it does the article he is writing about. . . . If any ordinary copy-writer . . . waste-basketed in a jiffy." Hubbard, of course, wasn't any ordinary copywriter, and in answering this critic's query ("Have advertizers become hypnotized by the frowsy Fra . . . ?"), he needed to do little more than refer to the theme song ("Personality") of Eva Tanguay, another raucously successful public figure.

For years, Hubbard had enjoyed the relief and the change of pace and of status that getting home from a trip had given him. Now the ad business was bringing a considerable number of these "outland" pressures right into his tower sanctuary, and in his last years he may have yearned for legitimate reasons to spend more of his time in the adjacent outdoors. At any rate, one of his last big projects was to experiment with a year-round Roycroft School.

The inadequacies of conventional education, of course, had been one of his favorite topics. "Schools and colleges are cumbrous makeshifts, often forcing truth on pupils out of season, and thus making lessons grievous." Not surprisingly, the core of Hubbard's ideal school would be honest labor, on the order of his own boyhood and the University of Hard Knocks: ". . . to keep the wood box full, to shovel snow, to clean up the front yard in the Spring, to make garden, bring in the eggs, milk the cow, break the colt." When he visited John Dewey's experimental school at the University of Chicago in 1901, he approved strongly of its learning-by-doing approach. But when he saw how much of it was "the same curriculum . . . that I had known in youth, I could not but smile. Prof. . . . Dewey, with his costly apparatus and heavy endowment, is merely trying to overcome the 'advantages' of civilization."

So his students would work. "To be healthy and sane and well and happy, you must do real work with your hands as well as with your head. The cure for grief is motion. The recipe for strength is action. Love for love's sake creates a current so hot that it blows out the fuse. But love that finds form in music, sculpture, painting, poetry and work is divine and beneficent. . . . A lover out of a job is a good man for a girl to avoid." As for what they would work at, there were the Roycroft Shops, the Inn, the woodlots, and the farms. This kind of schooling had been standard fare for his adult helpers from the beginning. His friend Reedy—for all his dissent to the *Message*—had been impressed by what he saw in East Aurora. "He is the one man I know of who makes anything like a success of his efforts to popularize work. Hubbard does something for these workers. He teaches them things . . . to see, to observe." As for the "head" part of this "head and hand" education, Alice was a gifted teacher, and Miriam, though still in her teens, had similar talents.

The school was advertised and experimented with for several years. There was some sort of informal sharing of ideas and personnel with the Interlaken School at Laporte, Indiana. (This was a venture by Dr. Edward Rumely—another Extraordinary Individual whose path had crossed with Hubbard's. His school mixed some elements of what would later be called progressive education, with a country setting, a work program, and a mixture of freedom and authoritarianism.) The nearest thing to a successful program at Roycroft seems to have come during the growing-harvesting seasons—so much so that the project became known as the Farm School. Reedy was enchanted with this swarm of youngsters who "groom horses, shear the sheep, feed the hogs, milk the cows, plant potatoes, pick currants, do all kinds of farm work joyously. You'll see them in the fields, with Hubbard at their head, laughing, shouting, dancing. They do the toil that fills the larder. And they pay Elbert Hubbard for the privilege of doing it. Isn't that lovely? Doesn't it remind you of Tom Sawyer's getting his pals to whitewash the fence for him? But that's Hubbard."

But apparently it took more than this to make a school. For one, it would have taken some intellectual work, in season or not. The winters are long in the Buffalo area. And there were state requirements for schools—and those ridiculous child-labor laws. Though Hubbard told Reedy, in 1912, that he expected the school to be the principal monument to his memory, it turned out to be more complicated than he had thought when he wrote (in 1903) about Starr King: "Where did this dry goods clerk get his education? Ah, I'll tell you—he got his education as the lion's whelp gets his. . . . The lion-nature gets what it needs with its mother's milk and by doing." So the school didn't reprieve him from his desk for long. And it was too bad, really, because Hubbard was often at his best with other people's children. He didn't patronize or bully; he entered their own spontaneous world, and they got the benefit of his evocative charm without its defensive complications. It was standard practice to look for missing East Aurora children first of all in the Fra's office. Some aspects of his playing Uncle

Elbert were part of his manorial pose, of course. East Aurora babies named "Elbert" or "Elberta" received five-dollar bank accounts, and there were many.

It also might have been more appropriate and useful had he been able to run out his life span in a Roycroft Shop more like its early William Morris pretensions, and without his public involvements. That world of big business with which he had so fiercely identified was moving rapidly away from his ken. Though he wrote a lot of pretentious essays about System in Business in his last years, system of any kind was hardly his best field.

The degree of system at Roycroft was indicated in one of Bert's reminiscences. Power for half a dozen printing presses came from a small steam boiler for which Bert was then engineer-in-charge. One morning he fired up without first filling the boiler. After he discovered the oversight and had killed the fire and started over, he had a boiler that spouted steam at every joint. Bert remembered an old handyman remedy for leaky cisterns, and began feeding the boiler with bran and cornmeal, which swelled and filled the leaks. Just as he was feeling that maybe he was getting things under control and the presses could roll, his father came charging in. An extravagant waste of expensive horsefeed, he snorted, and shortly came back from the barn with a basket of manure and floor litter. This noble mixture kept the boiler more or less intact, and aromatic, until repairs could be made.

One of the last portraits

16

Last Journey

MEANWHILE, back in the outside world there was this incredible war. In the first weeks after the lights went out, Hubbard tried to treat it as nonsense by Old World despots—stupid and annoying but hardly worth a civilized American's serious attention. In the November 1914 *Fra,* he compared the war to the Hatfields and McCoys: "a family feud . . . all the crowned heads of Europe are related." And the *Philistine* for the same month carried a lead article entitled "America's Chance." It announced that "Fate has eliminated America's commercial competitors. The world is ours. All we have to do is just shake the tree." But this offhandedness faded, and within two months he was emerging from shock. "The human race seemed sure of itself. Its mind was opening . . . art, science, invention, had glorified man—lifted him to the Matterhorn of Highest Hope. Then conceive the inconceivable. . . . Realize the unbelievable . . . no romance or heroism in this war."

"The war will progress from horror to horror," said Hubbard, "and with it the protest, disgust and anger of the people will deepen." The historians who have pegged Hubbard as an apologist for reaction have not noticed it, but the shock of the war also seems to have released him from his compulsive partnership. "Big business has been to blame in this thing," he said, "let it not escape this truth—that no longer shall individuals be allowed to thrive through supplying murder machines to the mob." In this same passage he went on to what was, for him, a remarkable concession: "And anyway, Socialism doesn't believe in spiked helmets—I apologize."

From this time on, there was a distinct flavor of Savonarola in Hubbard's references to big business. He warned his very own ad clubs not to take themselves too damned seriously. Pomposity, bureaucratic stuffiness, and "the business intellectic" began to annoy him, and he accused the mighty Pennsylvania Railroad of "begining to look like an old man who shaves once a week with a dull razor, who has forgotten how to use a toothbrush, who fails to shine his shoes, and has spots on his vest that make him look like a Swiss cheese." It was "a railroad without a heart, so big that it is going down by the head. You speak to any of the sub-officials and they tell you they have no authority to act, and will refer you to a man in Philadelphia or New York whom you can never meet, and if you write him, he icily refers you back to his subordinates." And the moralist in Hubbard pulled out all the stops in commenting on a businessmen's banquet in Great Barrington: "These great men . . . insisted on importing three professional femmelettes. Oho, also aha. . . . All bald heads were kissed. . . . The president of a National Bank . . . got his face properly slapped . . . to the great delight of the assemblage. . . . Do these things stimulate trade and foster civic pride? Not exactly; they merely mirror bad taste. . . . Businessmen above all other persons should set an example of right living."

Hubbard picked his scapegoat for the horrors of this war quite a bit in advance of most of his countrymen. Most people expected a short war, and there had been little taking of sides in the fall of 1914, when Hubbard wrote "Who Lifted the Lid Off Hell?" and answered his question: ". . . William Hohenzollern . . . a withered hand and running ear, a shrunken soul, and a mind that reeks with egomania. He is a mastoid degenerate of a noble grandmother. He is swollen, like a drowned pup, with a pride that stinks. . . . Our hearts are with the Germany of invention, science, education, skill—but not with the War-Lord." This was a pale shadow of what was to come later, but at the time it seemed recklessly partisan. It cost him ten thousand *Philistine* cancellations and a heavy-footed reply from George Sylvester Viereck's *Vaterland:* "In the period of Jurassic rocks, the festive diplodocus and megatherium, Elbert Hubbard attracted some attention. . . . this swamp-puddler and offal-infector . . . Whereupon he wiggled his playful tail, inflated himself with the poisonous exhalations of sewer, soil-pipe and sink, and breathed contagion upon the little world which chose to indulge his harmless antics. . . . today the name of Elbert Hubbard is only a vanishing echo . . ." Hubard's reply was surprisingly mild: "This hot endeavor to shift the war from Europe to East Aurora will fail." And later, "I'm neutral, I am. I don't care who licks Bill Kaiser . . . you needn't reach for the bung-starter—please observe that I have the ice pick."

As the spring of 1915 approached, the Hubbards decided to go abroad. The Roycroft enterprises were doing well, and Hubbard probably wanted to see for himself what was going on in that violent other continent. ("I am ex-officio General Inspector of the Universe, with power to investigate everything and report on anything in any way I choose, as long as I do not violate the Pure-Food Laws, or jump too hard on Brandeis.") He wrote a friend that he would "store the information in my head so as to escape the censor." There were a few arrangements to make. In 1913, Hubbard had been convicted of sending "filthy" matter through the mails—the "whirling-spray affair" joke in Chapter 13 was the basis for one of the counts in the indictment—and this stood in the way of his getting a passport. An appeal to President Wilson resulted in a pardon, with just time enough to book passage to England on the *Lusitania.*

After a cheery gathering of the Roycrofters, in which the reins were handed over to Bert, Elbert and Alice left for New York. The approaching sailing of the *Lusitania* was surrounded by rumors and anonymous warnings to passengers that they had better cancel their passage (as well as the published warning of the German Embassy to all Americans to stay off ships going to the war zone). Hubbard had pooh-poohed any talk of danger, though he had written to the same friend, "I may meet with a mine or submarine over there, or I may hold friendly converse with a bullet in the trenches." He seems to have planned to go to Germany, and he may have thought vaguely that he might be carrying a message to the Kaiser. He told reporters that he didn't know but what the Kaiser would be willing to talk to him and that such a meeting might even lead toward peace. He also said that he had no intention of fighting for space in a lifeboat. He exchanged greetings with Melville Stone as Stone was leaving the ship. Stone's son Herbert, of the *Chap-Book* and Stone & Kimball, was a passenger. Hubbard said to Stone, "Well, if they sink her . . . I will have a chance some day to meet the Kaiser in hell."

Very little is known about the actions of the Hubbards in the eighteen minutes of chaos between the explosion of the torpedo and the final plunge. They were seen standing together on deck, as passive as spectators. A friend told them to wait there while he went for lifebelts. On the listing, disorganized ship, this took him several minutes, and he couldn't find the Hubbards when he got back. Another survivor remembered that he had seen them go into a cabin and close the door. The final issue of the *Philistine* treated this as deliberate self-sacrifice—there was no room in the lifeboats, and Alice couldn't swim (though the lowering of lifeboats was such a shambles that many survivors had never been close to one). For years, many disciples were certain the Kaiser had ordered the sinking as a personal reprisal.

At home, the shock was severe. There were hours of waiting, as rumors and counterrumors filled the emptiness. Bert steadily refused to look at the greater emptiness: "My father's not dead, nor Alice Hubbard. . . . They must have been saved." The East Aurora switchboard blinked and buzzed most of the night.

But finally, as the grim salvage in Queenstown was sorted out, there was no further reason to hope. The Hubbards gathered for a private farewell service—Bertha was there; Miriam had come home from college; the sisters and their families assembled. Prayers, the Twenty-third Psalm, readings from *In Memoriam, Crossing the Bar,* and Hubbard's own conclusion to the Beethoven *Little Journey:* "He was what he was because he endured. He grew strong by bearing burdens. All things are equalized, and by the Cross is the world redeemed. God be praised! It is all good." Hubbard's mother grieved uncontrollably for days. Dr. Silas kept his composure, but "his soul was already wandering on the borderland of the Unknown."

There were also practical decisions to be made: publication schedules, advertising contracts, payrolls to be met and bills to pay. Young Bert took firm charge, and the wheels turned. He issued one final number of the *Philistine,* made up largely of what could be fairly described as his own Inaugural Address. In fact, the transition period had much of the hushed solemnity, the rallying of loyalties, and the dedication to carrying-on that follow the passing of a chief of state. Bert's succession statement was modest —"I am plain Bert Hubbard"—and his pledge to keep things going (with his father looking down from above to say "Good boy . . .") was simple and rather touching.

Hubbard's estate was estimated at $397,845, Alice's at $35,753. The wills of both divided their estates equally between Bert and Miriam. (Sanford had taken off for the West soon after his father's remarriage, and drifted and hoboed around Idaho, Montana, and Washington for several years. He came back in 1915 and was in charge of Roycroft buildings. Later, he made a modest success of his own business: building and selling log cabins for hunting lodges and camps.) Both wills requested cremation.

As the weeks passed and those thousands of letters came in, it was obvious that more was involved than the abrupt passing of a notorious eccentric. The letter writers were of many kinds: small-business proprietors, corporation executives, fraternal organizations in convention assembled, celebrities, and people, people everywhere. Something important had gone out of their lives, and they had to somehow express their loss. The man who had spent so many years in a public display of his identity-questing had not found it. But he had become part of the identities of an extraordinary number of other people.

Even Billy Sunday was shaken. "One man is gone who fought me hardest. Elbert Hubbard never had a good word to say for me. But I'm willing to forgive and forget. He was a bright man—one of the brightest men—and I take my hat off to his intellect." Walt Mason of Emporia, one of the early, rhyming-prose columnists, wrote a charming little piece which began: "Down to the depths went Elbert Hubbard, with smiling eyes that knew no fear, and all the lovely mermaids rubbered, and Neptune shouted, "See who's here!' " There were memorial services in many cities.

The public memorial services at East Aurora were impressive and full of eloquence, but there was something odd about their featuring Michael Monahan as the principal speaker. In the fourteen years since he had stood in the Opera House and denounced his recent employer and "his insane course, public and private," Monahan had become a literary figure in his own right. He may have visited East Aurora during those years, but I found no record that Hubbard received him as a friend. What the record does show is that Hubbard's hatred for Monahan was deep and lasting. In Hubbard's private language, Monahan was the "Black Dwarf," and the angry references to him kept cropping out in the *Philistine*. Hubbard seemed especially incensed whenever Monahan was starting a new journal, as in the August 1904 *Philistine*—"chipmunk magazines founded by impecunious and vituperative Black Dwarfs." Clearly, Monahan had gotten under his defenses more than most, and Monahan with access to print was a continuing threat. ("When a man has tired out the patience of a score of employers, and run the gamut of goosedom, it is not charity for his friends to dole out money that he may perpetuate his drool in print. Mental monstrosities should be sequestered. . . . when the readers of a periodical regard it as an emetic, it is time that the editor followed their example and threw up the sponge.") In the middle of an article on the Mormons in 1903, Hubbard took time out to reassure himself that "Black Dwarfs who vomit forth vituperation are unsafe authority. These all hate themselves and think it someone else they despise. We smile."

At about this same time, Hubbard had given his public a very oblique view of his quarrel with Monahan. In writing it, he dragged in Reedy ("Barrabas Bill") as a sort of stand-in for himself. Readers who lacked the key must have been puzzled.

The vital question in America seems to be this: Is Barrabas Bill sincere?
    . . . when he hired the Black Dwarf to Boswellize him, and the B. D.,

instead of fulfilling the contract, hired a hall and averred that Bill was a D. B., and explained further that he (the B. D.) had supplied the phosphorous for the Ozark Shop and that as he was going away the Whole Thing would tumble, I stood by Bill . . .

Women's clubs declared shrilly that Bill was a Mean Ol' Thing, and moreover Wasn't Nice, I still took no stock in the reports. I refused to believe the tales, although my Better Nature told me they were true, for it is the peculiarity of purity that it can always scent the wrongdoer from afar . . .

There has always been a suspicion of pose about Bill, and the Black Dwarf says that on close acquaintance the suspicion is confirmed. Some have said that Bill was a fakir, but I have contended again and again that if he was there was plenty of precedent for it. For any man to be absolutely honest, thus making himself conspicuous, is an absurd bit of megalomania, and most certainly Bill has been guilty of no such indiscretion.

So the "Black Dwarf" was the man who was invited back to memorialize Elbert Hubbard. Some sort of lurking ambivalence about the departed may have been at work among the new governing powers at Roycroft.

Monahan did his best to bury the old quarrel (". . . estranged . . . by circumstances which need not be recalled"), to blame much of it on others ("actively served and diligently promoted by our common friends"), and to put a curse on future historians ("I can only hope that no ill-conditioned person may take it into his head to reprint any words of mine put forth long ago in anger and bitterness.") But Monahan was not unhappy to have the last word, and his memorial address was definitely not discipleship:

On our first meeting I noticed something about him that smacked of the country parson. He once told me that the Bible and Emerson were the only books he had ever read *for the love of them.* . . . There was a mystic in Elbert Hubbard, suppressed or subordinated in those later years when, responding to the conditions of his public fame, he lived his life too much on the outside and aimed consciously to hold the crowd. This mystical note was strong in the man on his first appearance as a writer, and I think for his better audience it has always been the heart of his appeal.

And he had no praise at all for Hubbard's long warfare with religious orthodoxy: ". . . the world is somewhat wider than East Aurora, and the heart of man has cravings that cannot be appeased by the Gospel of Roycroft." It was also plain that Monahan had his doubts about the Roycroft enterprises surviving much beyond the memorial services, but he let them be washed away in his rhetoric.

In letters, in newspapers and magazines, many other onetime friends and enemies took their turns at a final summing up. As Monahan said, "That Elbert Hubbard was a many-sided man is shown by our anxiety to analyze him." Richard Le Gallienne—who had spent two summers at Roycroft as Hubbard's guest when he was homeless and down on his luck, but still "looking more like a poet than perhaps any man has ever looked"—found "the best thing about Elbert Hubbard" to have been the "playboy quality. He was good fun."

On a bed-rock of shrewd Yankee farmer was superimposed a composite, rather than a complex personality. . . . something of a Methodist preacher . . . freethinker . . . itinerant printer and journalist . . . a little of the strolling player, something of the cowboy, and very much of the old-fashioned medicine man.

Hubbard had "deserved a better brand of disciples," Le Gallienne said, instead of ". . . an unfair percentage of the half-baked and the hysterical." And "it would have done him no harm sometimes to heed his critics. He saw too many half and quarter truths . . . and his mistake was to endorse them all . . ."

Reedy sent a generous tribute, but he had pretty much said his say on the Hubbards three years before:

For eighteen years I have been pestered by people anxious to know what I think of Elbert Hubbard. . . . For the same period I have had to bear with fervent persons who wrote to tell me that Hubbard is a fraud, a faker and other things. In all that time I have never met any one who had a particle of proof that [Hubbard] was not on the level . . . no fraud . . . but is a benefactor, a maker of men.

Other people are doing the work for Hubbard. They know it. They rejoice to see him "get away with it" . . . for Hubbard gives them something: a little fun, visions of beauty and usefulness, love for better things, help to the self-made man, beginnings of a higher education. There is no getting away from this fact about Hubbard . . . he's helping a whole lot of people to think, and they will think, after a little, for themselves.

. . . every day Hubbard does something for somebody and somebody for something. Thus works out his glorious motto: "Be kind—but get the mazuma."

To this might be added an earlier Reedy judgment: "It is my firm belief that he has started more people to thinking in the last fifteen years than any man who has been talking or writing, or both, in this country, not even excepting Theodore Roosevelt. The only fault most people find with Hubbard is that he isn't something other than he is."

As the Roycroft enterprises continued without their founder, it became clear that their principal asset was the Hubbard-oriented momentum in peoples' minds—this reluctance to close the books on what had been a vivid and complex element in their own lives. People went right on buying books with the magic name in the title (people whose attics were stacked with piles of old *Philistines* and *Fras*). The presses kept running, and the Hubbard words—like interchangeable parts—kept reappearing in new arrangements. Order and continuity had never been characteristics of either Hubbard's writing or the Roycroft archives, but as the editors worked and reworked the files, the results became more and more of a hodgepodge. The point of no return was reached with *The Note Book of Elbert Hubbard*. In two hundred double-column pages heavily splattered with red initial letters, the random-selection sentences and paragraphs were fitted like masonry blocks. A handsome book, and as impossible to read consecutively as a Sears, Roebuck catalogue. Context and relevance steadily drained out of the material as these new permutations came forth.

Occasionally, unexpected complications also came forth, such as Benjamin De Casseres and his attorneys. One volume of *Selected Writings* was titled *Olympians* (subtitle: "Tall, sun-crowned men"). It contained thirteen essays. Ten of them, said De Casseres, were entirely written by him, and he had the records to prove it. After two years of negotiation, he received a cash settlement and assignment of the copyrights. *Olympians* was withdrawn. (Later, the Roycroft–William H. Wise Company team that was handling the posthumous publishing brought out a new edition of *Selected Writings*. To make things easy for bibliographers, they substituted a new collection titled *Olympians*.)

De Casseres was a New York City bohemian and a disciple of Nietzsche. At one time he had been a Hubbard follower, and wrote that Hubbard was having a "greater influence than Emerson, Thoreau or Whitman . . . writes English fluently but Americanese brilliantly." He also wrote that the *Philistine*—along with such works as *Ghosts, Zarathustra,* and *Timon of Athens*—was the fruit "of a sublime rage, a perfect frenzy of contempt, hatred and militant spite." This characterization sounded more like De Casseres's own writing. One of his essays in *Olympians* was on "Diabolistic Idealists" and the phrase was typical. For about twelve years, he had sent occasional essays to Hubbard, and Hubbard had occasionally sent back a small check and tossed the manuscript into the Roycroft hopper. Eventually it would appear in the *Philistine* or the *Fra,* usually unsigned. And when the *Selected Writings* were being selected, how was anyone to know? Obviously, there was no way to tell—except to read the material. De Casseres's prose was full of Gothic extravagance and frenzy, and most of his literary reference points were contemporary European. In any extended passage, De Casseres resembled Hubbard about the way Gabriele D'Annunzio resembled Oscar Ameringer.

The De Casseres affair was one of many arguments about who really wrote what in the Roycroft publications. With his disdain for the academic, and his playfulness and arrogance, it was not surprising that Hubbard regarded scholarly niceties as petifogging nonsense. Here is the note he appended to a quotation: "The italics are ours, having been purchased of the American Type Founders Co., at 40¢ per lb., 2 per ct. off—10 ds." Even an erratum slip had to be a comic production (it is fair to say that errata slips were not used unless they could be played for laughs):

The author of LITTLE JOURNEYS doubtless is a worthy Person, & because he has maligned me in the Public Prints is not the sole reason why I call attention to the fact that a statement on Page 30 is misleading, tho literary. Abraham Lincoln, Alfred Tennyson, Charles Darwin and William E. Gladstone were born in 1809. Robert Browning was born in 1912.

ALI BABA
Roycroft Shop, East Aurora, Feb. 10, 1900.

One of Hubbard's literary jokes was "The Essay on Silence"—a neatly bound pamphlet of blank pages. The Roycroft pilgrims used it as an autograph book; Hubbard declared it his best book; and the advertising pages of the *Philistine* had a field day with it: "has been translated into fifty-seven languages and dialects. It has been reprinted over fourteen thousand million times. Nothing ever written by any author, living or dead, has had so wide a circulation. Such is the felicity of the language in the original, that it loses nothing in the translation."

This aspect of Elbert Hubbard shaded from such monkeyshines as these, through a variety of practical joking in print, into the outright plagiarism of which he was often accused. One of his friends, O. J. Laylander, had showed him a copy of a letter by an Iowa lawyer. The letter was a flowery brush-off of a mistress—"And so farewell and farewell." Apparently it was considered a daring piece of verbal eroticism, and was circulated from hand to hand by the literary sporting set. Today it seems about as pornographic as the Bobbsey Twins. Hubbard, without asking anyone's permission, printed the letter in the *Philistine* under the head "An Unpublished Letter of Lord Byron." Quite a little storm blew up, with Byron scholars debating its authenticity, others claiming that Hubbard had written it himself. In July, 1908, the letter turned up again in the *Philistine,* "by request." This time it carried a prefatory note: "In answer to many questions as to where the original was found, I will say it was discovered under a Cabbage Leaf in the Roycroft Garden . . . by Ali Baba." A favorite Hubbard game was to print little narrative—"wholly fictitious"—items about his friends, and send proofs to *their* friends.

Another piece of leg-pulling was the publication of a "Translation from the Japanese" of *A Message to Garcia.* This was presented in the February 1910 *Philistine* as "a Translation from Japanese into English by Yone Kichikaschi of the University of Tokio." Just by internal evidence, this was pure hoax. "Law of averages" emerged from the alleged double translation as "law of marriages"; "fellows" and "frowsy ne'er-do-wells" were both rendered as "peasants," and "the survival of the fittest" became "the survival of those who have fits," while "was I hired for that?" and "getting the 'bounce' Saturday night holds many a worker to his place" were verbatim. This little item was good for many laughs, and was one of the Hubbard pieces in demand as advertising giveaways with business-house imprints. The Library of Congress has a copy of a Wanamaker Stores Edition carefully safeguarded in its Rare Books Collection. The American public had been much taken with the quaint little Japanese during the Russo-Japanese War, and Wallace Irwin's *Hashimura Togo* stories were having a vogue as humor.

We get into something more serious when we look at the charges of plagiarism brought against Hubbard. In a later postscript to his Memorial Address, Monahan rendered a mixed verdict. "Perhaps no man . . . has been so persistently, and not seldom unjustly, accused of stealing the thoughts and even the expressions of others. Truth is, the Fra never could acquire a due respect for quotation marks; never could see the iniquity and, in the long run, the suicidal error of purloining the fruit of another man's brain. . . . I wish he had let it alone." According to Shay, Hubbard appropriated a breakfast-table notion of Le Gallienne's, "to write an Apology for Living— an apology to his wives, sweethearts, bailors, tailors, editors, creditors." The thought probably came from the depths; Le Gallienne's load of unmanageable debt—both human and marketplace—was formidable. Hubbard's use of the idea appeared in the *Philistine* and led to a terminal quarrel— Le Gallienne leaving for New York after raging in and out of East Aurora and Buffalo for most of a day and trying to goad Hubbard into physical combat. There were other incidents, major and trifling. When Hubbard was caught red-handed, he might write the accuser a letter, such as the one "in which he acknowledges the appropriation and use of certain matter and invites the writer 'to come up to East Aurora and spend a weekend at his own expense and have a good laugh over it,' signed 'Lovingly, Elbert.' "

All through his writing life, Hubbard was hypersensitive to the question of originality-plagiarism, but he never seemed sure just where the lines should be drawn. He had been conditioned by Emerson—"The nobler the truth or sentiment, the less imports the question of authorship"—to regard the whole matter as just as much a hobgoblin of little minds as was consistency. As early as *Forbes,* he was asking, "What matters it who voiced it first, so long as 'tis truth?" And an early *Philistine* (1896) remarked that "Certain of the truths herein set forth have been expressed before, but not well." Some of Le Gallienne's fury had probably been brewing ever since 1896 when Hubbard had accused him—all in good fun, of course—of getting his *Quest of the Golden Girl* from an earlier book. Hubbard seems to have thought plagiarism was a general correspondence of theme or plot. His first reference (1897) to Reedy was: "As a plagiarist he is as splendid as Shakespeare—seizing his own by divine right wherever he finds it." Many of the things he gleefully cited as plagiarism in others were not even close enough to call paraphrases.

In 1900 Hubbard had remarked that "Steele absorbed everything, digested it, and gave out the good as his own, innocent and probably unmindful of where he got it. This accounts for his wonderful versatility: he made others grub and used the net results." The following excerpts are in chronological order. They show humor, defensiveness, and some simple perplexity:

The rest of this chapter is Heine's. I make the explanation because the passage is so well known that it would be both indiscreet and inexpedient for me to bring my James to bear and claim it as my own—much as I would like to.

Of this I am very sure, in the Pre-Raphaelite Brotherhood there was no lack of appreciation for Raphael. In fact, there is proof positive that Burne-Jones and Madox Brown studied him with profit, and loved him so wisely and well that they laid impression paper on his poses. This would have been good and sufficient reason for hating the man; and possibly accounts for their luminous flashes of silence concerning him.

I am a grafter. I graft pippins on crabby russets as a business. I send my thoughts out everywhere seeking my own. And these good things are for you, all I want is the exercise. You may have the pippins. . . . But mebbe you don't like pippins?

The paraphrase is always a compliment, and is never well done excepting by a man who loves the original and is a bit jealous of him. There is no copyright on an idea, no caveat can be filed on feeling, and at the last there is no such thing as originality, excepting as a matter of form.

I think he saw this proposition in THE PHILISTINE, but just where I got it I do not remember. However, I merely express the thoughts of many good people.

I am an intellectual grabheimer, from Grabville, Grab County. I watch for the divine spark and seize it, transmuting it into words. I take a feeling, and make of it a thought. Always and forever I am on the lookout for ideas, thoughts, jokes, plans, schemes—not to mention lofty aspirations and divine impulses. But I help myself only as I pass ideas along.

A great debate raged until 1915 and after as to just who had written this:

If a man can write a better book, preach a better sermon or make a better mouse-trap than his neighbor, though he build his house in the woods, the world will make a beaten path to his door.

Hubbard used the quotation several times—it is in the *Fra* for November 1908—and attributed it to Emerson. There was a scurrying-about of Emerson scholars, trying to authenticate it. Emerson's works yielded a couple of approximations of the idea but no mousetraps.

If the single man plant himself indomitably on his instincts, and there abide, the huge world will come around to him.

If a man has good corn, or wood, or boards, or pigs to sell, or can make better chairs or knives, crucibles or church organs, than anybody else, you will find a broad, hard-beaten road to his home, tho it be in the woods.

For a time Hubbard was noncommittal to inquiries as to where he had found the mousetrap, and I do not find that he ever claimed it as his own in so many words. But after the search had been under way for some time, his staff editor, John T. Hoyle, replied to an inquiry that "Elbert Hubbard evolved that Emersonian dictum from the depths of his own cosmic consciousness."

The "Lexicographer's Easy Chair" of the *Literary Digest,* then conducted by Dr. Frank H. Vizetelly, took up the quest, and advised its readers to forget Emerson and look for the source in Hubbard. But scholars found the item, credited to Emerson, in an anthology called *Borrowings,* compiled by Sarah S. B. Yule and published in 1889. Mrs. Yule claimed to have copied it down from an Emerson lecture in San Francisco or Oakland in 1871. The "Lexicographer's Easy Chair" got back in the game in the May 15, 1915, issue—the sinking of the *Lusitania* the week before had revived the con-

troversy. The "Easy Chair" had a letter from East Aurora (author not cited):
"We know of no quotation which has caused as much controversy as this
now famous 'mouse-trap' quotation. *Mr. Hubbard is the author."* The "Easy
Chair" discredited Mrs. Yule because she hadn't cited time and place and
because her anthologies were full of inaccuracies. Apparently it took as a
clincher a letter from Hubbard that stated: "The fact that *The Philistine*
was started in 1895 has nothing to do with the mouse-trap quotation. I was
born in 1856 and began writing hot stuff when I was four years old." So
the "Easy Chair" awarded authorship to Hubbard and tried to close the
books on the mousetrap.

There is nothing in the record to indicate that Hubbard published
anything except the parody sermons before 1891. My guess is that he picked
up the mousetrap from an inspirational compilation by Orison Swett Marden
entitled *Pushing to the Front,* published in 1894. The Marden book has
the mousetrap and presumably got it from Mrs. Yule. Hubbard had read
Marden's book—he called it "absurd and jejune," and said that "he had
better get in line and wait his turn." In the June 1912 *Philistine,* Hubbard
denied that Emerson had written the item—also that it made sense. "What
difference—that mouse-trap guff isn't true anyway. The world will never
make a path to your door unless you advertise. It may also be well to have
an automobile meet all trains and a free lunch served on the front porch."

It is noticeable that a half-apologetic, half-defiant note appeared in
his later references to Emerson and plagiarism. The *Roycroft Dictionary*
defined Charity as "a thing that begins at home, and usually stays there.
Bracing up Ralph Waldo Emerson's reputation by attributing to him literary
mousetraps which he should have made, but didn't." And an advertisement
for *A Thousand and One Epigrams,* in the June 1911 *Philistine,* rambled
on at length:

Mr. Hubbard, like all writers of epigrams, has attributed some of his good
Class A product to other writers. For instance, he was once writing about The
Roycrofters, and having in mind the number of visitors who come to see us,
he wrote this: "If a man can write a better book . . ."

It was a little strain on his ego to let this thing go under his own stamp,
so he saved his modesty and at the same time gave the epigram specific gravity,
by attributing it to Ralph Waldo Emerson.

The world took it up, and Emerson's writings have been scoured with
fine-tooth combs in the endeavor to locate this particular epigram, when it is
simply one of the things that Emerson would have said if it had occurred to
him . . .

Mr. Hubbard may have found a few mental mavericks in Emerson, which in moments of aberration he has branded his own; but if so, the debt is more than offset by things which he has attributed to Emerson that Emerson never wrote.

This has the look of Felix's prose, but it also looks inspired. The giveaway, of course, was that no reference to Roycroft visitors could have been written before Mrs. Yule's publication date of 1889. The *Philistine* for September 1902 had a long article that set out to deal with "that which is called plagiarism." It went all around Robin Hood's barn but it never quite squared off at its subject. Much of it was devoted to playing with a Hubbard conceit he called "kabojolism," defined as "attributing to another Good Stuff which he never expressed." But it concluded: "The suggestion of one who has dallied both with plagiaritis and kabojolitis would be the advice of Ali Baba to the young Athenian who wanted to borrow twenty-five obuli so he could wed: DON'T."

With all this postmortem controversy to help, the Hubbard words kept rolling into the market through the 1920's. The Roycroft periodical did less well. Felix succeeded to the editorial chair of the *Fra,* with bathetic results. (Felix's book on Hubbard was published in 1926. It sold around 40,000 copies, solidified a lot of the Hubbard mythology, and probably encouraged historians to consign the whole Hubbard story to oblivion.) The printing plant, and some of the craft manufacturing, flourished for some years under Bert's management—often doing more gross business per year than during Hubbard's life. But the whole enterprise began to run down, and it finally stopped during the Depression. Bert had contracted the *Fra* to *Roycroft,* then to *The Roycrofter,* then to *Elbert Hubbard's Roycrofter.* The final issue (September 1932) showed Bert to be a sadly puzzled man: struggling to solve the Depression by inspirational thoughts about the gold standard, credit, and interest rates. He tried to make a heroic figure out of Herbert Hoover—"He has been purged in the fires of a series of crises. He has found himself—and in the finding, America has found its leader"—and he prophesied new confidence, more credit, and "an ever-widening stream" of foreign gold flowing back to the country. "In the face of these far-reaching developments," he asked, "What do Governor Roosevelt's promises matter?" And the back-cover display of this last issue was a tombstone inscription for "F. DeLano de Roos, Creator of that Famous Phrase—'The Forgotten Man'—and one of the first to honor its wearing (For details see Newspapers of November 9, 1932)."

Publishers' Weekly for August 13, 1938, reported the sale of the

Roycroft Shops under court order, and editorialized, "Today the Roycroft books receive scant attention . . . as they stray into the second-hand shelves, but forty years ago they were proudly lying on the parlor tables of the rich and near rich as a mark of culture."

Since then there have been reminiscences, one inadequate biography, a steady attrition of the Hubbardisms in collections of familiar quotations, the occasional recording of disdain by historians, and not much more. Even the frantic prospecting for doctoral-thesis material has largely passed up the Hubbard lode—understandably: it looks like a slag heap, and a generation of scholars trained to relate to respectable authorities is unlikely to see much profit in a subject so far outside the academic framework.

In the late 1890's, the *Chap-Book* carried an essay by John Jay Chapman:

... the elemental parts of a man's mind and the fragments of imperfect education may be seen merging together, floating and sinking in a sea of insensate egotism and rhapsody, repellent, divine, disgusting, extraordinary . . . the man was a poseur, a most horrid mountebank and ego-maniac . . . he did to civilized society the continuous compliment of an insane self-consciousness in its presence. . . .

He belonged to that class . . . who are always particularly self-centered, autocratic, vain, and florid—the class of quacks. There are, throughout society, men, and they are generally men of unusual natural powers, who after gaining a little unassimilated education, launch out for themselves and set up as authorities on their own account. They are, perhaps, the successors of the old astrologers, in that what they seek to establish is some personal professorship or predominance. . . .

He had the bad taste bred in the bone of all missionaries and palmists, the sign-manual of the true quack. This bad taste is nothing more than the offensive intrusion of himself and his mission into the matter at hand.

Chapman felt strongly about his subject, whom he also credited with genius, spontaneity, and "flashes of reality." The picture is a little overblown, perhaps, but doesn't it sound like a portrait of Elbert Hubbard? It wasn't. It was Walt Whitman. The point is that in outlining the characteristics of "the true quack," Chapman was describing a nineteenth-century American type—one of the most fascinating and symptomatic types—and his description fitted quite a few individuals. Whitman may have been preeminent, but Hubbard was not the least of the others.

This "true quack" was the product of many forces: of outsiderdom in that "civilized society" which seemed so solid to Chapman and was actually so shaky; of the ferment of newness and the apparent vanishing of age-old limitations on aspiration and achievement; of puritan intensity and Protestant individualism; of pride and glory. In Hubbard's case we definitely come back to Glory. Chapman put it very well: "the offensive intrusion of himself and his mission into the matter at hand." This was Hubbard, at his best and at his worst.

And yet these "quacks" were an elemental force. There was a quality of prime mover in them. Others who were more judicious have been forgotten, while the second and third generations are still picking themselves up from the odd corners into which they were swept by the prime movers. These prime-mover types are less common today, or perhaps they are merely less effective, more isolated; most of us are the type in whom, as David Riesman has said, "all voices echo." There may not be enough elbow room anymore for the prime movers to operate—either physically or psychologically. Certainly the prime mover puts his neighbors under a strain. This is one of his hallmarks—he becomes an emotional obsession to everyone close to him. But this is not so much because he is many-sided as because his relations with other people are one-way operations. ("Jesus had twelve disciples. One-fourth of these proved untrue to him; one betrayed him with a kiss; another denied him with an oath; a third doubted him—all stood afar off on that night of death. But these are not facts about Jesus—they are facts about the disciples."

This one-way pattern had complex roots, of course, but in Hubbard's case there was a rather simple reason why he never sorted out the many selves he turned up in his identity-search. He was afraid to. At least once, he saw this clearly. In referring to "that fool wish of Bobby Burns," he said, "Let a man once see himself as others see him, and all enthusiasm vanishes from his heart; and when that is gone he might as well die at once."

We have peeled this onion about as far as makes sense. William Marion Reedy, who shared the same times and who went somewhat farther than the second mile with Elbert Hubbard, made a typically generous last judgment: "Mr. Hubbard represented nothing but the individual man standing squarely on his feet and looking life in the face—and that is everything— all there is." At his best, Hubbard did just that. But the years from Grover Cleveland to Woodrow Wilson were a long, bumpy time for anyone to stay squarely on his feet. Elbert Hubbard shifted his stance no oftener than the America he lived in, perhaps, and he looked life in the face as and when he could. No other country—and no other period in this country —could have produced anyone quite like him.

17

Afterword

THE FIRST ENTRY of Elbert Hubbard into my awareness came when I found a few of his Roycroft publications around the house during my growing up. It was a rented house, or part of a house, but it always held a great deal of reading matter. The books included large, heavy ones by people with names like Peter Kropotkin, Herbert Spencer, Benjamin R. Tucker, and Alexander Berkman. I also remember a paper-covered book with a lot of boldface printing in it. The title was *War, What For?* and there had been a period after the first big war with the Germans when that book had been kept hidden behind a row of others in the glass-doored bookcase. I understood it to be important that such people as policemen should not know it was there.

When we moved, which happened twice, I helped put all this reading matter into and out of wooden boxes, and I found things I hadn't seen before. Besides the books, there were many small magazines, without pictures, with titles like "Mother Earth" and "Lucifer." The Hubbard items turned up in one of these movings, and about all that I remember is that they looked different. They had red ink as well as black, and cartoons, and both words and printing seemed to vibrate with a special kind of excitement. At that time, I never did decide exactly what they were about or where they fitted—as between reading that gave me strong notions about things and reading that I gave up on quickly. My parents shrugged, or made faces, when I asked about these Roycroft pamphlets, and I decided that if I were ever to learn more about the excitements I found in them, I would have to do it on my own.

I realize now that I not only came late to an awareness of Elbert Hubbard (he was going down on the *Lusitania* at about the time I was learning to read) but also that my early perspective on him was unusual. In my parents' world, "radical" was a term of honor, not easily come by. And it was obvious that Hubbard didn't qualify. More than this, he seemed to be in some especially reprehensible category. My parents had not been to East Aurora, but they had friends and acquaintances who had, and my parents' contempt for Hubbard had the authority of nearly firsthand experience.

It should be explained here that my parents seldom talked to anyone who lived on the same street with us but that people kept coming to visit us—from remote parts of the city or from other cities. There seemed to be a network of these people, and one of the puzzles of my childhood was what made them special. Each one seemed to look, and sound, different from all the others. Some made a fuss over me, and brought me presents. Some ignored me, or talked about me as something interesting but not really there. The one thing they all did without exception was to talk. They talked loud and they talked late, and when a lot of them talked together they got excited and made speeches. There wasn't much I could follow in this talk, but I did notice that "the state" kept coming up, and I did sense that they weren't talking about Ohio.

As I grew older and sorted out some of these early perceptions, I learned that my parents called themselves philosophical anarchists. My father had come from Germany as a boy, and everything he knew and thought had been personally extracted by him from public libraries, from his own experiences, and from his special friends and acquaintances. My mother came from Massachusetts, and something of Emerson, Margaret Fuller, and Bronson Alcott came too. Her father—a tyrannical little man, a failed farmer, and a Civil War veteran—had driven all three of his children into rebellion, flight, and freethinking, with my mother their early ringleader. My parents had met in Cleveland, both of them people of consequence in their radical circle. Their standing was further enhanced when they formed a "free union," which was to last many years and to include an older brother and myself as exhibits. And since the state had not been consulted in this arrangement, my brother and I bore our mother's surname, and we had considerable explaining to do.

The point of this personal history is that Elbert Hubbard had been a disturbing, and often a liberating, element in the lives of many conventionally raised people a generation or two ahead of mine. But I came at him from the other direction. From the point of view of my parents and their circle, he was a renegade—someone who *should* have found his way to their total emancipation and doctrinal purity, but who had dropped out for sordid, mercenary reasons. I filed away this judgment as probably the way things had been, but I kept running into more excitements and puzzles that came from, or related to, this man Hubbard.

For one, I became a journeyman printer with a growing interest in what made for excellence in typography. This was at the end of the 1920's and into the thirties, and my daily experience was with the tastelessness of much of the printing I worked on or saw being produced. I was also exposed to models of classical elegance from such centers as The Printing House of William Edwin Rudge, and to the modernisms coming from Germany. I also spent hours in secondhand bookstores, where Roycroft books kept turning up on the cheaper shelves. These books had some of that remembered excitement in their design and printing. Often enough, I thought them bizarre and blatant, but they showed experiment and boldness to have been going on at a time when most American books were stodgy. This began another line of interest leading back to East Aurora.

Still later, I did a lot of reading in American history and letters. I was shaping up my own scheme of things then, and it wasn't philosophical anarchism. Hubbard continued to intrigue me. I was learning more about what had been going on during his lifetime, and I ran into more references to him. No two people—whether professional historians or literary figures writing their memoirs—seemed to see him in quite the same way. If there was a common element among the chroniclers and commentators who dealt with Hubbard, it seemed to be a flavor of emerging from shock—of having been brushed and shaken by some elemental force and being variously bemused, grateful, annoyed, and furious. When an opportunity came to spend several concentrated months on anything at all, I chose to spend them digging into the Elbert Hubbard story. I tried to sort out whatever facts and events I could establish, to see what kind of pattern they made, and to untangle some of the contradictions that were everywhere in the record. All of this—in some sort of responsible relationship to the history of the period —turned out to be a rather large project for a nonprofessional. But I went on chewing; in fact, I tried, in a previous draft, to do far too much—to wrap up, with no loose ends, every major facet of Hubbard's life and work in an equally tight context of American history. This was a mistake: it was not only beyond my competence; it assumed a tidy, rational penetrability of both lives and history that just isn't to be had. The present draft leaves more to the reader. It may be thought of as a do-it-yourself Elbert Hubbard kit. Hubbard's own life had the same bits-and-pieces quality, and perhaps some of that catalytic force that affected thousands of his contemporaries will emerge here and there.

There has been an honorable place in American history for the maverick intellectual—the nonaligned individual who sought his own meanings and values and who turned out to have a lot to say to his neighbors after all. It has always been a difficult role, beset by all the miseries and pathologies to which Man Alone is so susceptible. The wastage of life and talent can be appalling. And today, with academic disciplines ever more specialized, and mass-media Games ever more intrusive and compelling, such a role may seem obsolete if not downright impossible. But the need is greater than ever, and certainly the number of young opt-outs who may someday find their way back home with important tidings for the rest of us is increasing. Elbert Hubbard at least approximated this function, in a period which also had a high incidence of alienation and unassimilated change. His performance had little of the stubborn purity of Thoreau's long dissent or of Emerson's high flying, but Hubbard's posturings and his occasional pratfalls have a fascination, and perhaps a value, of their own.

In his relation to society, Hubbard may be thought of as starting from a central position, moving to an embattled outsiderdom, and later becoming the center of a little society of his own making—with mixed but powerful repercussions in the larger society. As the text should have made clear, this is only one of the many ways of considering Elbert Hubbard. It has been an important one to me, however, because I started from an extreme outsiderdom and have moved inward. Understanding Hubbard seems to have been an important element in understanding myself. This Afterword seems to be the place (and the only place) to call attention to my own background and to clue the reader in on the particular biases that may have resulted.

My explorations have been carried on during a time in which the question of whether any viable larger community can exist much longer in America has become increasingly insistent. This is not a question that will be answered here, but there are interesting and perhaps helpful similarities between Hubbard's time and the present.

In both periods, people who were different have confronted larger numbers of people who have felt strongly about being the same. Also in both periods, the rebel has seen the Others as faceless aggregations of conformity. But there have been differences too. Hubbard and his followers saw the gap between themselves and the Others as largely a matter of brains and enlightenment. ("In a country town the person who thinks, instinctively hunts out the other man who thinks—granting the somewhat daring hypothesis and that there are two of them"—Byron [1900] *I.I.*) The freethinkers were the vanguard; given time and good works, the others would get there too.

Today, this part of the picture has become fuzzy. Brains and a sort of enlightenment have become widespread; you could almost say that all men are born wise guys. But faith in reason as a tool for change in human life has become dim. To be with it now seems to require that one *stop* thinking and turn on other levels of awareness. And rather than seeing itself as a vanguard, the under-thirty cult has wiped out its own future by its own definition.

Another difference between then and now is that the prevailing culture of Hubbard's early years was solid—was everywhere and was massive. Rebellion wasn't simply a matter of defying the Baptist preacher or the squire or the local Anthony Comstock. The Others included practically all relatives, neighbors, countrymen. The power over the individual of what-simply-wasn't-done was enormous. When Carol Kennicott went scampering and whooping down that winter street in Gopher Prairie, curtains twitched all along the block. She faced a long term in purgatory, or worse, with no way out, and she knew it. This heavy weight of the Others was oppressive. But it also provided an assured longtime vocation for those who felt called to fight it.

For many people today, individual behavior has become so boundlessly free that all those choices are getting to be a drag. Large areas of society and tradition are so feeble there is little satisfaction in rebelling against them. There are other areas, of course. Draft boards symbolize one such, and for many young people this blacks out their whole sky. For those no longer young, there are still the Internal Revenue Bureau, the Narcotics Squad, and the dandelions in the lawn. The poor and the colored have barricades of their own. But things can change quickly, and some of today's walls might tumble down too suddenly to sustain full-length careers.

Elbert Hubbard established his right to wear his hair long, with an outlandish hat on top of it. He made jokes about Billy Sunday's God. But it is to be noted that he didn't let his hair grow until he had money in the bank and was on no man's payroll. When he was publicly marked down as a moral transgressor, he was put through a powerful wringer, and he emerged with extensive contusions and abrasions, at least. They wouldn't let him print dirty words; and Alice had to defend *her* right to wear bloomers in public.

It would be a gross oversimplification to bill Elbert Hubbard as a nineteenth-century hippie. An outsider he certainly was, and a protester. And there is something very contemporary in his search for identity. As this Afterword was being drafted, a writer in the *New York Review of Books* noted that "we have so often seen expression turn into unwanted evangelism and have discovered that he who tries, publicly, to find himself also finds the engulfing temptation, almost the necessity, of self-exploitation" (Elizabeth Hardwick, October 12, 1967). This observation about today comes close to summarizing one aspect of the Elbert Hubbard story of yesterday. But a dropout Hubbard wasn't. Nor did he ever find the world of things, communicable ideas, and people inferior to chemical distortions of his cortical pathways. Perhaps the training in the University of Hard Knocks that he was always bragging about did have its points.

The most important continuity between Hubbard's nonconformity and today's dissent may be simply that he existed and they exist—the heartening fact that there have always been, and still are, stubborn souls who refuse to be considered as members of something they haven't joined. This is a massive cliché, perhaps, but it may be as close to the realities of then and now as this trip will take us.

There are smaller similarities to be found between the two periods. Anyone who thinks, for example, that intellectual "probes" and "mosaic" writing are purely products of the electronic age might browse through a few *Little Journeys* or *Philistines*. The medium was type, letter by letter, line by line, but the message was a long way from being linear. Today's advanced thinkers sometimes find weathered footprints preceeding them into what they thought to be virgin wilderness. In the August 1967 *Atlantic,* novelist John Barth discussed "The Literature of Exhaustion"—the writer "in an age of ultimacies and 'final solutions.' " One of these ultimacies seems to be the celebration of Nothing: "How about an empty, silent stage, then, or blank pages—a 'happening' where nothing happens, like Cage's *4' 33"* performed in an empty hall?" Mr. Barth, or perhaps his editor, added a footnote to "blank pages" which reads "An ultimacy already attained in the nineteenth century by that avant-gardist of East Aurora, New York, Elbert Hubbard, in his *Essay on Silence.*"

If Hubbard had been one of those who know who they are, and where their work lies, he might have left a record clear to read and all of a piece. Instead, he navigated under sealed orders, which were never opened. His life doesn't define anything much, but perhaps it does illuminate. And that can be useful today, too.

SOURCES AND LEFTOVERS

SOURCES THAT are cited more than once are listed below. They are referred to in the "Notes to Chapters" by the authors' last names only (except that *Impressions* by Elbert Hubbard, II, is referred to by title, and his father's article in *Cosmopolitan* is designated by the name of the magazine).

The other citations from Hubbard are more complicated. He constantly cannibalized his own work. Similar or identical passages are often to be found in the *Philistine,* the *Little Journeys,* later in the *Fra,* in pre-1915 volumes of collected writings, and even in the advertising. And the various posthumous rearrangements are often an unmapped jungle. In most cases, an issue of the *Philistine,* or one of the *Little Journeys,* is the original source, and the *earliest* use found is the one cited. The occasional citation from the *Note Book* or the *Selected Writings* is an admission by the author of his failure to spot and document an earlier source (or to keep track of it through movings and rewritings). To simplify and shorten the Notes, the *Philistine* is abbreviated to *Phil,* with the publication date; *Little Journeys* citations are given as *LJ,* with the name of the putative subject and the year of publication.

ALLEN, FREDERICK LEWIS. "Elbert Hubbard," *Scribner's Magazine,* September, 1938.

BALCH, DAVID ARNOLD. *Elbert Hubbard: Genius of Roycroft.* New York, Frederick A. Stokes, 1940.

The only book about Hubbard that tries to put together an orderly total picture. It contains valuable details, and it sorts out some of the mythology. But it has little depth, and is incredibly coy about Hubbard and Alice Moore. It draws heavily upon Heath and Shay and it documents very few of its statements.

CRAMER, C. H. *Royal Bob: The Life of Robert G. Ingersoll.* Indianapolis, The Bobbs-Merrill Company, 1952.

HEATH, MARY HUBBARD. *The Elbert Hubbard I Knew.* Roycroft, 1929.

The indispensable source for material on Hubbard's parents, family life as a child, and his pre-Roycroft period. Mrs. Heath makes no attempt to follow her brother's public career, but her book is an excellent treatment of exactly what its title covers.

HUBBARD, ALICE. *Life Lessons: Truths Concerning People Who Have Lived.* Roycroft, 1909.

Seven widely discursive essays on Susan B. Anthony, David Swing, Mary Wollstonecraft, Robert Louis Stevenson, Friedrich Froebel, Henry D. Thoreau, and Elizabeth Cady Stanton.

HUBBARD, ELBERT. "A Social and Industrial Experiment," *Cosmopolitan,* January, 1902.

One of the few instances of Hubbard writing directly for someone else's publication. The article is an important source for Hubbard, and Roycroft, history and legend.

HUBBARD, ELBERT, II. *Impressions.* Roycroft, 1921.

An important source. Bert's reminiscences, reprinted from the *Fra.*

HUNTER, DARD. *My Life with Paper: An Autobiography.* New York, Alfred A. Knopf, 1958.

KEMP, HARRY. *Tramping on Life: An Autobiographical Narrative.* London, Boni and Liveright, 1922.

A lively account of Kemp's wandering adventures in the early years of the century. Many public figures appear in the narrative, but under fictitious names. Hubbard is "Roderick Spalton," proprietor of the "Eos Artwork Studios."

MONAHAN, MICHAEL. *Nemesis.* New York, Frank-Maurice, Inc., 1926.

Contains Monahan's Memorial Address delivered at East Aurora in July 1915, with some editing and afterthoughts.

POND, MAJOR J. B. *Eccentricities of Genius: Memories of Famous Men and Women of the Platform and Stage.* New York, G. W. Dillingham Company, 1900.

It classes Hubbard not under "Orators," "Literary Lecturers," "Author Readers and Lecturers," or "Humorists," but as "Miscellaneous" (along with Henry Watterson, William E. Gladstone, P. T. Barnum, George H. Daniels, and others).

REEDY, WILLIAM MARION. *The Feather Duster or, Is He Sincere?* Roycroft, 1912.

Also contains essays by Harold Bolce, Benjamin De Casseres, and Brainard L. Bates. The important one is Reedy's.

SHAY, FELIX. *Elbert Hubbard of East Aurora.* New York, William H. Wise & Company, 1926.

Valuable material, scattered through a hodgepodge of impressionistic reminiscences.

SULLIVAN, MARK. *Our Times: The United States, 1900–1925.* 4 vols. New York, Charles Scribner's Sons, 1927–1935.

Journalistic history, but an excellent source for the events, popular preoccupations, and the feel of the period.

WOLF, FRED WILHELM. *William Marion Reedy, a critical biography.* Ann Arbor, University Microfilms, 1954. Publication 7180. A Vanderbilt doctoral dissertation.

NOTES TO CHAPTERS

1. INTRODUCTION

The story about the demolishing of Hubbard's birthplace and the rescue of his memorial plaque is in the Bloomington, Illinois, *Daily Pantagraph* for January 6, 1954. The plaque was in the McLean County Historical Society building in 1956.

Life being "a zigzag course" is in the Michael Angelo *LJ* (1899). Harry Lauder's remark that Hubbard wore his makeup on the street is quoted in the *Fra* for December 1913.

2. FAMILY, 3. BOYHOOD, 4. SUCCESS STORY

Unless otherwise noted, the factual material and quotations in these chapters are from Heath.

Sullivan's reference to nineteenth-century American education as an adjunct to religion is in Vol. II, pp. 85–86. The Ingersoll references are from Cramer.

Hubbard's elegy to the country boy is from the *Cosmopolitan* article. Mozart and horses are in the Mozart *LJ* (1901). The Manhattan ball game is in Shay.

The drummer in the new vest first appeared in the *Phil* for March 1903.

The "spring bottom pants" are in Vol. 14 of *Selected Writings*. Hubbard's "went westward' saga is in his *Cosmopolitan* article. Hubbard the cowboy is in Monahan, the British *Who's Who* in Shay.

Snapping the head off the world is in the John Hancock *LJ* (1898).

The "Jack and Jill" sermon appeared in the Morris, Illinois, *Herald* in 1881. There was much more of it. After blessing the Lord because the title was not "Jill and Jack," he went on: "I thank the Giver of all Good that it does *not* read so . . . St. Paul gives us some very valuable hints for the proper management of women, and if I did not know that St. Paul was writing the words of inspiration, I might be tempted to ask (since he was an unmarried man, and it is not recorded that he went much in society), why should St. Paul look out of his bachelor's garret and tell *me* what is the proper sphere of woman, why should he give *me* instruction, I who have buried two wives, happily divorced three more, and am now enjoying domestic strife with another—why should he give *me* instructions? . . ." An interesting harvest of latent content might be gathered.

Details on the Larkin sales premiums are from Balch.

There is some interesting material on Hubbard and Frank Lloyd Wright in *Frank Lloyd Wright: A Study in Architectural Content* by Norris Kelly Smith (Englewood Cliffs, N.J., Prentice-Hall, 1966). The two met and they had arguments, with Hubbard apparently taking a stand for the freestanding individual as against Wright's (then) more conservative position.

5. REBIRTH

Alice's discovery of George Eliot (and of novels, which she had been "informed many times . . . were a fearful waste of time, and, moreover, of intrinsic evil") is related in the *Fra* for February 1910. Reedy's description of Alice is in the *Feather Duster.*

Ingersoll's letter to Hubbard about *The Man* is in *The Letters of Robert G. Ingersoll,* Edited with a Biographical Introduction by Eva Ingersoll Wakefield (New York, Philosophical Library, 1951).

Hubbard's letter to his mother announcing his "most important move" is in Shay, and part of it is in Balch. For some reason it is not in Heath, which is the source of the other family letters quoted in this chapter. Both the Mencken and Riis remarks are taken from Sullivan, Vol. I.

Harvard's Widener Library has an essay titled "Victorian Rebel," by Herbert L. Ley, Jr., which was submitted in an American Civilization Prize Essay contest in 1941–1942. It gives the dates of Hubbard's brief appearance on the college records.

"Please Be Seated" is in the *Phil* for December 1900.

Hubbard's college-life daydream in *Forbes of Harvard* might fairly be summed up as saying, "I was one of the boys. I *was!* . . . And who needs it?"

The *LJ* on Morris (1900) has a curiously aloof and synthetic flavor—as if Hubbard knew he was committed to an attitude of worship but was no longer quite sure why. The November 1905 *Phil* carried a quite different story of his visit to Morris. In it, he tells of going to hear Morris lecture in Hammersmith one evening ("Bernard Shaw told me"). He has trouble finding the place ("which Morris?") and when he does get there it is "a little hall, built as a lean-to against Kelmscott House . . . a single kerosene lamp . . . on a table." When Morris appears, he is "big, bold and shaggy" and he lectures his audience (a mere dozen slum-dwelling workingmen) on "The probable effects of color, as used in house decorations, on human character."

Judgments of skill in fiction have changed greatly. Today, many critics

(critics?—many high-school students) would call the ending of *No Enemy* overblown tripe or worse. But the New York *Herald*'s reviewer called the book "well written from beginning to end," and Francis Melville, in the November 1894 *Arena* said, "The end comes in tragic manner, but is worked over with rare skill and fidelity to the possible." Here it is:

(Himself and the blind heroine are approaching an open ferry slip, carrying a basket of flowers.)

"Straight ahead they walked, hand close pressed in hand. They were approaching the edge of the dock, five steps from the brink, four, three, two, one—!!!

"The guard came back.

"'I thought I heard a woman scream,' he muttered to himself. 'It must have been only the wind sighing through the shrouds of yonder ship.'

"He took the lantern, and holding it over the dock, peered down into the water ten feet below.

"'Flowers, flowers at this time of year, and floating in the water! I have seen flowers in gardens, flowers at banquets, flowers at weddings, flowers on graves—ah, there is the boat now. She must have been blocked by the ice.'"

Well? . . . (me, too). But here is what Stephen Crane said about this passage: "Your flowers on the water—Good God, that is magnificent!—a thing I felt in the roots of my hair. Hell and Blazes, but I do envy you that paragraph! . . . The book strengthened me and uplifted me." (Quoted in Shay.)

6. GROWING PAINS

The description of the little magazines as "a revolt" is from Gelett Burgess in the *Lark,* quoted by Sidney Kramer in *A History of Stone & Kimball and Herbert S. Stone & Co. with a Bibliography of their Publications 1893–1905.* (Chicago, Norman W. Forgue, 1940.)

Burgess also said that the little magazines were a "riot of decadence . . . a craze for odd sizes and shapes, freak illustrations, wide margins, uncut pages, Jenson types, scurrilous abuse and petty jealousies, impossible prose and doggerel rhyme."

Hubbard's quotation (from "a paper published at Red Oak, Iowa") about the *Philistine* being a student publication was quite possibly one of his jokes. It has his style, and several of his pet phrases are in it. I think he wrote it himself.

Hubbard's late reminiscence about the origin of the *Phil* is in the

June 1912 issue (17th Anniversary Number). His moving from myth back to reality was unusual, but he followed it with a plunge back into myth. "In order to keep the boy busy who had been hired to kick the Gordon, it was proposed to print a book." The first *Philistine* was printed by the Pendennis Press, not by Hubbard, and the book wasn't printed on a Gordon. Still, he couldn't resist that lovely trade expression "to kick the Gordon" (which meant operating a platen press by pumping a treadle with one leg while feeding sheets in and out with both hands—a complex performance, seldom seen anymore).

Frederick Lewis Allen's characterization of the "limp leather style" is in his *Scribner's* article. He characterized the Roycrofters as "disappointed poets, eccentrics, cranks . . . they labored joyfully in a spirit something like that of the dafter progressive schools of the nineteen twenties." As for Hubbard, Allen found him "a bundle of paradoxes" who "had ideas, a lively impertinence, and a knack for pungent expression." And he summed up the Hubbard legacy as "the memory of a buoyant and electric personality."

I am indebted to Richard G. Underwood, director of Syracuse University Press, for the information on Will Ransom. Underwood worked with Ransom during Ransom's last years at the University of Oklahoma Press.

Hubbard did give the Morris-oriented purists some reason to scoff. The *LJ* on Erasmus says: ". . . as an authority on books Erasmus can still be read. He it was who fixed the classic page margin—twice as wide at the top as on the inside; twice as wide at the outside as the top; twice as wide at the bottom as the side. And any printer who varies from this displays his ignorance of proportion" (1908). I haven't seen any Roycroft publications that followed this formula.

The item about Kipling's lawsuits is in the *Literary Digest* for July 1, 1899.

Hubbard's reference to the "mouth-breathers" telling him to get his hair cut is in the *Phil* for April 1904. "Covering his thinkery" is on p. 183 of the *Note Book.*

Hubbard's letters to Harte proposing the collaboration were quoted by Harte in his account of the quarrel in *The Critic* for May 23, 1896. Hubbard's account is in the *Phil* for January 1899.

The entries in Bert's "Log" are quoted in *Impressions.*

The joke about carving George Eliot's name on the door of his room is in Shay. "Bulling the market for boulders" is from the *Cosmopolitan* article.

The Roycroft article in *Catholic World* was in the September 1901 issue, by Anna B. McGill. It also quoted the following, from an unidentified "new magazine":

> "Dear printers," said Fra the Philistine
> (And he smiled like the cherubim Sistine),
> "Learn to work without wages
> Like monks of Dark Ages,
> Then shall we make books that are pristine."

The story of "John" holding the horses is in Kemp.

". . . writing . . . to a woman of Brains" is in the October 1904 *Phil.*

Reedy, in the *Feather Duster,* said the early Roycroft operated by "the genius of chaos."

"Literary men do not quarrel more . . ." is in the *Phil* for August 1904.

Crane's letter, written before the Philistine dinner (and indicating puzzlement about the whole thing), is quoted in *Stephen Crane: An Omnibus,* by Robert Wooster Stallman. (New York, Alfred A. Knopf, 1952.) Frank Noxon's reactions to the dinner are in a letter dated December 7, 1926, to Max J. Herzberg (quoted in *Stephen Crane's Love Letters to Nellie Crouse,* Edwin H. Cady, Ed., Syracuse, 1954). Claude Bragdon's memories of the dinner are in "The Purple Cow Period: The 'Dinkey Magazines' that Caught the Spirit of the 'Nineties,'" *The Bookman,* July 1929. Hubbard's comments on Crane's writing are in the Chopin *LJ* (1901). Crane's letter to "My dear Hub" is quoted in Stallman, above, as is "when I think of you, I rejoice . . ."

7. FRA ELBERTUS

Bryan's dialogue with the New York *Press* is recorded in Sullivan, Vol. I, pp. 305–306.

According to Shay, Hubbard's favorite everyday hat contained a gold pin, engraved with "Man Can Achieve What Man Can Conceive."

"No man can live in a village and illumine it . . ." is in the Goldsmith *LJ* (1895). Mrs. Grubbins appeared in the *Phil* for February 1899. The flareup over his comments on the troubles of the local preachers is in the *Phil* for April 1897. The salute to the "pimpled knave" is in the *Phil* for April 1898.

"Filtered through himself" is from Reedy. "What is the use of writing many volumes . . ." is in the *Phil* for February 1898. Goods in the show window came a month later. The "fine intoxication" is in the Milton *LJ*

(1900), as is the "masterly mind." "The man who caters to the public . . ." is in the Paganini *LJ* (1901).

". . . jocund day . . . tiptoe on the mountain top" is in *Time and Chance* (also, more or less, in *Romeo and Juliet*).

Hubbard's writing-craft admonishments are from: *Phil*s June 1896 and February 1896; *No Enemy, Phil*s for March 1897 and October 1896.

Joining up with the "Great Ones gone" is from the *Phil* for April 1898.

"When a man and a woman . . ." is in the *Phil* for January 1900.

Alice's caveats on propinquity are in *Life Lessons,* p. 145, her remarks about Mrs. Stanton on p. 149.

Hubbard's joke about the father of Little Lord Fauntleroy is in the October 1895 *Phil.*

Bert's comments on his father as taskmaster are in *Impressions.*

The "come-outers" are discussed in the Elizabeth Fry *LJ* (1897), and Brook Farm in the Thoreau *LJ* (1904). Rural genius and the cause of ignorance are from the Jane Austin *LJ* (1897). Joseph Parker appears in the *Phil* for September 1896, and "all foolish schemes of philosophy" in the *Phil* for April 1910.

The Bloomington reporter's story on the Hubbard lecture is in the *Daily Pantagraph* for March 19, 1901.

The man of Christ consigning Hubbard and his works to hell via the sewer was reported in the Indianapolis *News* and displayed in the ad section of the June 1911 *Phil.* "Poison in sugar-coated pills" came from a Methodist minister quoted in the Cincinnati *Enquirer* of August 22, 1910, and was also featured in the *Phil.*

The sneers of the *Chap-Book* at popular education are in the October 15, 1867, issue.

Socrates, Claudius, Nero, and Comte are in the Great Philosophers series (1904) of *LJ.* (Claudius and Nero are in the one on Seneca.) Krutch's comment is in his review of Felix Shay's book in the *Nation* for August 4, 1926. Reedy on the half-baked is in the *Feather Duster.*

The Abbey-Putnam-Hubbard story is in *Memories of a Publisher, 1865–1915,* by George Haven Putnam. (New York, G. P. Putnam's Sons, 1915.)

Hubbard's reference to "the literary and philosophical hill tribes" is in the Plato *LJ* (1908), his reference to Whitman in the *Phil* for November 1911, and his recipe for having "something worth writing about" in the *Phil* for January 1913. The pedagogues got their lumps in the November 1902 and Samuel Johnson in the September 1906 *Phil*s.

8. MESSAGES

In my last year of junior high, my English and homeroom teacher was a refined, imposing, and slightly addled lady of advanced middle age. One of her principles of pedagogy seemed to be that her duller students could be galvanized into brilliance if she singled them out for sudden notice and glory. When the time came for the class to elect a president or a student-council representative, she would pounce on some class nonentity in the back rows, drag the wretch to the front, and deliver a eulogy of his or her unsuspected talents and virtues. Then she would call for election by acclamation, and we would mutter and oblige.

She read the *Message to Garcia* aloud to us one day, with full elocutionist treatment. Then she called on an adenoidal class butt named something like August. "August is my Major Rowan," she told us brightly, while August stood with his jaw hanging. "I can always count on August to *Carry the Message.* . . . August, will you please find the janitor and tell him I wish to see him?"

August gulped and took a step or two, and then made the day bright and joyous for us all by blurting, "Where is he at?"

The actual history behind Hubbard's essay has been spelled out by Stewart Holbrook in *Lost Men of American History* (New York, The Macmillan Company, 1946). Few people, of course, saw the *Message* as history, through Stephen Crane did, because he had been reporting the war and knew the facts. He wrote Hubbard: "I object strongly to your paragraphs about Rowan. . . . He didn't do anything worthy at all. . . . Besides he is personally a chump. . . . When you want to monkey with some of our national heroes you had better ask me, because I know and your perspective is almost out of sight." (*Stephen Crane,* by John Berryman, William Sloane Associates, 1950, p. 245.)

The minority report on the *Message* by George Heafford of the Milwaukee & St. Paul was quoted by Reedy. Reedy's comments are in "A Message to Hubbard," St. Louis *Mirror,* June 15, 1899, later reprinted as the first of the *Mirror Pamphlets.*

Hubbard's insistence that the *Message* was not to be considered his best writing is in his *Cosmopolitan* article. His letter to Walter L. Brown of the Buffalo Public Library is quoted from a photocopy of the original (generously sent me by Mr. W. B. Pleadwell of Buffalo, who has been collecting material about Hubbard for many years).

Hubbard's sentence about the *Message* leaping hot from his heart is quoted, without a source, in Balch. The revised version is in the *Cosmo-politan* article. Bert's correction of the record is in *Impressions.*

"Work stops bickering . . ." is from the St. Benedict *LJ* (1908). The set piece framed in today's FBI offices ("If you work for a man, in heaven's name . . .") is from an inspirational pamphlet appropriately titled "Get Out or Get in Line." (By February 1908 it had sold over a million copies as a reprint.)

"When you revolt . . ." is in the *Phil* for September 1908. "Blessed is the man who has found his work" was Carlyle's before it was Hubbard's.

De Casseres's hailing of "The Man with the Hoe" is quoted in Sullivan, Vol. II, p. 240.

The story of Hubbard and Ali Baba in the Waldorf is in Shay.

See the bibliographical listing following these Notes for data on Albert Lane's biography of Hubbard.

Miriam Allen de Ford's phrase is in a letter to the author.

Major Pond's comments are from his book. Bert's remark is in *Impressions.*

Reedy's comments on Hubbard's brashness and diffidence are in the St. Louis *Mirror* for April 19, 1900. His later discussion of the "suspicion of pose . . ." is in the *Feather Duster.*

The biographical details on Reedy are from Wolf.

Hubbard's words about "love-children" are in the *Phil* for April 1897. They were followed in August 1904 by this: ". . . the word 'illegitimate' is not in God's vocabulary, since He smiles on the love-children as on none other. If you know history, you know this: that into their keeping God has largely given the beauty, talent, energy, strength, skill and power, as well as that divinity which confuses its possessor with Deity Incarnate." Harry Kemp thought Miriam ". . . a wonderful girl. She had shining, abundant hair, and a face rendered superlatively beautiful by the glowing of vivacity, understanding, feminine vitality behind it and through it, like a lamp held up within."

Documentation of the events surrounding Hubbard's divorce has not been attempted beyond the key facts and dates. This book has never been intended to be a detailed biography, rather a study of a man's involvement with—and influence upon—some of the larger changes taking place in his time and his country. The events of his life have been treated in terms of their apparent importance to that involvement and that influence.

One of my sources is a newspaper clipping dated December 9, 1902. The clipping was generously lent to me by Mr. Garth Cate, who was one of Hubbard's lecture-tour managers. Mr. Cate was not sure of the source of the clipping. Datelined Buffalo, it announced Bertha's suit for divorce, naming Alice Moore as corespondent. "The suit is the outcome of an action brought in the Supreme Court here some time ago by W. W. Woodworth, an attorney of this city, in which he sought to recover from Hubbard a large sum alleged to be due for the support and maintenance of a child born to Miss Alice Moore, a sister of Woodworth's wife. Miss Moore alleged that Hubbard was the father of her child, and charged that Hubbard had lived with her at Denver, Col., and in Massachusetts.

"The bringing of this action led to the publication in the *Philistine* of a denunciation by 'Fra Elbertus' of lawyers in general, whom he characterized as a class of persons who have but two objects in life, grand and petit larceny" (*Phil*, November 1901).

The Woodworth suit was settled out of court September 30, 1902 (date from Mr. Pleadwell, see above). Apparently it had been filed (and the scandal had become public knowledge) late in 1901. At least part of the time between her leaving Hubbard and getting her divorce, Bertha Hubbard lived with the John Larkins, Hubbard's oldest sister (according to the clipping).

Monahan's Opera House speech is in the Buffalo *Express* for February 7, 1902. The complaint to Reedy about "Mine, but mutilated!" is in Wolf.

9. HOW CAN SIN BE SIN?

The "all-around rogue" reference is from the Kansas City *Independent*, and is quoted in Shay. Hubbard printed some of these comments in the *Phil* for January 1903, including the one from the New York *Sun*. His reference to the "fat and harmles poodle" is in the Velásquez *LJ* (1902), and his reflection about the public relishing someone's "grief, woe, disgrace" is in the *Phil* for January 1903.

Paul Mavity's "Little Journey" was issued in 1904, printed by Westminster Press of Franklin, Indiana. After much lambasting of the fallen, Mavity concluded, "I am inclined to think that at bottom Mr. Hubbard's taint is not so much impurity as genius-worship."

Hubbard's "If your friend reveals his humanity and the rabble forsake him" is part of a passage which comes about as close to pleading as he ever did. ". . . stand by him . . . your neighbor is the man who needs you. . . . When sympathy finds vent in vengeance and love takes the form of strife, who can say where it will end!" (September 1902 *Phil*) His reference to the "good many people in my own town" was in the June 1902 *Phil*. This rapid veering from misery to jauntiness and back again runs through this whole period. In August of 1902, the *Phil* observed that "You can vanquish your foes alone, but you will need help when it comes to withstanding your relatives."

The letters to his mother and to Mary are in Heath. The statement about antipathetic temperaments is quoted in the newspaper clipping from Mr. Garth Cate cited in the notes to the previous chapter.

"The true solace for all private troubles" was displayed on the cover of the December 1902 *Phil*, the month of Bertha's divorce suit. "Disgrace consists in . . ." had preceeded it by over a year (September 1901 *Phil*). "Never explain . . ." is also from the September 1901 *Phil*, and it was featured, by itself, on several *Phil* covers. It has a close relationship to a passage in the February 1902 issue: "If you are defamed, let time vindicate you— silence is a thousand times better than explanations. Explanations do not explain. Let your life be its own excuse for being—cease all explanations and all apologies, and just live your life."

"Just how much discord . . ." is from the Whistler *LJ* (1902), undoing Calamity is in the Schumann *LJ* (1901), and "How can sin be sin . . ." in the August 1902 *Phil*. There is one other sentence from the *Phil* that would round off this section neatly: "When one reaches the so-called jumping-off place of despair, he discovers that, by God's providence, the world is round." Except that the date for this is 1897 and his major jumping-off places were still to come. And unfortunately for logical progression, the *Phil* that proclaimed that the great man was seizing the horn and blowing it forevermore came a month before the issue that almost begged his neighbor to stand by him.

The congratulatory letter to his parents is in Heath.

That "great and exalted love," with its habit of fading and fleeing, stayed on Hubbard's mind for several years. In 1897 he ascribed the passage to Comte. In 1902, it was used again as "a certain writer has said . . .", and elsewhere he used it without quotes in several variations and contexts.

In 1931, Harvard's Widener Library received a printed leaflet entitled "A loose leaf from Judge Henry Neil's Magazine, East Aurora, N.Y. The True Romance of Alice in Wonderland, by Judge Henry Neil. Father of Mothers' Pensions. Listed by the Council of Librarians as one of the ten best authors." It seems to be a compilation of anti-Hubbard and anti-Alice gossip then current. (Elbert II stated, in a letter to the author, that Neil stayed in East Aurora only about a year, in 1931–1932.) The leaflet starts:

"Alice came to East Aurora, N.Y. about forty years ago to teach in the high school. She was a red-headed Alice. Unlike most school teachers, who have much intelligence but little 'IT,' this Alice possessed both traits to a marked degree, and she used both to the utmost limits of her power. . . ." It goes on with a scurrilous version of the Hubbard–Alice Moore affair. Its only importance seems to be as an indication of some of the kinds of legend and gossip persisting in East Aurora over fifteen years after the *Lusitania* was sunk.

Alice's discussion of Mary Wollstonecraft and her anguish is on pp. 74–75 of *Life Lessons*. The story of Hubbard's tangle with Fred Gardner is in Shay. The information on the marriage is from the New York *Times* for January 21, 1904.

The quotation from Opie Read was reprinted in the September 1912 *Phil.* Sanford's haircut is related by Kemp. Bert's reminiscences are in *Impressions*. The Reedy item is in the *Feather Duster*.

"No man can deceive his children . . ." is in the Jane Austen *LJ* (1897). "It is a great thing to teach" is in the Bellini *LJ* (1902).

Hubbard's letter to Pond is in Pond's book, p. 368. His later announcement that he was about through with lecturing is in his *Cosmopolitan* article. The "monastic impulse" is discussed in the Luther *LJ* (1903). The "jiner instinct" is in the Schumann *LJ* (1901). A year later (Whistler *LJ*, 1902) brought the "mix and mingle" alternative.

10. MORTGAGE–BURNING

Dard Hunter's comment on Alice is in his book.

Reedy's reactions to *White Hyacinths* are in *Reedy's Mirror* for July 18, 1907, and were reprinted in the 1907–1908 Roycroft Catalog. A Hubbard remark in the Comte *LJ* the year of his second marriage may also have been pertinent to *White Hyacinths*: "Comte was always much impressed by intellectual women. His wife had given him a sample of the other kind, and caused him to swing out and idealize the woman of brains."

The "meek and lowly" priest was identified as the Reverend Father Judge, writing in *The New World,* Chicago, November 25, 1905. Billy Sunday's reply to Hubbard was credited by the *Phil* to the Rockford, Illinois, *Register-Gazette.*

Billy Sunday and such crusading agnostics as Ingersoll and Hubbard really needed each other. Hubbard (*Phil,* April 1908) referred to "The old orthodox idea of God still taught by Sunday . . . is that He was a paranoiac, suffering from fatty enlargement of the ego, with everything His own way, and responsible to nothing and nobody, making laws but to break them, and creating millions of human beings but to damn them. My conception is, that at least, God is a gentleman."

There was merriment about 1912 when a Decoration Day address by Sunday in Beaver Falls was shown to be almost identical with an 1882 address by Colonel Ingersoll. Cramer (pp. 98–99) says, "Sunday claimed that he had never read a line of Ingersoll in his life, but that 'folks' sent him clippings from time to time and someone must have contributed 'considerable clippings' from Ingersoll."

The "what are you going to give us in return" item is from the King Alfred (1904) *LJ*. The "so-called infidel" in the Socrates (1904) *LJ*. "Dogma has less place . . ." is from the Burke (1903) *LJ,* and "a certain type of religion fits a certain man . . ." from the Humboldt (1905) *LJ*. The Spinoza (1904) *LJ* contains the remarks about "the destiny of the liberal church."

"Life is a paradox. Every truth . . ." is a risky quotation to use because it is part of a long disquisition in the *Phil* for October 1910 that was not written by Hubbard, but by Benjamin De Casseres. The quotation, however, is from the first two paragraphs of the article, which, with the third paragraph (which has Hubbard's style well branded on it), seems to me almost certainly a Hubbard introductory note taking the curse off the Nietzschean harangue that followed.

"Nothing matters and no difference" comes from the *Phil* for September 1910, and "Religion is in the heart of man" from the Marcus Aurelius (1904) *LJ*.

Alice's "to express the best within us" definition is on p. 54, and her exasperation with a being who was prone to wander is on p. 74 of *Life Lessons.*

Hubbard's story about proposing a Temple of Man for East Aurora is in the *Phil* for January 1902. His reference to "plain hypocrites and grafters" is in the November 1911 *Phil,* and the men's clubs and bishops in the Beethoven (1901) *LJ*.

The "unknown cause" is from the November 1905 *Phil*. Hubbard's "Corner Grocery Infidel" had his earliest appearance in the *Phil* for December 1897. The quotations on "everything lies in the mass" and "to be scientific" are in the *Note Book* on pp. 84 and 162.

"The idea that a person after having a certain disease" is from the *Fra* for May 1909 and "People who live rightly" in the February 1911

Phil. The discourse on vaccination is from the December 1906 *Phil.* The roguish reference to Nature is in the December 1897 *Phil.* Alice's formulation comes from p. 54 of *Life Lessons.*

Hubbard's 1905–1906 lecture schedule is in the January 1906 *Phil,* his joke about introductions in the *Phil* for October of the same year, and the "Bishop of all Outsiders" designation in the *Phil* for that December.

Dard Hunter's stained-glass windows are discussed on pp. 33–35 of his book, and his adventure with Miss Morris on pp. 35–36. Hubbard's remarks about the growth of his printing plant are in the *Phil* for December 1914.

Dard Hunter's "octopus" design is related on pp. 42–43 of his book. In the June 1908 *Phil,* Hubbard said that the Standard Oil executives had "great practical shrewdness combined with minds that, so far as abstract truth is concerned, are simply prairie-dog towns." He used the same phrase in the Mary Baker Eddy *LJ* (December 1908).

11. ART AND GLORY

Monahan's rhyme was part of a larger effort, printed in *The Phoenix* for October 1915 as part of his Memorial Address:

When you get to Buffalo
And the Pan America show,
Leave the brawling hippodromes
With their parti-colored domes.
Leave, oh leave the wicked Midway
Greased as 'twere the Devil's skidway.
Leave the cabbies and the fakers
And the mob of loot-partakers—
Make a drive for East Aurory
Where we work for Art and Glory!

Come you once, you'll come again-a
On the W N Y & Penna.
There's a one-hoss train doth sneeze her
Devious way to Ebeneezer,
Springbrook, Elma, Jamison Road,
(None of these is Fame's abode)—
Now the little narrow gauger
Snorts and screams as to assuage her
Bursting joy—'tis East Aurory,
Where we work for Art and Glory!

"Art is not a thing separate and apart" is in the Mozart (1901) *LJ.*
The quotation about allowing religion, and so on, to creep into working
hours is from *Time and Chance.* "Any man who does not enjoy . . ." is in the
Phil for August 1911.

The picnickers having to wade the creek is in Heath. The story about
clothes making the man is in Shay, as is the account of Felix's coming to
East Aurora, and of the Carnegie *LJ.*

". . . famous ones as surely eight feet tall" is in the Alfred Russell
Wallace (1905) *LJ.* The other definitions of genius are in the *Phils* for
June 1903, November 1905, and February 1909.

"Hike for respectability . . ." is from the *Phil* for February 1909.
Climbing a tree occasionally is from the Wagner-Nietzsche (1904) *LJ.* A
rather nice leftover that fits here is from the July 1904 *Phil:* "Be very
careful how you go into the Best Society. I know a man who ventured in,
once, and sank over his ears. We got him out, but he was never any good
afterwards."

The "voluptuary of labor" is from the Mozart (1901) *LJ.* Visitors
who "were willing to do anything but work" appear in the *Cosmopolitan*
article.

The reference to the great man being great only from a distance is
from the *Note Book,* p. 67; "life never did, nor can . . ." is from the *Note
Book,* p. 124. "To center on science . . ." is from the Comte (1904) *LJ.*

"The man of masterly mind" comes from the Leonardo (1902) *LJ.*
Emerson's soft-handedness is from the Mary Shelley (1897) *LJ.*

The "bold men who have blazed . . ." are celebrated in the *Phil* for
November 1908 in announcing the forthcoming *Little Journeys to the
Homes of Great Business Men.*

The *Phil* for July 1904 saluted Booker T. Washington as an 'instrument of deity." Hubbard once wrote to Brand Whitlock suggesting a Tom
L. Johnson for President campaign. Whitlock's reply is in *The Letters and
Journal of Brand Whitlock,* edited by Allan Nevins (New York, D. Apple-
ton & Company, 1936), pp. 87-88. ("I have been for Johnson for President
for a long time, but I don't think we can land him because he has too big a
job in Cleveland. . . . I am not sure that it is not a bigger job than the
Presidency.")

Felix's remarks about "The Wise Member of the Perfesh" are on a
page of the August 1909 *Phil* headed "Advertising Diplomacy." Hubbard's
early heresy about advertising was in the *Phil* for April 1906. Felix's story
about the making of the Roycroft Catalog is on pp. 293–294 of his book.

Alice's description of the Realist is from pp. 123–124 of *Life Lessons*. Felix's story of his "only passing-serious" quarrel with Hubbard over the prohibition parade is on pp. 295–297 of his book.

O'Sullivan discontinuing his ads received notice in the *Fra* for February 1909, and he got his punishment in the following July issue.

Bert, in *Impressions,* is the source for the Roycroft shops making a workday of New Year's. Hubbard's words on the troubles of "the man who attempts to better . . ." are in the September 1904 *Phil.* The child-labor incident is in the *Phil* for November 1907, and Harry Kemp's report on pp. 191–192 of his book.

12. BECAUSE I COULD

The June 1910 *Fra* was billed as "The Vaudeville Number," and carried Hubbard's account of his adventures and his triumph. Some of the items he omitted are to be found in an article by Arthur Hopkins in the October 1937 *Ladies' Home Journal.*

As a young man, Hubbard had dreamed of being an actor (". . . committed most of 'Hamlet' to memory with an eye to the stage"—*Cosmopolitan* article), and he found an enormous challenge and satisfaction in his tour. The announcement in the May 1910 *Fra* of the coming "Vaudeville Number" was fervent. "To stand in the glare, unarmed save for your wit and gesture, before two thousand indifferent people, to play upon them, to sound their stops, to appeal to that great, common heart-throb of humanity which ebbs and flows through us all, to get their response—that breathless silence, followed by a roar and rumble of prolonged applause—to bow yourself off the stage and be called back, and yet again called back, until the orchestra chops off the tumult—this is a gratification—a wild, weird intoxication, which once tasted is never forgotten."

Alice's essay on entertaining Great Men is in the *Phil* for January 1907. Hubbard's charging an extra fifty dollars for the ordeal of the spare room is from "I Managed Presidents," by S. Russell Bridges, as told to Kurt Singer, *South Atlantic Quarterly,* July 1951.

Both Amy Leslie's remarks and Hubbard's response are in the *Phil* for November 1899. Hubbard as the VIP on the train is recorded in the *Phil* for April 1914. From today's perspective, Hubbard's reference to "the coon" is shocking. It should be remembered, however, that at, and beyond, the turn of the century, stereotypes were almost the only reference points to Negroes that were available to many people in the North. The passions of the Civil War had faded, and the Negro himself been quietly sacrificed to political expediency. As far as the northern popular mind could see (Hubbard and most of his audience included), the Negro had just begun to move from the quaint, picturesque, and barely human qualities of E. W. Kemble's darky drawings to a new level of *comic* stereotype. The minstrel show was part of this pattern. Another example may be found in Booth Tarkington's *Penrod,* with its simple, nonmalicious description of the three colored brothers who became Penrod's neighbors. They are portrayed as really admirable characters, who put to ignominious flight a "tough guy" who has mesmerized Penrod and who tries to bully the brothers as "nigs." But the brothers' names are Herman, Sherman, and (start laughing) Verman. ("Verman, he tongue tie.")

There was no "prejudice" in today's emotion-laden sense in this sort of thing, nor in Hubbard's expecting Felix to keep him supplied with "coon stories"—at which he laughed immoderately. There was a large degree of stupidity, and a simple inability to conceive of a Negro as an individual, full-scale human being.

As has been noted, Booker T. Washington was a Hubbard hero and Tuskegee almost the only college for which he had a good word. At least once, Hubbard gave the visiting President Washington the full celebrity treatment at Roycroft, including lunch with himself and Alice (Felix was invited and found excuses; Dard Hunter was invited and attended). Theodore Roosevelt, in 1901, had entertained the same Washington at lunch in the White House, and hysterical outrage had exploded in the southern press. (Sullivan called it "one of the most talked-of luncheons ever eaten in America" [Vol. 1, p. 562]).

"Recently, on a trip to California . . ." is in the June 1903 *Phil,* and the New York street-corner story in June 1915.

Reedy challenging Hubbard to get his hair cut is related by Shay.

The "All is one . . ." formulation is in the Haeckel (1905) *LJ,* as is the "self-lubricating" universe and the other references in this paragraph. "When you place a creed . . ." goes back to the Milton (1900) *LJ.* "Anchorage . . . God's great open sea" was also an early one, from the December 1902 *Phil.*

Dr. Eliot's address on "A New Religion" is in the May 1910 *Fra* and Hubbard's comments in the *Fra* for September 1909.

Prof. Faulkner's judgment is in his *The Quest for Social Justice,* Vol. XI of *A History of American Life* (New York, The Macmillan Company, 1943). Hubbard's snooting of the New Thought convention was reported by Harold Bolce in his article in *The Feather Duster.* "There are two kinds of thought . . ." is in the Hypatia (1908) *LJ*, and "that peculiar proclivity" in the *Phil* for April 1905.

The story of the portrait of Mrs. Eddy is in Shay.

Hubbard's invocations of intellectual integrity were frequent. In writing about revival meetings (July 1905 *Phil*), he said, "To pretend to believe a thing at which your reason revolts—to stultify your intellect—this . . . is the unpardonable sin." He also defined the unpardonable sin as "the disposition to evade the payment of small bills" and "neglecting to close the screen door."

"The gods have gone . . ." is from the Moses (1908) *LJ*. "That is good which serves" is from the Coleridge (1900) *LJ*, as is the "We no longer accept . . ." that follows it. The "Credo" is in *The Philosophy of Elbert Hubbard* (a posthumous paste-up job). The "working system" is in the *Phil* for May 1911.

"Health and prosperity are not pure blessings . . ." is from the Tennyson *LJ* (1900), success as "a subtle connivance . . ." is in the February 1906 *Phil*, the "Dead Sea of neutral nothingness" in the Burns (1900) *LJ*, and religion pure "only in poverty and persecution" in the Elizabeth Fry (1897) *LJ*.

"That quality of mind which constructs . . ." is from *Man of Sorrows* (a Hubbard version of the Gospels), pp. 24–25. "We fight on forever and fail" is in the *Note Book*, pp. 120–121. The spirit of man living again is from the Chopin (1901) *LJ*, and man being hurried out of life in the *Phil* for July 1907.

13. THE NEW WOMAN

All the quotations from Alice Hubbard in this chapter are from *Life Lessons*. Hubbard's strictures on "the average Christian household" are in the Rothschild (1909) *LJ*. The "one out of five" is in the *Phil* for February 1903. Reedy's remark about Hubbard's "one great discovery" is in *The Feather Duster*. Hubbard's reference to "one-half the race . . ." is in the *Phil* for January 1912, and the cake burnt on the bottom February 1908.

". . . women are seldom wise . . ." is from the Burns (1900) *LJ*. "No man ever did a great work" is from the Herschel (1905) *LJ*, and the "women who live in history" from the June 1899 *Phil*, while "no woman is either wise or good until . . ." comes from the Browning (1900) *LJ*. The "punk outfit" is in the *Phil* for November 1908, and the modern girl, including the Gibson Girl, appears in the *LJ* on Dante and Beatrice (1906).

"The Pretty Woman" and "Women under 30" are from *Phil*s for January 1913 and March 1897. This latter also has the "secrets of the confessional . . ." "No sane dentist" is from the Byron (1900) *LJ*, and "The Queen of the Porch" from the October 1904 *Phil.*

Hubbard may have borrowed the queen of the porch from Stephen Crane, who had a similar phobia and referred in a letter to "those hunks of women who squat on porches of hotels in summer and wherever their eye lights there blood rises. . . . This lady in her righteousness is just the grave of a stale lust and every boy in town knows it." (Quoted in Stallman.)

The reference to the woman hater is in the Socrates (1904) *LJ*. The verse about the New Woman was quoted from *Ad Sodales* by Frank Taylor, Blackwell, Oxford in the *Chap-Book* for October 15, 1895. The two Monahan items are from *The Phoenix* for June and November 1915. The Reedy quote is from Wolf.

The *Chap-Book* article on "decent literature" was by Hamilton Wright Mabie, and appeared in the January 1, 1896, issue.

An account of Moses Harmon going to jail for publishing an article on birth control is in Stewart Holbrook's *Lost Men of American History* (New York, The Macmillan Company, 1946). Hubbard's "whirling-spray affairs" joke was in the *Phil* for June 1911. It was one count of an indictment against him in 1913 for sending "filthy" matter through the mails.

Sullivan's observation on "Bok jokes" is from p. 395 of Vol. I. The *Phil* for December 1908 carried Hubbard's sneers at Bok's "Awful Something." The *Harper's Weekly* account of the audience at *Damaged Goods* was by Ethel Watts Mumford, in the October 1913 issue.

Hubbard's crying out that "there should be no such thing as divorce" is cited in Health. His comments on Mormon polygamy are in the *Phil* for August 1903.

All of the quotations from Elinor Glyn about her book are from her autobiography, *Romantic Adventure* (New York, E. P. Dutton & Co., 1937), quoted by permission. American letters had had a native foretaste of the Elinor Glyn type in 1883 when *Poems of Passion* (very young, very romantic) by Ella Wheeler Wilcox set off an unholy scandal.

The November 1916 *Fra* carried "The Independent Woman" by Marjorie Sutherland and "Woman and the Emotions" by Margaret Ashmun.

14. BIG BUSINESS AND MORE OF IT

Hubbard's reference to "our own Teddy" is in the September 1899 *Phil.* James J. Hill's lament is from a private letter quoted by Sullivan on p. 415 of Vol. II.

The New York *Times* for January 28 and 29, 1915, carried the story of the hearings of the Federal Commission on Industrial Relations, and my quotations are taken from there. *Harper's Weekly* carried "Elbert Hubbard's Price" in its January 30, 1915, issue. Hubbard's invocation of the "Rockefeller head with the Mother Jones heart" is in the April 1915 *Fra.* "The disgrace which comes . . ." was Hubbard's own comment (January 1900 *Phil*) on Mark Twain's attack on Christian Science. Hubbard's letter to Hapgood is in Shay.

That Federal investigation had a sideshow that has an ironic flavor today. The Commission heard from such liberals as John Haynes Holmes, who viewed with alarm the creation of the early philanthropic foundations (especially the Rockefeller Foundation). Holmes and others felt strongly that these huge aggregations of tainted money were a menace to freedom and democracy—that they could not help but entrench capitalist plutocracy and subvert the people's advocates.

"I Am an Anarchist" was in the *Phil* for November 1899. He referred to himself as a Fabian socialist in the *Phil* for December 1903. His reference to private toll roads is in the *Phil* for December 1907.

"The Christian men to whom God . . ." is quoted by Sullivan on p. 424 of Vol. II. Hubbard's attempts to define government are in *Selected Writings* and the *Note Book*. "People who do not readily pass under hypnotic control" is in the *Phil* for March 1900.

"The judgment of the incapable many" is in the *Phil* for February 1904. "All men are created . . ." is in the *Phil* for November 1897.

"This inert, greasy, obese thing . . ." is in the *Phil* for December 1904, "democracy as applied by the beneficent Strong Man" in the *Fra* for November 1914, and the "Nice Man by the name of Harry Peck" in the February 1898 *Phil*.

"Supervision . . ." is on p. 40, and "the rule of the walking delegate" on p. 134 of the *Note Book*.

The Theodore Roosevelt quotation comes from his speech August 31, 1910, at Osawatomie, Kansas, on "The New Nationalism." Hubbard's speculations on the future of anarchism and socialism are in the May 1910 *Phil*. Reedy's interpretations are in *The Feather Duster*. Hubbard's slightly premature vision of a "new deal" and his irritation at "the stupidity of big business" are in the *Phil* for September 1914. His attempt to disassociate himself from "grinding the public," and his plea to businessmen to be humanitarians, are in the *Phil* for July 1913. Reedy's "Stand Pat" joke came in 1912.

"It will not do" and "I object to the accusation" are in the *Phil* for March 1913. His ". . . philosopher may at times be a chucklehead" is in the July 1908 *Phil.*

The references to Brandeis are in the *Phil*s for July 1914 and July 1913.

15. VESTIBULE TO PARADISE

"Keep it going til I come back" is in Shay.

The reference to Alexander Woollcott is in Samuel Hopkins Adams, *Alexander Woollcott: His Life and His World* (Reynal and Hitchcock, 1945). The Burton Rascoe reminiscences are from his *Before I Forget* (New York, Doubleday, McClure & Company, 1937).

The charade with Edwin Markham is related in the *Phil* for October 1899. "Is Niagara Falls sincere . . . ?" is in the *Phil* for November 1907, and the catechism from the Boston lady in September 1912. Tom Johnson's comment was featured in the ad pages of the *Phil* for December 1907. Frederick C. Howe's visit is from his *The Confessions of a Reformer* (New York, Charles Scribner's Sons, 1925). That Johnson carried the Hubbard motto card is stated in Elizabeth J. Hauser's Introduction to Johnson's *My Story* (New York, Huebsch, 1913).

The anecdotes featuring Felix Shay are from his book. Dard Hunter's edition of one copy is related on pp. 41–42 of his book.

The Blaisdell ad is in the *Fra* for April 1910, the life insurance puff in Equitable Life Assurance ad in the same issue, and the Burroughs ad a month later.

Felix's advice to the Advertiser is in the September 1909 *Phil.* Hubbard's reference to Felix's leaving is in Vol. 14 of *Selected Writings,* pp. 192–193. "Advertising is fast becoming a fine art" is on p. 66 of the *Note Book,* and his plug for the ad clubs is in the May 1914 *Phil.* His plea for education of the incompetent many by advertising is in the September 1914 *Phil.*

The Reverend Seal's disapproval was quoted in the *Phil* for January 1912. The heretic in *Printer's Ink* was quoted, and squelched, in the March 1911 *Phil.*

"Schools and colleges are . . . makeshifts" and the later reference to getting education "as the lion whelp got his" are from the Starr King (1903) *LJ.* The University of Hard Knocks curriculum was spelled out in the *Phil* for February 1914. The reference to the John Dewey School is in the *Phil* for February 1901.

"To be healthy and sane" is on p. 38 of the *Note Book*.

Dr. Rumely's school is described in Albert Edward Hamilton, *The Real Boy and the New School* (London, Boni & Liveright, 1925). Reedy's comments on the Farm School (and on Hubbard's success in popularizing work) are in *The Feather Duster*. Reedy also had fun with his host with this:

"We were riding in his auto to Buffalo. 'This is a great potato country,' he said, with an all-inclusive gesture, 'All that field there to the left is potatoes.'

" 'Why, no, Elbert,' said Mrs. H; 'those are beans.'

" 'So they are,' said he mildly.

" 'And I said nothing, but my mind was busy cogitating the consequences to the Hubbardian world if I should make public the fact that the great projector of the farm school doesn't even 'know beans.' ' "

Bert's adventures with the boiler are in *Impressions*.

16. LAST JOURNEY

The January 1915 *Phil* carried Hubbard's second thoughts about the war, including his anger at big business and his apology to the socialists.

The call-down of the Pennsylvania Railroad is in the *Phil* for September 1914, and the disapproval of the businessmen's banquet with "femelettes" in the March 1915 *Phil*.

"Who lifted the Lid . . . ?" is in the October 1914 *Phil*. The quotation from Viereck and the replies to it are in the *Phils* for December 1914 and February 1915. This same Viereck delivered a Fourth of July Address as an invited speaker at the Roycroft convention in 1917. Reedy used considerable restraint in commenting that Viereck was "not a good drawing card in the circumstances" (*Fra,* July 1917).

"I am ex-officio General Inspector" is in the *Phil* for July 1914. Hubbard's plan to "escape the censor" was in a letter to E. W. Edwards of Cincinnati, and was quoted in the New York *Times* of May 9, 1915.

The events surrounding the sinking of the *Lusitania* are from *Impressions,* Heath, the final issue of the *Phil,* and *The Last Voyage of the Lusitania* by A. A. and Mary Hoehling (New York, Popular Library, 1957). Billy Sunday's memorial remarks are reported in the New York *Times* for May 10, 1915. The Walt Mason verse is in Shay. The filing of the Hubbard wills and the size of the estates were reported in the New York *Times* for June 8, 1915, and December 17, 1915.

Monahan's memorial address does not appear in the Roycroft volume of speeches, letters, and other tributes (*In Memoriam, Elbert and Alice Hubbard,* 1915). Apparently he held on to it for his own uses, and reserved his rights to revise and extend his remarks. It appears in his magazine, *The Phoenix,* for June 1915, and later in *Nemesis.* (Some of the eulogistic portions did appear in the July 1915 *Fra.*) In his rather ambivalent speculations about the future of Roycroft, Monahan wished young Bert well, but noted that "his father who never willingly divided authorship or prestige with anyone took no great pains to prepare him for the intellectual succession."

Le Gallienne's epitaph is in the Roycroft *In Memoriam* volume. The reference to Le Gallienne as "looking more like a poet . . ." is quoted from Grant Richards's Preface to Le Gallienne's *From a Paris Garret* in *The Quest of the Golden Boy,* Richard Whittington-Egan and Geoffrey Smerdon (American edition 1962, Barre, Mass., Barre Publishing Company).

Reedy's "For eighteen years . . ." is in *The Feather Duster,* his earlier comment on Hubbard having "started more people to thinking . . ." was reprinted from *Reedy's Mirror* in the *Phil* for December 1909.

A letter from Benjamin De Casseres in the *Saturday Review of Literature* for March 16, 1940 (after the publication of Balch's book), reasserted his claims to authorship. Balch had quoted two passages that were not Hubbard but De Casseres, and their author put it plainly in his letter: "before any one else writes a life of Hubbard or quotes him he had better look into the authorship of what was printed in the *Philistine* and the *Fra.*"

Elbert Hubbard, II, generously furnished the author with material on De Casseres, including a list of the portions of the early printings of the *Selected Writings* and the *Note Book* that De Casseres claimed and that were omitted from later printings. Excerpts from correspondence were included. Here is one of the first (De C. to E. H.):

"Now what is the good of me (the greatest writer in the world) going on turning out my spiritual guts on paper if I can't make a little money out of it?

"The enclosed go for fifteen dollars apiece. Of course, they are worth fifty dollars apiece, but I give them to you at a minimum because you have been O pretty good to me and because you are poor."

In returning one of these manuscripts (titled "The Affirmative I"), Hubbard said, "It is all right, too, but you know I am writing a lot of rubbish myself on things that nobody knows anything about."

Many of De Casseres's letters emphasize his being "financially embareassed," and once he referred to "my little Bastards, who have not where to lay their heads." Hubbard's replies seen guarded and almost formal by contrast, and De Casseres appeared to enjoy needling him: "Really, Pop, don't you think it's worth a five or ten over our scale? Of course, I know you'll tone it down a little, but you are getting too damn respectable. I'll go to jail for you any old time."

Elbert II gave it as his opinion that De Casseres was the only writer from whom material was bought and printed without signature—also that Hubbard bought most of it because he was sorry for the man.

Hubbard's joke about "The italics are ours" (*Phil* for May 1897) was a joke for printers. The *Phil* avoided using italics because in those days of hand-set type, interpolating italics was a nuisance.

The "Letter of Lord Byron" first appeared in the *Phil* for June 1901.

The story of Le Gallienne's final quarrel with Hubbard is in Shay. Hubbard's playful accusations of plagiarism in the *Quest of the Golden Girl* are in the *Phil* for April 1897.

The Hubbard quotations bearing on plagiarism are from: Paganini (1901) *LJ,* Raphael (1902) *LJ, Phil* July 1902, Burke (1903) *LJ*—sentence starting "The paraphrase is always"—the rest of the paragraph is from Comte (1904) *LJ, Phil* June 1908, and *Phil* April 1910.

Hubbard once quoted Alva Adams as writing: "The world has only produced three makers of epigrams who were supremely great. These are Solomon, Shakespeare and Elbert Hubbard. And Hubbard is the greatest of all. Hubbard, however, had this advantage—he wrote last!"

The two Emerson warm-ups for the mousetraps are from *The American Scholar* and Vol. VIII, p. 28, of *Works.*

The source for Hubbard's editor claiming the mousetrap for his boss, and for Vizetelly raising the odds against Emerson (also for the earlier citation of Hubbard's invitation to a plagiarism-sleuth to come have a good laugh over it) is "More About the Mouse Trap," Burton Stephenson in *The Colophon,* Vol. 1, 1935, pp. 71–86.

Vizetelly had reason to question Mrs. Yule's reliability. Hubbard printed the last four lines of Henley's *Invictus* in a hand-lettered display on a *Philistine* back cover (February 1902), without mentioning title or author. Mrs. Yule picked them up for a new compilation entitled *For Thy Good Cheer,* and credited them to Hubbard (Stevenson, as above).

In the unlikely event of anyone undertaking more exhaustive Hubbard researches, I offer a further lead on his "kabojolisms." Many of Hubbard's pronouncements on psychology and sex are credited to one "Dr. Charcot." (At least one Charcot quotation is elsewhere attributed to G. Stanley Hall.)

The *Fra* for April 1908 (the first issue) has a by-lined article ("By Dr. Jean Charcot") entitled "How to Live a Hundred Years" that has what looks like Hubbard's style all through it. There was a Dr. Jean Charcot (1825–1893) who was a French neurologist and an early teacher of Sigmund Freud. How much Hubbard picked up from the real Dr. Charcot, where he found it, and how much Dr. Charcot was another Hubbard front (like Ali Baba) could be an interesting exploration, if unlikely to stagger the mass media.

The long, solid success of the Roycrofters under Bert's direction was mentioned in a letter from him to the author (September 23, 1958).

The Chapman essay is in the *Chap-Book* for July 15, 1897. It prompted several replies. One, by Maurice Thompson (August 1, 1897), rather agreed with Chapman, and it has a sentence that might also have been applied to Hubbard by one of his enemies: "No man ever had such a reservoir of unfiltered, unsterilized, and altogether amazing egotism upon which to draw for floods of resonant and high-rolling absurdities."

Hubbard's remark about the twelve disciples is in the *Phil* for January 1903. The "fool wish of Bobby Burns" is in the *Phil* for November 1898.

Reedy's epitaph was printed in the *Fra* for August 1915. Hubbard's own instructions for his "tombstone" (the *Fra,* October 1914) were: "Simply put these words, 'He made them laugh, and he made them mad— but he made them think.' "

The following sources have some interest. They have not been cited in the Notes to Chapters.

BOOKS AND ARTICLES

ALLEN, FREDERICK LEWIS. Review of Balch's book in *Saturday Review,* February 24, 1967.

ANGERT, EUGENE H. "Is Mark Twain Dead?" *North American Review,* September, 1909.

A complicated spoof that elaborates the notion that Twain died in Switzerland in 1906 and his publishers hired Hubbard to keep the pot boiling with the book on Christian science.

BATES, BRAINARD LEROY. "A Day at the Roycrofters, Their Shop."

Included in *The Feather Duster* (see Reedy in source list preceding Notes to Chapters). A hero-worshiping piece, but it has a description of the equipment of the Roycroft printing plant.

BEER, THOMAS. *The Mauve Decade.* New York, Alfred A. Knopf, 1926; Vintage paperback, 1960.

Contains an account of a call on Hubbard by one Charles Maurice in 1899.

FLOWER, BENJAMIN O. *Progressive Men, Women and Movements of the Past Twenty-five Years.* Boston, New Arena Publishing Company, 1914.

Brief reference to Hubbard's association with the *Arena* group.

FOWLER, GENE. *Minutes of the Last Meeting.* New York, The Viking Press, 1954.

Contains secondhand (and badly garbled) comments on Hubbard and Roycroft by a Detroit meat-packer named Ben Marx; also material by and about Sadakichi Hartmann, a bohemian of enormous inner-circle notoriety. Hartmann, who had stayed at East Aurora, is quoted as saying that Hubbard "was a person of great magnetism, of restless energy, clever, and alert. It was impossible to down him, but intellectual somersaults seemed to be his particular gift; and he was like a two-headed monster, with each of the heads smiling, one at the other."

FRENCH, GEORGE. In *The American Printer,* April 1902.

A critique of Roycroft bookmaking. It discusses the rumor (which pops up in several places) that Roycroft limited and numbered editions sometimes had a separate series of numbers for each section of the country.

GRIFFITH, WILLIAM, editor. *The Elbert Hubbard Book.* Racine, Wisc., Whitman Publishing Company, 1934.

A cheap and sleazy compilation.

HARTT, ROLLIN LYNDE. "Elbert Hubbard," *The Critic,* November, 1899.

A long, solemn appraisal by a man who had been impressed by *A Message to Garcia* ("the one morsel of unquestionably great work"), and hoped that "it means for him an end of trifling and the beginnings of serious endeavor."

LANE, ALBERT. *Elbert Hubbard and His Work.* Worcester, Mass. Privately printed, 1901.

Interesting as an early attempt to understand Hubbard and his place in American society. It was written in 1901 at the peak of Hubbard's first stage of public acceptance (after the *Message* and before the scandal). Lane's point of view is broadly conservative, and he largely accepts Hubbard's public front of this period at its face value. The book contains excellent photographs, and bibliographies of both Hubbard's writings and Roycroft publications through 1900.

SINCLAIR, UPTON. *The Brass Check: A Study of American Journalism.* Revised edition, April 1931 (original edition, 1920). Published by the author, Pasadena, California.

Not exactly a Hubbard fan, Sinclair has a chapter titled "The Elbert Hubbard Worm." After quoting some of Hubbard's playful aspersions on *The Jungle,* Sinclair demands, "Can it be possible that any one is deceived by this insane rant and drivel?"

TASSIN, ALGERNON. *The Magazine in America.* New York, Dodd, Mead, 1916.

A fanciful and not always reliable account of the *Philistine,* the *Lark,* and the other little magazines of the 1890's.

VAIL, R. W. G. "A Message to Garcia" A Bibliographical Puzzle. *Bulletin of the New York Public Library,* February, 1930.

An attempt to sort out the printing history and successive editions of the *Message.*

NEWSPAPER STORIES AND UNSIGNED ARTICLES

The Bloomington (Illinois) *Daily Pantagraph* (file in the McLean County Historical Society) has occasional references to its native son. One such, reporting a visit to his parents in 1899, said that Hubbard's "great desire for learning led him to desert the plow for the school room, and after graduating from Harvard College, he entered the literary field for honors."

Current Opinion, April 1923. "A Writer Who Made America Think."

A routine and laudatory summary. It contains the somewhat premature judgment that Hubbard "was not accepted in his lifetime by the literary Brahmins, and is not accepted by most of them even yet. If the time is already here when their approval or disapproval seems unimportant, it is because he has won, over their heads, the kind of victory that ensures immortality." William H. Wise was president of the Current Literature Publishing Company, which issued *Current Opinion.* This article may have been a buildup for the posthumous Hubbard books published by Wise.

Literary Digest for April 22, 1899, has an account of the instant success of the *Message.*

Springfield (Ohio) *Daily News* for May 27, 1923.

Carries reminiscences by a man named Potter, secretary to the late John Bryan, of Yellow Springs. Bryan was a freethinking eccentric, with money and considerable local fame. Hubbard referred to Bryan in the *Philistine* several times, and apparently stayed with him during some of his lecture tours.

MAJOR PUBLICATIONS
IN THE ELBERT HUBBARD OUTPUT

PERIODICALS

The *Philistine*. First issue: June 1895. Last issue: July 1915. Issued monthly;
6 months per volume.

The *Fra*. First issue: April 1908. Last issue: August 1917. Issued monthly;
6 months per volume.

The *Roycroft Quarterly*. Issued once, May 1, 1896 (a Stephen Crane issue).

"LITTLE JOURNEYS TO THE HOMES OF THE GREAT"

VOL. I. *Good Men and Great*. Putnam, 1895.
(George Eliot, Carlyle, Ruskin, Gladstone, Turner, Swift, Hugo, Words-
worth, Thackeray, Dickens, Goldsmith, Shakespeare)

VOL. II. *American Authors*. Putnam, 1896.
(Putnam reissued an 1853 series, then titled *Homes of American Authors*.
Hubbard contributed one number, on Whitman.)

VOL. III. *Famous Women*. Putnam, 1897.
(Elizabeth Browning, Mme. Guyon, Harriet Martineau, Charlotte Brontë,
Christina Rosetti, Rosa Bonheur, Madame de Staël, Elizabeth Fry, Mary
Lamb, Jane Austen, Empress Josephine, Mary Shelley)

VOL. IV. *American Statesmen*. Putnam, 1898.
(Washington, Franklin, Hamilton, John Adams, Hancock, J. Q. Adams,
Jefferson, Webster, Clay, Jay, Seward, Lincoln)

VOL. V. *Eminent Painters*. Putnam, 1899.
(Michael Angelo, Rembrandt, Rubens, Meissonier, Titian, Van Dyck,
Fortuny, Scheffer, Millet, Reynolds, Landseer, Doré)

VOLS. VI AND VII. *English Authors*. Roycroft, 1900.
(Morris, Browning, Tennyson, Burns, Milton, Johnson, Macaulay, Byron,
Addison, Southey, Coleridge, Disraeli)

VOLS. VIII AND IX. *Great Musicians*. Roycroft, 1901.
(Wagner, Paganini, Chopin, Mozart, Bach, Mendelssohn, Liszt, Beethoven, Handel, Verdi, Schumann, Brahms)

VOLS. X AND XI. *Eminent Artists*. Roycroft, 1902.
(Raphael, Leonardo, Botticelli, Thorwaldsen, Gainsborough, Velásquez,
Corot, Correggio, Bellini, Cellini, Abbey, Whistler)

VOLS. XII AND XIII. *Eminent Orators*. Roycroft, 1903.
(Pericles, Antony, Savonarola, Luther, Burke, Pitt, Marat, Ingersoll,
Patrick Henry, Starr King, Beecher, Phillips)

VOLS. XIV AND XV. *Great Philosophers.* Roycroft, 1904.

(Socrates, Aristotle, Spinoza, Seneca, Aurelius, Swedenborg, Kant, Comte, Voltaire, Spencer, Schopenhauer, Thoreau)

VOLS. XVI AND XVII. *Great Scientists.* Roycroft, 1905.

(Copernicus, Newton, Herschel, Galileo, Humboldt, Darwin, Haeckel, Linnaeus, Huxley, Tyndall, Wallace, Fiske)

VOLS. XVIII AND XIX. *Great Lovers.* Roycroft, 1906.

(J. and S. Wedgwood, Wm. Godwin and Mary Wollstonecraft, Dante and Beatrice, John S. Mill and Harriet Taylor, Parnell and Kitty O'Shea, Petrarch and Laura)

VOLS. XX AND XXI. *Great Reformers.* Roycroft, 1907.

(Wesley, Henry George, Garibaldi, Cobden, Paine, John Knox, Bright, Bradlaugh, Parker, Cromwell, Anne Hutchinson, Rousseau)

VOLS. XXII AND XXIII. *Great Teachers.* Roycroft, 1908.

(Moses, Confucius, Pythagoras, Plato, King Alfred, Froebel, Booker T. Washington, Thomas. Arnold, Erasmus, Hypatia, St. Benedict, Mark Baker Eddy)

VOLS. XXIV AND XXV. *Great Business Men.* Roycroft, 1909.

(Robert Owen, James Oliver, Stephen Girard, Albert A. Pope, H. J. Heinz, Philip D. Armour, Mayer Rothschild, James J. Hill, John Jacob Astor, August Schilling, John Wanamaker, Andrew Carnegie)

BOOKS

The Man. A Story of Today. New York, J. S. Ogilvie, 1891.
One Day. A Tale of the Prairies. Boston, Arena Publishing Company, 1893.
Forbes of Harvard. Boston, Arena Publishing Company, 1894.
No Enemy (but Himself). New York, G. P. Putnam's Sons, 1894.
The Legacy. Roycroft, 1896.
Time and Chance: A Romance and a History: Being the Story of the Life of a Man. Roycroft, 1899. Also a revised edition by G. P. Putnam's Sons, 1901. (This was Hubbard's "life" of John Brown; the Library of Congress has it catalogued as fiction.)
The Man of Sorrows. Roycroft, 1905.
White Hyacinths. Roycroft, 1907.

These, I believe, are the major items. There were many regroupings, new editions, and new combinations of old material under new titles. Both Roycroft and Putnam editions of *Little Journeys* are to be found after 1900.

Index

Abbey, Edward, 85
Ad Clubs, 188, 193–94
Adams, Alva, 239
Advertising, 4, 132–33, 186–87, 188–89
Allegheny College, 8
Allen, Frederick Lewis, 59, 64, 220
Andrews, Elisha B., 83
Arena, the, 49
Armour, Philip D., 169

Baba, Ali (Anson A. Blackman), 65–66, 92, 125, 183, 201, 206
Baer, George F., 175
Baptist Usage, 16
Baseball, and Hubbard, 17–18
Bible: Hubbard family, 16; in 19th-century U.S., 15, 27, 115
Birth control, 159–60
Bloomington, Ill., 2, 7, 82, 150
Bok, Edward, 55, 160–61
Bragdon, Claude, 68
Brandeis, Louis D., 179, 195
Brown, John, Hubbard book on, 4, 39, 76, 78
Bryan, William Jennings, 30, 71–72
Buffalo, N.Y., Hubbard's parents in, 9–11; Hubbard move to, 30
Burnett, Frances Hodgson, 79
Business and businessmen, and the *Message,* 89; as a Hubbard market, 120–21; *Little Journeys* about, 128; as heroes, 130–31, 174; as outsiders, 130; Hubbard fronting for, 167–72; disillusion with, 193–94

Calvinism, 10, 114
Carlyle, Thomas, 62–63, 224
Carman, Bliss, 67
Carnegie, Andrew, 128
Catholic World, 65, 221
Chap-Book, the, genesis, 54; circulation, 58; scorn for popular culture, 83; on "decadent" literature, 159; on feminism, 157, 158, 159; Chapman essay from, 207; mentioned, 61

Chapman, John Jay, 207–8
Charcot, Dr. Jean, 77, 132, 239–40
Chautauquas, 55–56, 181
Child labor, 135–36
Children, in 19th-century U.S., 154
Christian Science, 146–47
Christmas, in Hubbard childhood, 19
Church trials, 16–17
Circus, the, 18
Civil War, 12
Colorado coal strike, 170–72
Comstock, Anthony, 159, 160
Concord, Mass., 46
Connor, Jerome, 65
Cosmopolitan, 83
Crane, Stephen, 68–69, 219, 223, 234

Damaged Goods, 161
Daniels, George H., 88
De Casseres, Benjamin, mentioned, 91, 228; comments on Hubbard, 200; writings ascribed to Hubbard, 200–201; correspondence with Hubbard, 238–39
De Ford, Miriam Allen, 93
Debs, Eugene V., 72, 177
Denslow, W. W., 65
Dewey, John, 189
Divorce, Hubbard attitude to, 161–62
Dooley, Mr. (Finley Peter Dunne), 146

East Aurora, 4, 34, 69, 73–74, 93–94, 100, 115, 142–43, 190–91
Eddy, Mary Baker, *see* Christian Science
Education, in Hubbard boyhood, 14–15; Hubbard's philosophy of, 124, 189–90
Eliot, Charles W., 144–45
Emerson, Ralph Waldo, 27, 46, 94; 130, 144, 146, 198, 204–6
Emerson College of Oratory, 41, 64
Epitaph, Hubbard's, for himself, 240
Evolution, theory of, 28–29, 115

Faulkner, Harold U., 145
FBI offices, Hubbard quotation in, 91
Feminism, 48, 77–79, 153–60, 164–65

Fletcher, Horace, 184–85
Flower, Benjamin Orange, 49, 241
Fly Leaf, the, 54, 61, 62
Forbes of Harvard, 47–49, 50, 78, 182, 203
Fosdick, Harry Emerson, 9
Fra, the, 63, 131–32, 164–65, 186
Frederic, Harold, 18
Freud, Dr. Sigmund, 150
Froebel, Friedrich, 132

Gardner, Fred, 103
Gaspard, Jules Maurice, 146
Germ theory, Dr. Silas and the, 20, 117
Gibson Girl, the, 156
Gilder, Richard Watson, 55
Glyn, Elinor, 162–64
Goldman, Emma, 78, 157, 170, 177–78

Haeckel, Ernst, 143–44
Hapgood, Norman, 172–73
Harmon, Moses, 159
Harte, Walter Blackburn, 54, 61–62, 67
Hartmann, Sadakichi, 241
Harvard College, 41, 43-48
Heafford, George H., 89
Hill, Adams Sherman, 45
Hill, James J., 169
Holbrook, Stewart, 89
Holmes, John Haynes, 235
Hopkins, Arthur, 140
Horses, Hubbard and, 17, 34, 35–36
Hovey, Richard, 67
Howe, Frederic C., 184
Howells, William Dean, 55
"How I Found My Brother," 39, 150–51
Hubbard, Alice Moore, background, 37; Hubbard's early references to, 37–38, 48–49; feminism and, 37, 48, 77–78, 153–54, 155; and *The Man,* 40; and *Forbes of Harvard,* 48–49; and Miriam, 50, 54, 103; as audience for Hubbard, 66; on marriage, 77; lawsuit, 97, 102–3, 225; marriage to Hubbard, 103, 109; Hubbard tributes to, 110; on religion, 114–15; on science, 118; writings in the *Fra,* 132; on entertaining Great Men, 140; on bloomers, 141–42; will and estate, 196
Hubbard, Bertha Crawford, marriage to Hubbard, 33; mentioned, 38, 58, 101, 124, 130, 196; estrangement from Hubbard, 76–77, 95, 97
Hubbard, Charlie, 7, 10–12, 151
Hubbard, Daisy (Anna Mirenda), 12, 14, 25, 33, 44, 46, 47, 48
Hubbard, Elbert, appearance, 4–5, 26, 30, 32, 60–61; and art, 123–25; and book design, 58–60; as businessman, 86, 120, 126; clergy, battles with, 82, 111–12; and disciples, 105–6, 127; European trips, 49–50, 62–63, 194–95; federal conviction, 195; government, attitudes to, 175–77, 188; greatness, pursuit of, 129–

131; identity quest, 1–3, 5, 26, 27, 30–31, 36, 39, 41–42, 43, 46–47, 49–50, 53–55, 56–58, 61, 62–63, 66–67, 69, 74–75, 81–82, 84, 103, 106–7, 120–21, 123–24, 143, 152, 196–97, 208; "Is he sincere?", 183–84; as lecturer, 93, 106–7, 118; memorial services, 145, 196, 197, 198; newspaper comments on, 99, 101, 104, 110–11; occupational mythology, 30; as outsider, 43–46, 50, 54–58, 62, 81–82, 118, 124, 130, 189–91, 207; parents, relation to, 12, 20, 21, 22, 41–42, 100, 101–2, 117, 151–52; and plagiarism, 98, 200–201, 202–4, 206, 239; as popular prophet, 39–40, 43, 53, 72–73, 82–84, 123–24; posthumous letters from public, 5, 196–97; practical jokes, 65, 125, 201–2; quarrels, 61, 67–68, 97–98, 202; and radicalism-reform, 71–72, 91–92, 120–21, 130–31, 167–79; religious formulations, 111–16, 143–150; scandal and divorce, 49–50, 75–77, 95–98, 99–102, 224–25; soap business, 22, 25, 26–27, 30–31, 34, 41; vaudeville, 139–40, 231; will and estate, 196; and women, 32, 33, 38, 39–40, 48, 77, 78–79, 84, 130, 155–57, 162–63, 164, 217; work, and philosophy of, 21, 91, 189–90; writing style, 32–34, 40, 45–46, 75, 85–86, 179–80
Hubbard, Elbert II, mentioned, 34, 62, 104–5, 126, 127, 151, 195, 196, 238; on father as Boss, 80; on the *Message,* 90; on father's "nerves," 94; boyhood memories of father, 104–5; adventure with boiler, 191; on *Lusitania* sinking, 196; management of Roycroft, 196, 206
Hubbard, Elias, 8
Hubbard, Hannah Frances (Mrs. John Larkin), 7, 11, 13, 22, 26, 41, 225
Hubbard, Honor, 12
Hubbard, Juliana Frances, personality and family, 9–10; marriage and children, 10–12, 13, 19, 21–22; mentioned, 16, 196; the theatre and, 26; at Roycroft, 92, 151–52
Hubbard, Justus, 8
Hubbard, Katherine, 50, 63, 97
Hubbard, Mary (Heath), birth, 12; mentioned, 14–15, 25, 34, 35, 49; religion and, 15; visit to Buffalo, 31–32; on scandal, 100–101; on brother and God, 114
Hubbard, Miriam, 50, 97, 103, 143, 190, 196, 224, 225
Hubbard, Ralph, 34, 97
Hubbard, Sanford, 36, 104, 196
Hubbard, Dr. Silas, in Bloomington, 7; in Buffalo, 7; in Hudson, 7–8, 11; family background, 8; education, 8–9; in East Aurora, 8, 92, 152; marriage, 10; religion, 10, 16–17, 18, 20; Civil War and, 12; eccentricities, 13–14, 19–20; on germ theory, 20, 117; mentioned, 196

Hubbard, Solomon, 8, 10
Hunter, Dard, on Alice Hubbard, 109; dining-room windows, 119; May Morris lecture, 119; octopus cover, 121; mentioned, 106, 232

Illegitimate children, Hubbard on, 95, 224
Ingersoll, Robert G., quoted, 15, 29; lecture by, 27; popular appeal of, 29; mentioned, 143, 145

"Jack and Jill" sermon, 32–33, 217
Jenks, Tudor, 67
"John," 65
Johnson, Tom L., 131, 184, 230
Jones, Mother, 170, 171–72
Jungle, The, 169, 242

Kaiser, The, 194, 195
Kemp, Harry, arrival at Roycroft, 64–65; on Sanford Hubbard, 104; ambivalence to Hubbard, 105–6; on Alice, 109; on working conditions at Roycroft, 136–37
Kimball, Ingalls, 54
Kipling, Rudyard, 60
Krutch, Joseph Wood, 84

Ladies' Home Journal, see Bok, Edward
Lane, Albert, 93, 241
Larkin, J. D., & Co., 34, 36, 41
Larkin, John, 22, 30, 36, 41
Lauder, Harry, 5, 140
Le Gallienne, Richard, 60, 199, 202
Lease, Mary Ellen, 79
Leslie, Amy, 140–41
Lincoln, Abraham, 12, 176
Little Journeys, 4, 46–47, 49–50, 54, 83–85, 92, 119, 128–30, 174
Lusitania, 195, 204

McGuffey's Readers, 14, 89
Magazines, little, 4, 54–55, 219
Man, The, 38–41, 152
"Man with the Hoe," see Markham, Edwin
Mangasarian, M. M., 185
Marden, Orison Swett, 145, 205
Markham, Edwin, 91–92, 183
Mason, Walt, 197
Mavity, Paul W., 100
Memorial plaque, 2–3
Mencken, Henry Louis, 43
Message to Garcia, A, 58, 86, 87–91, 92, 95, 202, 223–24
Monahan, Michael, on Hubbard as cowboy, 30–31; mentioned, 62, 105, 107, 157, 237–38; Opera House speech, 97–98; at Memorial Service, 197–98; on plagiarism, 202; "Art and Glory," 123, 229
Monism, 143–44
Mormons, 162
Morris, May, 119
Morris, William, 3, 50, 58–60, 62, 119, 160, 218

Morrow, Marco, 67
Mousetrap controversy, 204–6
Muckrakers, 167–69
"Mudsock," 13, 42, 150–51

Nation, Carrie, 78
Negro, Hubbard attitude toward, 141, 231–32
New Thought, 145–46, 162
New Woman, the, see feminism
No Enemy (but Himself), 50, 53, 54, 152, 218–19
Nordau, Max, 158–59
Note Book of Elbert Hubbard, 5, 200
Novel-reading, taboo on, 18, 27, 218
Noxon, Frank W., 68

One Day, 42–43, 152
O'Sullivan's Heels, 134–35
Owen, Robert, 4, 124

Peck, Harry Thurston, 176–77
Pendennis Press, 54, 60
Pennsylvania Railroad, 194
Philistine, the, reception of, 4, 58; first issues, 55–58; circulation of, 55, 58, 92, 118–19; origin of name, 56; development of, 57–58; advertisers in, 64; contract with Fred Gardner, 103; contrasted with the Fra, 131
Phrenology, 8, 9, 20
Pond, Major James B., 92, 94, 106
Powderly, Terence V., 181–82
Putnam, George Haven, 85
Putnam's Sons, G. P., 54

Quimby, Phineas, P., 146

Radicalism, 71–72, 91–92, 169–70
Ranson, Will, 59, 220
Rascoe, Burton, 183
Reedy, William Marion, on Alice, 37, 110; appraisals of Hubbard, 84, 94, 199, 208; on the Message, 89–90; on Roycroft community, 94; life and career, 94–95; quoting Monahan, 98; on Hubbard and sons, 105; on White Hyacinths, 111; practical jokes, 139–40, 143; on feminism, 155; on Emma Goldman, 157; on Hubbard and business, 178, 179; on Farm School, 190; on Hubbard as popularizer of work, 190; on Hubbard blast at Monahan, 197–98; Hubbard reference to plagiarism by, 203; on Hubbard and Alice, 237
Reid, Opie, 104
Respectability, Hubbard on, 129, 230
Revival meetings, 15–16, 112
Reynolds, Stephen Marion, 184
Ricker, Marilla, 142–43
Rockefeller, John D., Jr., 170–72
Rockefeller, John D., Sr., 121, 170–71, 178
Rollins, Carl Purington, 60

Roosevelt, Theodore, 92, 167, 169, 177, 199, 232
Roycroft community, book printing, 3, 58–60; crafts, 3, 63, 123, 125; Hubbard proprietorship of, 4, 66–67, 69, 120–21, 133–37; buildings, 63, 64, 65; communal nature, 63, 64, 65–67, 80–81; in Hubbard lectures, 93–94; Hubbard performances with visitors, 105, 181–82, 184; under Alice, 109, 120, 133–34; child labor at, 135–37; summer conventions, 181–83; celebrities at, 183, 184–85; Farm School, 189–90; post-Hubbard history, 200, 206–7; sale of plant, 206–7; mythology about, 220
Rumely, Edward, 190, 237

Savage, Minot, 145
School, Roycroft, 189–90
Science, 28–29, 115–18
Shakespeare, 40, 75
Shaw, George Bernard, 60
Shay, Felix, mentioned, 26, 66, 141, 184–85, 202, 206; quoted, 64; initiation to Roycroft, 126–27; as ad man, 132–33, 187–88; Christmas catalog, 133–34; quarrels with Hubbard, 133–34; fasting, 185; trips to Chicago with Hubbard, 185–86; and "The Cigarettist," 186; leaves Roycroft, 187–88; mousetrap controversy and, 206
"Silence, Essay on," 201
Sinclair, Upton, 169, 170, 172, 242
Spencer, Herbert, 116
Standard Oil Company, 121, 167–68, 229
Stanton, Elizabeth Cady, 78
Stone, Herbert S., 54, 195
Stone, Melville, 195
Sunday, William A. (Billy), 112, 197, 227–28

Taber, Henry, 61, 67, 68
Tanguay, Eva, 140, 189
Tarbell, Ida M., 168, 172
Thompson, Maurice, 158, 159, 240
Three Weeks, see Glyn, Elinor
Titanic, sinking of, 169
Towne, Elizabeth, 145
Tramp lore, 50, 63
Trusts, 168, 173–75, 177
Tufts College, 92
Twain, Mark, 55, 235
Typographical Union, 134–35

"University of Hard Knocks," 31, 167, 189
"Unpardonable sin, the," 233
Utopian communities, Hubbard on, 81

Vaccination, 117–18
Venereal disease, Bok and Hubbard on, 160–61
Viereck, George Sylvester, 194, 237
Vizetelly, Frank H., 204–5

Walker, John Brisben, 55, 82–83
Washington, Booker T., 131, 232
Watson, Thomas E., 131
Weller, Justus, 22, 25, 29–30
Wendell, Barrett, 45–46, 53
White Hyacinths, 110
Whitlock, Brand, 230
"Who Lifted the Lid Off Hell?", 194
Wilde, Oscar, 139, 158
Wise, William H., Company, 5, 200, 242
Woodhull, Victoria C., 78
Woollcott, Alexander, 183
World War I, 180, 193, 195
Wright, Frank Lloyd, 36, 218

Yellow Book, the, 158
Yule, Sarah S. B., 204, 205, 239